Alternative Assessments With Gifted and Talented Students

Alternative Assessments

With Gifted and Talented Students

Edited by
Joyce L. VanTassel-Baska, Ed.D.

Prufrock Press Inc.
Waco, Texas

a service publication of

Library of Congress Cataloging-in-Publication Data

Alternative assessments with gifted and talented students / edited by Joyce VanTassel-Baska.
   p. cm. -- (Critical issues in equity and excellence in gifted education series)
  Includes bibliographical references.
  ISBN-13: 978-1-59363-298-4 (pbk.)
  ISBN-10: 1-59363-298-3 (pbk.)
  1. Gifted children—Identification. 2. Educational tests and measurements I. VanTassel-Baska, Joyce.
  LC3993.2.A48 2007
  371.95—dc22
                      2007034531

Copyright © 2008, National Association for Gifted Children
Edited by Lacy Elwood
Cover and Layout Design by Marjorie Parker

ISBN-13: 978-1-59363-298-4
ISBN-10: 1-59363-298-3

Prufrock Press Inc.
P.O. Box 8813
Waco, TX 76714-8813
Phone: (800) 998-2208
Fax: (800) 240-0333
http://www.prufrock.com

To my family, Lee and Ariel, who continue to support
and inspire.

Contents

List of Tables

List of Figures

Acknowledgements

I would like to acknowledge the support of Bronwyn MacFarlane and Elizabeth Sutton in their preparation of this manuscript. Their word-processing work was deeply appreciated.

—Joyce VanTassel-Baska

An Overview of Alternative Assessment Measures for Gifted Learners and the Issues That Surround Their Use

Joyce VanTassel-Baska

This book is the second in a series designed to emphasize critical issues in the field of gifted education. It has been developed to highlight alternative assessment approaches used for both the identification and assessment of learning outcomes of gifted and promising learners. The book explores the use of alternative assessments for identification, noting both strengths and weaknesses of various instruments. It also includes chapters that argue for the use of traditional measures—ones that have a rich history in psychometrics and high degrees of technical adequacy. The book also explores several alternative assessments for learning, found to be viable in measuring gifted student learning outcomes. These approaches are highlighted in separate chapters devoted to performance-based, portfolio, creativity, and product assessment models.

The intended audience for the book is the educational practitioner, charged with designing both identification and learning systems for the gifted. Researchers and school psychologists also would find the book of interest as a way to conceptualize the use of different types of assessment tools for different purposes. It also could be used by professors teaching gifted endorsement or certification courses, as it thoroughly addresses the standard on assessment (VanTassel-Baska & Johnsen, 2007).

An Overview of the Chapters

In the second chapter that follows, Bracken outlines the important aspects of nonverbal assessments as a way to enhance the identification of underrepresented groups and as a way of assessing g-factor intelligence through means other than verbal. He describes his Universal Nonverbal Intelligence Test (UNIT), which has been developed as both an individual and group test, as a tool to find students whose language experience may impede their capacity to perform well on a verbal test, as well as other populations whose disabilities may mask verbal performance. He also describes two studies using his Clinical Assessment of Behavior (CAB) as an efficient teacher assessment of gifted student behaviors found to be as effective as other assessment tools. He cautions against the use of nonverbal assessment as the only measure to employ in identifying gifted learners, but encourages practitioners to include such an assessment in their overall identification system. Suggesting that intervention should override prediction, he is less concerned about the mismatch between curriculum in schools and the types of items found on nonverbal tests. Finally, he strongly suggests that nonverbal tests tell us as much about g-factor intelligence as verbal tests.

The Lohman and Lakin chapter provides us with a vision of the power of domain-specific measures as important parts of any identification schema and challenges us to be cautious in using nonverbal measures in contexts that demand high verbal capacities, contexts that typically characterize gifted programs. Their analysis of the Cognitive Abilities Test (CogAT) as a viable measure for identification focuses on its structured utility due to verbal, mathematical, and nonverbal properties and three major procedures for use to include a broader range of students in gifted programs. Of special interest is the argument for using "opportunity to learn" groups such as second language learners as another reference group to consider in exercising judgments for selection. The authors also carefully explicate the problems associated with nonverbal assessment as a sole tool for identifying gifted learners, raising the issue of how practitioners use nonverbal assessment in the overall selection paradigm for gifted programs.

The Naglieri chapter argues strongly for the use of nonverbal assessment as a strong and substitutable predictor of general ability, not saddled with verbal mediation requirements that jeopardize the performance of minority and English-limited learners, and the poor. Citing studies conducted on his Naglieri Nonverbal Ability Test (NNAT), he suggests the power of nonverbal assessment in finding equal percentages of underrepresented populations from minority groups who would be eligible for gifted services. Naglieri also claims that nonverbal assessment contains no achievement factor that could distort scores and limit the performance of underrepresented groups. The issue of using nonverbal assessment as a sole screener for gifted programs, however, is raised by this chapter, with Naglieri suggesting it as an efficacious approach, given its proven effectiveness in the "screening in" of minority children. The chapter also raises important questions about the curriculum inferences that can be made from nonverbal test scores.

The Olszewski-Kubilius and Kulieke chapter presents the case that exists for the use of off-level assessments both to identify and assess learning among gifted youth. The chapter provides a rationale for off-level testing and provides the reader with a blueprint for the logic of it, complete with examples of such tests used in talent searches nationwide. Evidence for both the efficiency of the approach, as well as its effectiveness in finding the highly gifted, is systematically explained. Special care also was given to linking the meaning of the test scores to appropriate follow-up intervention in specific areas of aptitude. Concerns are noted, however, for the misinterpretation of scores by parents and professionals alike that sometimes interferes with using these tests in school contexts. Issues also emerge around the level of test expertise needed in order to work with off-level assessment tools and the myriad ways that interventions could be constructed.

The Ford chapter constitutes a manifesto on the need to identify underrepresented learners for gifted programs. She attacks both the educational establishment and the testing industry for not resolving the problems of finding more students of poverty and color through the use of nonbiased and appropriate measures. She also suggests that the use of tests by practitioners compounds the problem of the tests themselves. Ford provides a cultural framework for thinking about why Black children may respond differently to test items so that their scores are lower and offers a set of culturally sensitive assumptions about the role of testing in assessing ability. Finally, Ford outlines guiding principles that provide an equitable assessment approach for practitioners to follow. Clearly, this chapter raises the issue of bias in test construction, as well as test use for Black students who continue to be underrepresented in gifted programs.

The Feng and VanTassel-Baska chapter chronicles the 4-year use of performance-based assessments for the identification of more low-income and minority students in one state. Now adopted as part of the statewide identification protocol, performance-based assessment tasks, as a value-added component to ability and achievement tests, account for close to 20% more underrepresented populations being identified annually as gifted. The chapter provides a 3-year portrait of these learners' identification patterns, noting that while more were identified in the nonverbal area, the approach also found verbally able students not identified through traditional measures. The authors also track the results of performance task-identified students on the state's high-stakes test, noting that these students score below their traditionally identified counterparts in both math and verbal areas at levels of significance but not educational importance and that they rebound well in their strength area by the second year of testing. Issues of administration loom large, however, in using performance-based assessment, especially on a large scale. On a smaller scale, technical adequacy issues, especially interrater reliability, also pose real threats to the use of such measures.

The Sternberg chapter also explores a new use for alternative assessment as a value-added aspect of identification of gifted learners, exploring the employment of practical and creative performance-based assessment tasks as part of a college admissions process at a selective university. Rather than discontinue the use of the SAT, which he argues measures primarily analytical abilities, he and his Rainbow Project collaborators devised a system that added additional tasks to the college application form, resulting in finding more minority students who qualified for admission during the pilot year of the initiative. His pilot use of this multifaceted testing approach at grades 4–7 also is briefly described. Sternberg concludes his chapter by asserting the need to identify for diversity and to validate tests that are successful in doing so. Such a stance provides a strong purpose for identification, yet it is clearly different from our testing history that has sought to identify the students who are most advanced in cognitive development across and within areas of learning. The Sternberg chapter then raises an important issue about the core purposes of testing for gifted programs: Should diversity trump evidence of advanced ability?

The Robinson chapter provides an important cautionary tale about the use of alternative assessments. She clearly argues for the retention of more traditional tests as a way of ensuring that underrepresented populations are not overlooked in the identification process. In crafting her argument for traditional tests, she cites literature supporting the use of both aptitude and achievement tests to find students who already are demonstrating giftedness, the majority of students we seek to find. In identifying students of promise, she suggests that such tests may be useful but far from conclusive in locating these students, suggesting that traditional measures also need to be considered. An important issue raised in her chapter is that of the purpose for which the testing is done, noting the need to provide the optimal match between the tools employed to find students and the program provided to serve them. If giftedness is defined as advanced cognitive development, then we have many traditional measures that can identify it, according to Robinson.

The Rimm, Gilmore, and Silverman chapter explores nontraditional approaches needed to score current intelligence tests to ensure that gifted students are identified appropriately for programs. Citing several concerns, ranging from tests that do not provide enough ceiling to judge who is highly gifted, to being unable to judge twice-exceptional students on a discrepancy verbal-performance score, to the use of particular subtests to judge giftedness, the authors offer concrete strategies to school and clinical psychologists in how to score and index their results to ensure gifted students are able to demonstrate what they know and what they don't know. The need for broad dissemination of the authors' findings is paramount as gifted students are being underidentified, even when an individual intelligence test is being used.

The Cramond and Kim chapter provides a comprehensive overview of the use of creativity tests for identifying creative potential in students who would be promising candidates for gifted programs, along with a review of studies of creativity programs and their effects on learning. Citing both societal and personal needs for enhancing creativity, the authors share several examples of eminent individuals and young children who possess characteristics of creativity, yet are rejected in the societal context. The chapter reminds us of the importance of the development of creative abilities in all of our gifted learners and the need to broaden our use of tools to be sure creative students, who may not be as strong academically, are identified and nurtured in programs, as well as those learners with demonstrated exceptional ability in intellectual areas. An issue raised by this chapter is the relative importance of assessing creativity to ensure that students found through such measures are not excluded from gifted programs; however, a future question is raised regarding the nature of programs that best serve the creatively gifted. In a standards-based environment, how likely will the use of research-based creativity programs be? How much should creativity dominate academic programs?

The Johnsen chapter on portfolio assessment presents an even-handed look at the issues surrounding the use of portfolios to judge student learning. Included in the chapter is a set of procedures for thinking about constructing a portfolio, several models of types of artifacts to be included, and sample rubrics for judging them. The uses range from elementary student learning in core areas to graduate school candidates' mastery of core standards. The Johnsen chapter also carefully chronicles the research on portfolios, suggesting that we have limited data on their effectiveness as a measure of authentic learning, even as their use for this purpose expands. Of particular concern is interrater reliability and educational consensus on what elements should be included to adequately reflect the scope of learning within a given time frame.

The Renzulli and Callahan chapter explores the various dimensions of constructing and using product assessments to judge the nature of learning accrued by gifted students who create a viable Type III enrichment product as a part of their program. The authors review the literature on successful curriculum models for the gifted, all of which require student products as a part of the learning experience. Consequently, the use of a well-constructed product assessment would be essential for teachers to use in judging those products. Guidelines for the development and use of such assessments are included in the chapter, as well as a case study of one such instrument already developed and in use. The authors argue convincingly that product assessment provides the most authentic way to assess the real learning of gifted students even as they demonstrate the rather difficult process for validating a product assessment tool. Thus, the issue becomes one of choice—should practitioners create their own assessments of learning or rely on those that already meet technical adequacy considerations?

The VanTassel-Baska chapter explores the issues inherent in the construction and design of performance-based assessment tasks to judge gifted students' learning. The author argues for the use of such measures to assess the authentic learning of gifted students within subject-related domains. Criteria to consider in developing such assessments are included in the chapter, along with elementary and secondary models currently in use. The chapter challenges us to consider the labor-intensive nature of performance-based assessment development in contrast to the benefits accrued for enhancing instruction. As with product assessment, the question remains about the viability of new task construction when existing instrumentation may be used.

The concluding chapter provides a comprehensive model for thinking about the use of alternative assessments within a broader context of identification and learning results. Consideration of the issues raised in Chapter 1 is provided and described with the proposed model. An alignment to the National Council for Accreditation of Teacher Education (NCATE) standards on assessment also is featured and calibrated to the proposed model for schools. The chapter concludes with a call for closer attention to the system of assessment employed that links identification though program intervention to outcome assessment. Planning effectively for gifted programs clearly requires such thinking.

Issues in Identifying Gifted Students Through Alternative Assessments

There are many issues associated with changing an identification approach for gifted learners from one type of assessment to another. Although traditional assessments have historically employed group and individual intelligence and achievement tests as the "gold standard," newer approaches to assessment have moved away from using this combination as the exclusive way to locate gifted learners. Perhaps the most popular of these nontraditional approaches is the use of nonverbal tests that purport to find more equal representation of minority and English Language Learners than the more traditional measures. Yet, performance-based assessment and creativity tests have advocates, as well, for similar reasons—their capacity to find students of color and poverty. However, these new approaches bring with them their own set of problems in use and beyond in classroom practice.

One issue that alternative assessments for identification face is nested in the larger debate over domain-specific versus general ability. In order for schools to program effectively for students identified through nonverbal assessment, they must change their current program models, which are highly verbally loaded, to a more general curriculum base that includes mathematics, especially geometry, science, and other subjects requiring spatial intelligence such as art, architecture, engineering, and mechanics, as core parts of the curriculum. Because nonverbal measures are assessing primarily general intelligence, a broader application of academic achievement must be attempted through the curriculum.

With any test for giftedness, there is the issue of ceiling effect, the situation where there are not enough test items at the top of a test to discriminate effectively among top students. The use of off-level assessment helps this situation a great deal for highly gifted students; however, the data must be used to plan programs off level, as well, a situation not often occurring in school districts, even where the data are available for making decisions. Thus, alternative assessment can fall victim to lack of provisions at the program level that would make the testing useful.

Another issue in the use of alternative assessment for identification relates to the predictive validity of the measures for success in gifted programs. Although it is criminal to not include able learners in gifted programs, it also is criminal to place them in contexts where their chance of success is severely limited by factors beyond sheer ability such as functional level of skills within subject domains, motivation, and patterns of underachievement. Studies of such validity must be carried out on these measures to assess their viability in not just finding students but also seeing that they are properly serviced in programs.

In the case of creativity and performance-based assessment, there always is the issue of sufficient coverage of a range of abilities within and across domains to tap into the relevant skills for use in school-based programs for the gifted. Each type of test uses fewer items to assess learning, thus lowering the reliability of items, a chronic problem with creativity tests over the last several decades. Moreover, these types of assessment require more labor-intensive approaches to scoring in order to ensure interrater reliability.

Yet, creative ways of combining measures such as the Lohman and Lakin chapter suggest, as well as consideration of different measures altogether, such as Bracken's CAB, point the way toward improving identification through using alternative measures in combination with other proven approaches. Sternberg's value-added approach to the university admissions process is one model for applying alternative assessment sensibly to existing procedures, as is the South Carolina performance-task assessment approach.

Issues in Assessing Gifted Student Learning Through Alternative Assessments

Just as the identification of gifted students requires multiple criteria for selection, judgment about the learning of gifted students also must employ multiple measures. Ideally, a gifted program would collect multiple types of assessment data on students annually, as shown in Table 1.1. Standardized achievement test data should be collected to demonstrate appropriate levels of mastery within the ceiling effect range of the test at the upper end or actual mastery, using off-level advanced versions of the test. Performance-based assessment should be employed pre- and postintervention to demonstrate short-term gains on higher level task demands crafted for the gifted population. A multiyear design model could be employed to assess long-term gains on product-relevant skills such as problem solving and research. Finally, portfolio assessment could be employed to assess learning processes in key areas of work. For example, use of portfolios could show how and when the integration of specific scientific research processes began or how the writing process unfolded over a period of time. Because there is a paucity of literature on the effectiveness of gifted programs as measured through student outcome data, the need is great to see an emphasis in this area included in progress for the gifted at all levels.

Assessment of how a gifted program impacts learners also is one of the most important aspects of all program development work. It is at this level of analysis that one can begin to understand the learner's level of comprehension and knowledge of what we had hoped to teach. The purpose of the assessment process is really multidimensional. It provides insight into student progress in a curriculum and pinpoints future needs in a

Table 1.1
Types of Student Assessments for Gifted Programs

Type of Assessment	Application/ Purpose	Use in Gifted Programs
Standardized achievement tests (on-level)	Mastery-oriented	To assess current levels of mastery and ensure reasonable growth
Standardized achievement tests (off-level)	Mastery-oriented	To assess "real" gifted student achievement in an area
Advanced Placement/ International Baccalaureate (secondary)	Advanced mastery in subject areas	To assess levels of gifted students' advanced learning
Performance-based (all levels)	Pre-post or time series	To assess short-term growth in advanced skills and processes
Product-based (all levels)	Pre-post over multiple years	To assess enhancement of research and problem-solving skills
Portfolios (all levels)	Evolving competencies-based	To assess the process of learning as it unfolds in key dimensions

From *Designing and Utilizing Evaluation for Gifted Program Improvement* (p. 136), by J. VanTassel-Baska and A. Feng, 2004, p. 136, Waco, TX: Prufrock Press. Copyright © 2004 by Prufrock Press. Reprinted with permission.

curricular area for a learner. As such, it is a critical tool for ongoing curricular planning. Moreover, assessment data instruct us about how well our deliberate planning of programs has fared, providing data for decision making about program improvements needed to enhance gifted student learning.

Many educators decry the emphasis on standards and accountability measures in education because of their use as punishment for teachers, schools, and districts that don't measure up. But, the very real issues of individual student learning may still be swept under the rug through such large-scale efforts. It is especially difficult to track the learning pattern of our best learners in schools due to several issues.

One issue that makes it difficult to assess gifted student learning is the absence of appropriate standardized assessments for students who are already very advanced in a subject area. If students enter grade 4 already scoring at the 95th percentile on an in-grade reading assessment, no matter how strong the teacher or the curriculum, the learning result on that same measure will reflect only minor, if any, growth gains at the end of the year. The problem rests with the assessment, not the learner's growth. If the same type of assessment tool were used off-level, at least we could assess how much further beyond grade-level expectations a gifted student had progressed. Thus, off-level assessment represents an important direction for consideration in understanding gifted students' learning.

A second issue in assessing gifted student learning is the match between the content of the assessment and the content of student learning. Because programs for the gifted pride themselves on addressing higher level thinking, problem solving, and research in the curriculum, appropriate assessments for learning must tap into these skills, yet typical school assessment rarely addresses those areas. Thus, the use of other types of assessments to show growth is warranted. The most promising directions for such growth has been the employment of performance-based measures, portfolios, and product assessments that demonstrate how advanced students are progressing in these skill areas. Pre-post or time-series designs that can illustrate student change over time are the most helpful approaches for assessing specific high-level gifted curricular outcomes. Any of the approaches mentioned can be applied in such ways for student learning to be judged.

Another issue to be aware of in assessing gifted student learning is the propensity of this population to do well on

Table 1.2
Use of Alternative Test Assessment

Advantages	Disadvantages
Identifies more members of underrepresented populations as gifted than typically found on other test measures	Assesses g-factor general intelligence in the absence of domain-specific behaviors
Includes a broader range of students in gifted programs	Includes students whose academic skills often are limited in one or more areas, thus linking predictive validity for academic work and success
Provides a technically adequate measure of g-factor ability	Does not provide clear inference for curriculum planning

Note. Alternative test assessments include nonverbal measures.

short-term, content-based assessments, while demonstrating few important gains in higher level skills. Thus, assessment that only focuses on content learning to the exclusion of more transferable skills also may be limited in tapping into the nature and depth of gifted student learning. Product assessment tools may be important for purposes of demonstrating the depth of knowledge and skills attained at a given point in time. A drawback of this approach rests with the difficulty in determining good preassessment data within the same year. Rather than relying on a postassessment-only analysis, educators could collect product assessment data over 2 or more years in order to record meaningful growth gains through this approach.

In conclusion, alternative assessment provides very important avenues for understanding who the gifted are and what they can do. Advantages and disadvantages for the use of such measures are summarized in Tables 1.2 and 1.3. Table 1.2 outlines the advantages of using nonverbal assessment tests to identify gifted learners as related to their potential for identifying g-factor intelligence through a nonverbal modality and finding more underrepresented populations. Disadvantages relate to the

Table 1.3
Use of Nonstandardized Alternative Assessment Approaches for the Identification and Learning of Gifted Students

Advantages	Disadvantages
Domain-specific or topic-specific	Lack generalizability
Sufficient ceiling to assess authentic capacity and learning results of the gifted	Challenging to develop rubrics, score, and establish interrater reliability in respect to the resources needed
Opportunity to assess higher level skills of thinking, problem solving, and metacognition	Do not assess full range of skills to be taught within any domain or across domains
Can easily be linked to content standards for design	Difficult to demonstrate technical adequacy, given the narrower scope of tasks
Offer creative response mode, found effective in motivating underrepresented populations	
Offer diagnostic information for instruction	

Note. Nonstandardized alternative assessment approaches include performance-based assessments, portfolios, and creative products.

translation of nonverbal scores into usable data for program and curriculum planning and the problems associated with placing students who may lack threshold levels of functional skills in academic domains. Table 1.3 focuses on the advantages and disadvantages of other types of alternative assessments that may be used for identification and/or learning outcomes. These types of measures include performance-based tasks, portfolios, and creative products. Advantages of these alternative assessments rest in their strong diagnostic capacity for instructional decision making, given their domain-specific and authentic learning orientations. The open-endedness and higher level thinking and problem solving required of such assessments also enhances their use with gifted populations. Major disadvantages rest with their lack of generalizability across domains, the difficulties in establishing technical adequacy, especially interrater reliability, and the scope of skills that may be tapped.

References

VanTassel-Baska, J., & Feng, A. (2004). *Designing and utilizing evaluation for gifted program improvement.* Waco, TX: Prufrock Press.

VanTassel-Baska, J., & Johnsen, S. (2007). Teacher education standards for gifted education: A vision for the future. *Gifted Child Quarterly, 51,* 289–299.

Nontraditional Strategies for Identifying Nontraditional Gifted and Talented Students

Bruce A. Bracken

Assessing nontraditional students who come from cultur-ally diverse backgrounds, low socioeconomic households, or who have limited English language proficiency has long been a concern in psychology and education (Bracken & McCallum, 1998; Ford, 1996; Ford & Harmon, 2001; McCallum, Bracken, & Wasserman, 2001). With an increasingly large and diverse student body in U.S. schools, there has been a corresponding press for equitable assessment and representative identification of ethnic and racial minority students for inclusion in special education programs, including programs for the gifted and tal-ented. Additional efforts and new directions have been required to ensure that equitable assessment and identification practices are employed for all students in U.S. schools, especially for those nontraditional students who historically have been disen-franchised by the educational system. This chapter explores two innovative and promising strategies for accurately and represen-tatively identifying diverse populations of students as gifted and talented, while reducing the sometimes biased overlays of lan-guage, culture, and poverty.

Population Diversity

In 2000, U.S. Census Bureau data reports indicated that 31,844,979 Americans spoke English as a second language and almost 2,000,000 had no English-speaking ability (U.S. Bureau of the Census, 2000). Estimates derived for the 1997 reauthorization of the Individuals With Disabilities Act (IDEA; 1990) suggest that nearly one in three people living in the U.S. was from a Black, Hispanic, Asian American, or Native American sociocultural group. As the U.S. population crossed the 300 million mark, minorities collectively have become the majority, especially in large city schools. The 2000 U.S. Census identified minority students as comprising an overwhelming majority of the student population in Miami (approximately 84%), Chicago (89%), and Houston (88%). Moreover, students who are Limited English Proficient (LEP) comprise the fastest growing demographic group in the nation, with more than 200 languages spoken in the Chicago public schools alone (Pasko, 1994).

Given these population demographics, growing concern has been voiced over the discrepancies that exist in numbers of referrals and placements of minority children in special education programs (e.g., Ford, 1996; Ford & Harmon, 2001). Although Black and Hispanic students are significantly over-represented in special education disability categories, they also are significantly underrepresented in gifted education. Just as relatively few minority students are identified as gifted, even fewer twice-exceptional students are identified as gifted due to the masking overlay of disability and the compounding effects of singular reliance on language-loaded ability tests for identification purposes. Such over- and underrepresentation statistics led the 1997 reauthorized IDEA to admonish that, "greater efforts are needed to prevent the intensification of problems connected with mislabeling . . . of minority children" (p. 4).

Underrepresentation of students from diverse backgrounds in programs for the gifted has created a large reservoir of untapped and underdeveloped talent in U.S. schools

(Passow, 1991). To better address the problem of underidentification of minority students, Maker (1996) proposed that an altered conceptual framework for gifted identification might be needed to better reflect the changing values, beliefs, and demographics of American society and educational settings; that is, accepting and appreciating the diverse gifts and talents represented by members of a diverse population. Contributing to the effects of inequitable identification, however, is the lack of an agreed upon identification procedure or definition of giftedness, which is consistently the most frequently cited barrier to identifying, placing, and providing appropriate services to gifted students (Clasen, 1992; Clasen, Middleton, & Connell, 1994; Maker, 1996; Pfeiffer, 2003; Sarouphim, 1999).

Appropriate gifted identification practices are critical because equitable placement helps ensure fair access to services, programs, and resources to all students, which are both honorable goals and legal mandates. If identification of gifted students is to be comprehensive, accessible, and fair, then efforts to identify students should be broadened beyond current practices and systematically should investigate new, promising methods and procedures. To gain a broader perspective of students' abilities, schools must employ multiple measures and multiple respondents to gain and triangulate various perspectives contributing to the identification process.

Historical Perspective

During the foundational years of the field of gifted education, researchers such as Lewis Terman and Leta Hollingworth defined giftedness as raw intellectual power measured by intelligence tests or as simply IQ. The term *giftedness* was synonymous with *intellectual giftedness*. Those students who were admitted into this new "intellectual club" often were done so on the basis of their performance on the heavily verbal-laden Stanford-Binet Intelligence Scale or one or another form of the Wechsler Scales of Intelligence. As the field evolved, a sense of elitism and limited access to programming and resources began to become associated with giftedness. To be gifted meant one had to have superior English facility, despite the fact that many notably gifted contributors to our society came to this country as English Language Learners. Due at least in part to this perception of elitism, as well as social awareness and recognition of the inherent benefits of a diverse society, the field began to consider alternative, nonintellectual methods and procedures for identifying gifted students—procedures that were intended to broaden our conceptualization of giftedness beyond English proficiency.

The remainder of this chapter will assume that the reader shares the educational and societal goals of equity, fairness, equal opportunity, and valuation of the unique talents and characteristics of our diverse American population. This author believes that the past historical mistakes made at Ellis Island and during the Eugenics Movement belong in the past, and should not be repeated by narrow-minded, protectionist, exclusionary approaches to assessment and intervention. Although there remain some in education and testing who argue for a verbally elitist exclusionary doctrine in gifted education, this author does not see the value of such an ethno- or linguistic-centric approach.

This chapter will focus on several unique instruments that have evolved in an effort to respond to the public and professional call for the assessment of students' abilities in a fair and equitable manner. Two new instruments developed on a model of fairness will be explored, and other instruments will be mentioned in passing. The two primary instruments addressed in this chapter are the Universal Nonverbal Intelligence Test (UNIT; Bracken & McCallum, 1998), which assesses cognitive functioning from a nonverbal assessment paradigm, and the Clinical Assessment of Behavior (CAB; Bracken & Keith, 2004a), which assesses teachers' and parents' perceptions of students' behavioral functioning, including important behaviors associated with giftedness (e.g., social skills, competence, executive functioning).

Nonverbal Testing

Assessing the cognitive functioning of individuals who lack the manifest language to demonstrate their latent knowledge has been problematic for as long as clinicians assessed intelligence. During the early 1800s, French clinicians were among the first to assess and attempt to remediate the intellectual abilities of children with limited language. In the landmark clinical case, Jean Itard sought to assess the abilities of Victor, the Wild Boy of Aveyron, and determine whether Victor could acquire functional language (Carrey, 1995; Itard, 1932). In addition to Itard, additional historical figures have addressed the problem of assessing the intellectual abilities of children who could not or would not speak (e.g., Seguin, 1907). Seguin also is notable for his development of one of the earliest nonverbal ability measures, the Seguin Form Board. Itard and Sequin recognized the value and importance of verbal facility, in general, but were astute to recognize that not all individuals are capable of demonstrating their abilities best through a verbal mode.

Nonverbal tests have proliferated during the century since Itard's and Seguin's work as a result of significant advances in psychometric theory and their application to nonverbal assessment approaches. During the past 20 years, nonverbal ability tests have become especially useful in clinical and educational practices throughout the United States because of the rapidly shifting world population and the resettlement of immigrants into communities of all sizes throughout the country. Because of the effort to climb aboard the "nonverbal bandwagon," many language-loaded ability tests have applied the "nonverbal" moniker to performance tasks with verbal directions (e.g., Wechsler Performance Scale subtests). Ironically, most of these "nonverbal" tests continue to employ verbal directions and sometimes require verbal responses, as well (e.g., Reynolds & Kamphaus, 2005). As such, a nonverbal intelligence test with verbal directions administered to a person with limited English proficiency is as much a test of verbal ability as a group-administered test with written directions is a test of reading ability when administered to students with limited literacy skills. Such misnamed nonverbal tests assess construct irrelevant variables (e.g., language abilities, verbal comprehension) as much or more than the intended construct (i.e., general intelligence), which is just the unintentional measurement bias clinicians were attempting to avoid in the first place.

Because of emotionally charged reactions to legal and illegal immigration within the United States and consequent ethno- and linguistic-centric protectionist beliefs, some Americans have taken a view that a high level of English proficiency is the defining characteristic for being considered as gifted. Similarly, some researchers argue that English facility predicts academic achievement better than alternative assessment approaches (e.g., Lohman, 2006), and therefore verbal tests of ability should be the gold standard in the gifted identification process. Such an argument, taken out of the emotionally charged linguistic arena and considered within the visual modality, would suggest by extension that because sightedness is a good prediction of ability to read print and visually impaired students cannot read a written test without modification, those students are not as bright as visually sighted children who can read and score well on written verbal tests. Just as visual limitations do not define or set the limits of a person's intelligence, neither does his or her language or culture of origin.

Overlay students' language facility with race, ethnic heritage, socioeconomic status, parents' educational levels, number of family members living in the home, or whether one, both, or neither biological parents are rearing the children, and the sociocultural and educational situation becomes exponentially complex. The goal in education is simple: to integrate a diverse population of students, ensure that each student achieves his or her maximum potential, treat all students equitably and with sensitivity, and try our very best to *disprove* the predictive validity of any measure that asserts that a child will not achieve well.

Universal Nonverbal Intelligence Test

The Universal Nonverbal Intelligence Test (UNIT; Bracken & McCallum, 1998) has become a popular and internationally used individual, nonverbally administered test of general intelligence. Importantly, the UNIT is an entirely language-free, comprehensive test of cognitive ability; that is, the UNIT requires no receptive or expressive language from the examiner or the examinee for the administration of a diverse collection of subtests. Unique to the UNIT are the considerable technical adequacy and fairness data presented in the UNIT Examiner's Manual, with estimates of reliability posted by gender, race/ethnicity, exceptional/clinical students, and for important decision-making points (i.e., mental retardation and gifted levels of cognitive functioning). Additionally, the UNIT Examiner's Manual presents a wide array of construct, criterion-related, and content validity evidence, with considerable fairness evidence presented, as well. Because of its wide popularity as an individual clinical tool, a group-administered companion instrument has been developed and is currently being standardized (i.e., UNIT Group Ability Test [UNIT-GAT]; Bracken & McCallum, in press). The UNIT-GAT extends the desirable features of the individual test to a group-administration format for the purposes of screening large numbers of students (e.g., gifted screening) in an efficient manner.

Theory and Structure of the UNIT

The individually administered UNIT is a six-subtest comprehensive measure of intelligence that assesses four important areas of cognitive functioning, including working memory, reasoning, and symbolic and nonsymbolic processing. These four abilities are combined and overlay six individual subtests in an interlocking two-by-two model (see Figure 2.1). The UNIT includes three subtests on the Memory scale (i.e., Symbolic Memory, Spatial Memory, Objective Memory) and three subtests on the Reasoning scale (i.e., Cube Design, Analogic Reasoning, Mazes). Of these six subtests, three rely heavily on verbal mediation to solve the task and contribute to the Symbolic scale (i.e., Symbolic Memory, Objective Memory, and Analogic Reasoning), while the three remaining subtests include content that is largely nonsymbolic in nature and con-

	Memory Subtests	Reasoning Subtests
Symbolic Subtests	Symbolic Memory Objective Memory	Analogic Reasoning
Nonsymbolic Subtests	Spatial Memory	Cube Design Mazes

Figure 2.1. UNIT theoretical model and subtest assignment.

tribute to the Nonsymbolic scale (i.e., Spatial Memory, Cube Design, and Mazes).

The six UNIT subtests can be combined to form three distinct batteries, depending on the examiner's needs. The initial memory subtest and reasoning subtest form a two-subtest 15-minute Abbreviated Battery intended for intellectual screening. The first two memory and reasoning subtests create a 30-minute Standard Battery intended for placement and eligibility decision making. When all six subtests are combined, they comprise the Extended Battery, which requires about 45 minutes to administer and is intended for eligibility testing and providing additional diagnostic information. The UNIT scale compositions and scoring software allow for different combinations of subtests to form the Abbreviated and Standard batteries.

The UNIT was designed to provide a fair assessment of intelligence for all students, but especially minority children and children of poverty, who historically have been over- and underrepresented in programs for the mentally retarded and gifted, respectively (Rycraft, 1990). This issue of misidentification has become especially important given that the U.S. Office of Civil Rights has begun investigating school systems nationally for instances of gross over- and underrepresentation of students in special education programs (e.g., Ulik, 1997). In an effort to address the issue of fair assessment for children, regardless of their gender, race, nation of origin, or exceptional condition, the UNIT authors developed the test based on a model of fairness and included a chapter in the Examiner's Manual dedicated to fairness in testing. As a result of these efforts, the

UNIT subtests are 100% nonverbal, demonstrate excellent psychometric qualities, and are low in cultural content (i.e., depict common objects in test items).

Test characteristics such as those included in the UNIT development lead to fairer assessment of children for whom traditional language-loaded and culture-bound intelligence tests would be otherwise inappropriate. However, fairness cannot simply be claimed, it must be demonstrated empirically. As part of the empirical examination of UNIT fairness, every UNIT item was reviewed by a comprehensive "sensitivity panel" and subjected to extensive Differential Item Functioning (DIF) bias analyses as part of the developmental process. An independent DIF investigation was also conducted on deaf students, with favorable evidence in both instances and no items identified as being biased (Bracken & McCallum, 1998; Maller, 2000).

The UNIT has a normative sample of 2,100 children and adolescents, from ages 5 to 17 years, 11 months. An additional 1,700 students were tested for UNIT reliability, validity, and fairness studies. Average reliability coefficients for the four UNIT scales range from .86 to .91 across the Standard and Extended batteries, and the Full Scale IQ (FSIQ) reliabilities of the Abbreviated, Standard, and Extended batteries were .91, .93, and .93, respectively. Important for gifted identification, the UNIT Full Scale IQ reliabilities for gifted students are .93, .94, and .93, for the Abbreviated, Standard, and Extended batteries, respectively. The UNIT also demonstrates essentially identical reliabilities for White, Black, and Hispanic students.

Although large differences in mean scores between groups (e.g., males and females; White and Black students) are not an a priori indication of test bias, mean score differences and their implications are discussed frequently in both professional and lay media because of their personal and societal consequences. Consequential validity is the one form of validity generally not addressed or mentioned by advocates of the status quo in identification practices (Bracken, 2005). Therefore, in addition to the many fairness analyses cited in the UNIT Examiner's manual, UNIT consequential validity was assessed in matched sample comparisons of White students with Hispanic, Black, Native

American, Asian American, Pacific Islander, and bilingual children, and children residing in Ecuador. Additionally, mean score comparisons between a matched sample of deaf and non-deaf children are reported in the UNIT Examiner's Manual. As compared to traditional language-loaded intelligence tests, the sizeable reductions in the typical mean score discrepancies between the various samples when assessed on the UNIT appear related to the minimization of cultural content and the removal of language from the UNIT assessment process.

The UNIT manual also reports a validation study with 160 gifted students in which the UNIT produced significantly higher mean Full Scale IQ (i.e., 117.64) for previously identified high-ability students than a matched sample from the standardization sample (i.e., 104.14). Based on promising preliminary analyses, the UNIT was employed as one of two cognitive ability tests in a federally supported curriculum scale-up study, Project Athena (Bracken, VanTassel-Baska, Brown, & Feng, 2007).

UNIT in Practice and Research

The UNIT was employed in Project Athena, funded by a Jacob K. Javits grant administered through the U.S. Department of Education. The project is a demonstration intervention study, designed in part to scale up a nationally validated language arts curriculum designed for high-ability learners. As a curriculum intervention study, Project Athena employed an experimental research design that randomized the assignment of classrooms of students and teachers in grades 3–5 to comparison and experimental instructional conditions. The project was implemented in 15 schools, in 7 school districts across 3 states (Maryland, South Carolina, Virginia). One of the primary objectives for Project Athena was to develop and implement instrumentation sensitive to low socioeconomic learners for the purposes of identification and assessment of learning (i.e., equitable assessment and identification). The ethnic composition of the sample was diverse, with 43% White, 27.5% Black, 18% Hispanic, and 2.4% Asian American students participating. The remaining students (9.1%) were identified as Pacific Islander, Native

American, or "Other." Ethnic or racial minority students comprised 53.5% of the Project Athena student sample. Gender was approximately evenly divided within and across groups.

The two cognitive ability tests used in Project Athena included the Verbal and Nonverbal scales of the Cognitive Abilities Test (CogAT; Lohman & Hagen, 2001) and the Abbreviated battery of the Universal Nonverbal Intelligence Test (UNIT; Bracken & McCallum, 1998). Of interest in the project was the sensitivity of the two instruments for identifying gifted students, especially students from diverse cultural backgrounds.

Not all students were tested on both instruments due to variations in the research protocol across participating districts, student absenteeism, and so on. For those students who were assessed on both instruments, we found that by using two nonverbal measures of intelligence and one verbal measure, we identified nearly twice as many Title One students as gifted as compared to the school districts' identification procedures. Of 253 students identified as intellectually gifted using a standard score or IQ $\geq$ 120, 94 students had been identified by the school districts and an additional 159 were identified by the Project Athena assessments. Using a minimal cut-score of 130, a total of 64 students were identified, with 29 identified by the districts and an additional 35 identified by Project Athena. Importantly, for those students with IQs at 120 or above, when identified by the UNIT, 21% were Black; when the CogAT Nonverbal and Verbal scales were used, 8.8% and 9.8% of those identified were Black.

With respect to equitable assessment practices, the Project Athena identification measures nearly doubled the number of Title One students identified as intellectually gifted by including nonverbal tests of ability in the assessment process. When the UNIT was employed, the identification rate of Black students (i.e., 21%) nearly matched their representation in the overall sample (i.e., 27.5%). These research outcomes illustrate the benefits of combining two or more cognitive ability tests in the process of identifying gifted students and underscore the importance of including nonverbal ability tests in the process of identifying low-income students who are gifted. These results also highlight the importance of recognizing that *different* tests may help identify *different* students as gifted, even when the tests purport to measure the same general construct (see Bracken, 1988; Wasserman & Bracken, 2002, for a more detailed explanation of why similar tests may produce dissimilar results).

Clinical Assessment of Behavior

Historically, Durr (1960) lamented the lack of consensus in terminology and definitions related to giftedness and the lack of agreed-upon IQ cut-scores for identification. Durr additionally recognized that some researchers believed that IQ was a necessary but insufficient criterion for gifted identification, and he commented further that "Other writers define the gifted by scores on achievement tests. [But] here again, there is no consistent cutting point" (1960, p. 75). Since the 1960s, efforts to identify gifted and talented students have broadened beyond their performance on verbal ability tests (e.g., Ashman & Vukelich, 1983) and have begun to include additional procedures, such as teacher-completed rating scales. Among the earliest rating scales for gifted identification was the Scales for Rating the Behavioral Characteristics of Superior Students (SRBCSS; Renzulli, Smith, White, Callahan, & Hartman, 1976). The SRBCSS and similar scales were noteworthy because they added a formal third-party element to the identification process, believing that teachers could contribute meaningfully to the identification process.

During the three decades since the publication of the SRBCSS, the number of behavior rating scales used for the identification of gifted students has proliferated to more than 30 (Jarosewich, Pfeiffer, & Morris, 2002). Among the more widely used scales there generally is a broader range of behaviors assessed and a more contemporary conception of giftedness than was found among early rating scales. The most contemporary instruments, including the Gifted Rating Scales (GRS; Pfeiffer & Jarosewich, 2003) and the UNIT Gifted Screening Scales (UNIT-GSS; McCallum & Bracken, 2007), have extended the pool of quality scales even further and provide a comprehensive list of behavioral indicators consistent with various definitions of gifted and talented.

Because teachers frequently interact with and observe students in a variety of contexts, they are in a unique position to serve a central role in the identification of gifted students. Yet, concerns persist over whether teachers are qualified to make judgments about gifted students' behaviors. Rohrer (1995) expressed concern that teachers' preconceived notions of giftedness could preclude children with certain personality traits from gifted programs; however, Rohrer also found that teachers accurately recognized potential in students who would not be considered the stereotypical gifted student. Additional potential problems in the use of behavior rating scales include the possibility that teachers may be unduly influenced by scale headings, may be sensitive to item arrangement and organization, or may easily recognize item content and intent. Moreover, on most gifted rating scales teachers may distort their ratings (e.g., "fake good" or "fake bad"), depending on their feelings about the students they are rating.

A new instrument contributing to the assessment of gifted and talented students addresses all of these aforementioned practical and potential scaling problems. The Clinical Assessment of Behavior (CAB; Bracken & Keith, 2004a) is a comprehensive teacher- and parent-completed behavior rating scale for children and adolescents (ages 2–18 years). The CAB randomly distributes items consistent with gifted and talented behaviors across matched 70-item parent and teacher scales that assess both disordered and adaptive behaviors. Items on the CAB present behaviors from both a positive, as well as negative, orientation to help conceal their interpretive intent. Importantly, the CAB forms include no scale headings to identify relevant item-to-scale associations, adaptive and maladaptive items are mingled throughout the instrument, and the CAB includes two veracity scales designed to identify possible rater distortion. The CAB also includes a computer scoring system, which makes the scoring and interpretation process that much more accurate and objective (Bracken & Keith, 2004b).

The Clinical Assessment of Behavior-Teacher Form (CAB-T) assesses behaviors across 4 primary scales and 12 clusters. The CAB-T is a highly reliable and comprehensive measure of psychosocial adjustment for a broad age range of students (i.e., 5–18 years). The CAB Examiner's Manual presents convincing construct validity evidence (e.g., factor structure), strong concurrent validity as compared to the Behavioral Assessment System for Children (BASC; Reynolds & Kamphaus, 1992) and the Devereux Scales of Mental Disorders (DSMD; Naglieri, LeBuffe, & Pfeiffer, 1994), and diagnostic accuracy as shown in contrasted group studies.

The CAB parent- and teacher-completed rating scales can be used easily and inexpensively to complement existing instruments and procedures by providing objective third-party data on gifted student behaviors, data that have beneficial implications for school district identification protocols, professional development, and classroom practice. In two separate studies Bracken and Brown (2006a, 2006b) investigated the criterion-related validity of CAB-T ratings as a means of identifying gifted students. In the first study, the ability of the CAB to discriminate between students who were previously identified as gifted and talented and those students without identified exceptionalities was investigated. The second study investigated the extent to which CAB ratings of students' behaviors were consistent with the outcomes of two objective measures of cognitive functioning.

The first study, Bracken and Brown (2006a), provided preliminary support for the utility of the CAB Gifted and Talented adaptive cluster and other corresponding scales and clusters in the identification process. In this contrasted-groups investigation, 22 teachers and 2 administrators matched 45 students who previously had been identified as gifted under local district guidelines and procedures with 45 regular education students on the basis of grade, race, and gender. Importantly, the gifted students previously had been identified by means other than the CAB; that is, none of the students were identified as gifted on the basis of their performance on the instrument being studied. None of the regular education students were disordered or had been diagnosed as exceptional in any way. The sample included children and adolescents across the age spectrum from 5-year-olds (kindergarten students) to 18-year-olds (12th-grade students), and the subsamples were matched quite well on the basis of gender and race/ethnicity. The sample also was heterogeneous in terms of race and ethnicity, with approximately 13% of the sample representing Black, Asian American, or Hispanic backgrounds. All 24 raters were White.

Gifted and talented students' mean scores were not statistically different from the mean scores of nongifted students on scales measuring internalizing and externalizing problem behaviors or adaptive behaviors. As compared to their nongifted peers, the gifted and talented students also demonstrated significantly fewer behaviors associated with specific psychosocial disorders (e.g., conduct problems, bullying, aggression, anxiety, depression), as well as four educational exceptionalities (i.e., Attention Deficit/Hyperactivity Disorder, Autism Spectrum Disorders, learning disabilities, and mental retardation) and the total scale score (i.e., CAB Behavioral Index; CBI). Although the regular education students' clinical cluster scores hovered around the normative mean of 50, the gifted students' scores were one-half to one full standard deviation below the normative mean. These findings demonstrate that the gifted students were perceived by their teachers to be as well adjusted as or better adjusted than their nongifted peers.

Significant mean score differences were found between the gifted and regular education students on the Competence scale, indicating higher levels of perceived and rated competence behaviors among the gifted and talented students. The gifted students also demonstrated significantly higher mean scores on adaptive clusters in the areas of Executive Function and Gifted and Talented, with these mean adaptive cluster scores exceeding one standard deviation above the means of the regular education students. As such, the pattern of mean scores on the CAB-T scale and cluster ratings effectively discriminated between those students previously identified as gifted and talented and those nongifted students enrolled in regular education. Additionally, the pattern of clinical and adaptive scores, as well as the total

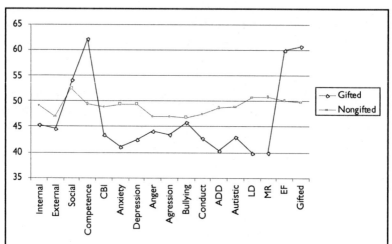

Figure 2.2. Graphical display of gifted and nongifted students' profiles on the CAB-T scales and clusters.

Note. Internal = internalizing; External = externalizing; Social = social skills; CBI = CAB Behavioral Index; Conduct = conduct problems; ADD = Attention Deficit Disorder; Autism = Autism Spectrum Disorders; LD = learning disability; MR = mental retardation; EF = executive function; Gifted = gifted and talented.

scale score (CBI) highlights that gifted and talented students' demonstrated overall better psychosocial adjustment than their nongifted peers.

Figure 2.2 presents a graphical display of the mean score differences between the gifted and nongifted students on each of the CAB clinical and adaptive scales and clusters. It can be readily seen that the gifted students were rated considerably higher (i.e., $d > 1.0$) on the Competence scale and the Executive Function and Gifted and Talented clusters. Also, it can be seen that the gifted and talented students evidenced fewer behavioral problems as compared to their peers. Importantly, this pattern is consistent with known characteristics and strengths of gifted students as compared to their nongifted peers.

As a follow-up to the initial contrasted-group study, a second study (Bracken & Brown, 2006b) was conducted on students who had been assessed on objective ability tests and were functioning at the gifted level, intellectually. The kindergarten through third-grade sample in this study was gathered in a large urban school district in Northern Virginia and a midsized rural

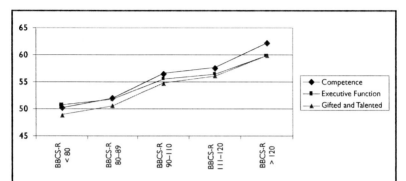

Figure 2.3. Graphical display of teacher ratings on CAB Competence Scale and Executive Function and Gifted and Talented Clusters according to assessed ability on the BBCS-R.

district in Coastal Virginia as part of Project Clarion. Project Clarion is a federally funded curriculum scale-up intervention project with science as its curricular focus. Several instruments were administered to participating students to gather baseline data during the project; this investigation includes all students who were administered one or both of two ability tests, the Bracken Basic Concept Scale–Revised (BBCS-R; Bracken, 1998) and the Naglieri Nonverbal Ability Test (NNAT; Naglieri, 1996). The second condition for inclusion in this investigation was that the students also had to have been rated by their respective teachers on the Clinical Assessment of Behavior (CAB; Bracken & Keith, 2004a). In total, 795 students had both BBCS-R and CAB scores, 752 students had both NNAT and CAB scores, and 465 students had scores entered for all three instruments.

To assess the ability of the CAB to differentiate different levels of cognitive functioning across the ability spectrum, the BBCS-R and NNAT distributions were divided into five ability levels (i.e., total test scores < 80; 80–89; 90–110; 111–120; > 120). As can be seen in Figures 2.3 and 2.4, the CAB ability scales/clusters create similar linear relationships whether the students' assessed abilities were verbal or nonverbal. This linear relationship demonstrates that teachers who complete the 5-minute CAB Teacher form accurately can describe students' ability-related behaviors. These findings also suggest that the

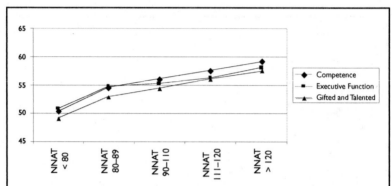

Figure 2.4. Graphical display of teacher ratings on CAB Competence Scale and Executive Function and Gifted and Talented Clusters according to assessed ability on the NNAT.

CAB appears to be useful for differentiating students' ability levels.

Of specific interest, however, was how teachers described high-ability students on the basis of the adaptive and maladaptive behaviors. Once students had been identified as "high ability" on either the BBCS-R (n = 65) or NNAT (n = 143) using a cut-score of 120 on the two objective measures, teachers' ratings of adaptive and maladaptive behaviors were culled and compared to students in the general population.

Students identified as high ability on either the BBCS-R or NNAT differed significantly from the general population on *all* CAB scales and clusters. Figure 2.5 graphically displays the nature of the differences between the high-ability students' behavior as compared to the general population normative sample mean T-score of 50. As can be seen in the two graphed lines, the high-ability students were perceived as having significantly better adaptive behaviors (i.e., social skills, competence, executive function, gifted and talented) and significantly fewer problem behaviors in all areas. These results are consistent with the Bracken and Brown (2006a) study, with the exception that social skills also were significant in this study. Teachers rated students who were identified as high ability on the BBCS-R generally higher on the CAB ability scales (i.e., competence, executive function, gifted and talented) than when the student

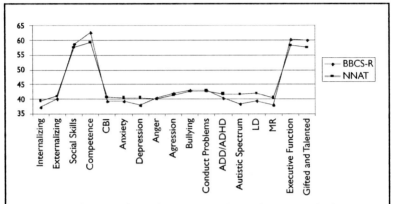

Figure 2.5. CAB profiles of students with total test standard scores > 120 on the BBCS-R (*n* = 65) or NNAT (*n* = 143).

Note. CBI = CAB Behavioral Index; ADD/ADHD = Attention Deficit Disorder and Attention Deficit/Hyperactivity Disorder; Autism Spectrum = Autism Spectrum Disorders; LD = learning disability; MR = mental retardation.

was identified as high ability on the NNAT, which suggests that teachers are more attuned to gifted students' verbal skills than nonverbal skills.

In combination, the two studies demonstrate that gifted students are rated as having higher levels of social skills and competence, executive functioning, and gifted and talented type behaviors than nongifted students on the CAB-T. Importantly, the CAB-T also showed that the gifted students overall had much better adaptive functioning and fewer problem behaviors than the typical student in the general population, thus supporting the literature that suggests that gifted students are generally as well-adjusted or better adjusted psychosocially as their nongifted peers (Caplan, Henderson, Henderson, & Fleming, 2002; Olszewski-Kubilius, 1995).

For many years, school districts have wrestled with better ways to identify gifted and talented students with brief, equitable, objective, and more inclusive measures, as well as simultaneously melding methods of identifying twice-exceptional learners into the overall assessment process. The CAB allows teachers of the gifted and talented the option for quick, easy, and comprehensive behavioral assessment of students between the ages of 5 and 18 years. The CAB-T provides the additional benefit of using a single instrument to identify both traditional and nontraditional gifted and talented students, as well as twice-exceptional K–12 gifted students.

The CAB-T demonstrates considerable potential for complementing extant verbal and nonverbal procedures employed in the schools for identifying gifted and talented students (e.g., cognitive and academic assessments), and it allows for meaningful triangulation of diagnostic information for improved and more comprehensive decision making. The CAB Teacher scale provides reliable and accurate third-party ratings of behaviors consistent with gifted and talented students, as well as yields an overview of each student's overall level of psychosocial adjustment. The CAB-T has the benefit of being easy to administer, brief, and computer scored and interpreted, and it has excellent psychometric properties for students ages 5–18 years.

Summary

This chapter described two nontraditional measures that hold promise for identifying gifted and talented students, especially those students who historically have been underidentified using traditional language-loaded procedures. The UNIT provides an assessment of students' cognitive functioning in a completely nonverbal manner, while also reducing cultural content. The UNIT has been shown to contribute to a significant increase in the numbers of identified low-income and minority gifted students.

As a 5-minute, teacher-completed behavior rating scale, the CAB illustrates the ability of teachers to accurately identify students' level of cognitive functioning across the ability spectrum and identify high levels of competence, social skills, executive functioning, and gifted and talented related behaviors. With diverse item content distributed throughout its scales, the avoidance of scale headings, the inclusion of two veracity scales, and its easy-to-use computer scoring software, the CAB provides an objective scoring, interpretation, and identification process.

As such, the nontraditional instruments and procedures addressed in this chapter, as well as others not mentioned due to space limitations, provide researchers and practitioners with additional promising methods for the triangulation of relevant information in the process of identifying traditional, twice-exceptional, or nontraditional gifted and talented students. Importantly, the alternative approaches addressed in this chapter emphasize an enlightened orientation to gifted identification and a flexible effort to fairly and equitably identify and include a more diverse student body in programs for the gifted—an orientation and approach that is sensitive to the consequences and limitations of relying solely on the ethno- and linguistic-centered, and singularly verbal proficiency orientations and approaches of the past.

References

Ashman, S. S., & Vukelich, C. (1983). The effect of different types of nomination forms on teachers' identification of gifted children. *Psychology in the Schools, 20*, 518–527.

Bracken, B. A. (1988). Ten psychometric reasons why similar tests produce dissimilar results. *Journal of School Psychology, 26*, 155–166.

Bracken, B. A. (1998). *Bracken Basic Concept Scale–Revised*. San Antonio, TX: Harcourt Assessments.

Bracken, B. A. (2005, November). *Identifying gifted students: Unintended self-reflection*. Paper presented at the annual meeting of the National Association for Gifted Children, Louisville, KY.

Bracken, B. A., & Brown, E. F. (2006a). Behavioral identification and assessment of gifted and talented students. *Journal of Psychoeducational Assessment, 24*, 112–122.

Bracken, B. A., & Brown, E. F. (2006b). *Use of the Clinical Assessment of Behavior Teacher Scale (CAB-T) to identify objectively identified gifted students*. Manuscript submitted for publication.

Bracken, B. A., & Keith, L. K. (2004a). *Professional manual for the Clinical Assessment of Behavior*. Lutz, FL: Psychological Assessment Resources.

Bracken, B. A., & Keith, L. K. (2004b). *CAB scoring program*. Lutz, FL: Psychological Assessment Resources.

Bracken, B. A., & McCallum, R. S. (1998). *Universal Nonverbal Intelligence Test*. Itasca, IL: Riverside.

Bracken, B. A., & McCallum, R. S. (in press.). *UNIT Group Ability Test*. Itasca, IL: Riverside.

Bracken, B. A., VanTassel-Baska, J., Brown, E. F., & Feng, A. (2007). Project Athena: A tale of two studies. In J. VanTassel-Baska & T. Stambaugh (Eds.), *Overlooked gems: A national perspective on low-income promising learners* (pp. 63–67). Washington, DC: National Association for Gifted Children.

Caplan, S. M., Henderson, C. E., Henderson, J., & Fleming, D. (2002). Socioemotional factors contributing to adjustment among early-entrance college students. *Gifted Child Quarterly, 46*, 124–134.

Carrey, N. J. (1995). Itard's 1828 memoire on "mutism caused by a lesion of the intellectual functions": A historical analysis. *Journal of the American Academy of Child and Adolescent Psychiatry, 34*, 1655–1661.

Clasen, D. (1992). Changing peer stereotypes on high-achieving adolescents. *NASSP Bulletin, 76*, 95–102.

Clasen, D., Middleton, J., & Connell, T. (1994). Assessing artistic and problem-solving performance in minority and nonminority students using a nontraditional multidimensional approach. *Gifted Child Quarterly, 38*, 27–37.

Durr, W. K. (1960). Characteristics of gifted children: Ten years of research. *Gifted Child Quarterly, 1*, 75–79.

Ford, D. Y. (1996). *Reversing underachievement among gifted Black students: Promising practices and programs.* New York: Teachers College Press.

Ford, D., & Harmon, D. (2001). Providing access to gifted education for culturally diverse students. *Journal of Secondary Gifted Education, 3*, 141–143.

Individuals With Disabilities Education Act, 20 U.S.C. §1401 et seq. (1990).

Itard, J. M. G. (1932). *The wild boy of Aveyron.* New York: Appleton-Century-Crofts.

Jarosewich, T., Pfeiffer, S. I., & Morris, J. (2002). Identifying gifted students using teacher rating scales: A review of existing instruments. *Journal of Psychoeducational Assessment, 20*, 322–336.

Lohman, D. F. (2006). Beliefs about differences between ability and accomplishment: From folk theories to cognitive science. *Roeper Review, 29*, 32–40.

Lohman, D. F., & Hagen, E. P. (2001). *Cognitive Abilities Test (CogAt), Form 6.* Itasca, IL: Riverside.

Maker, J. (1996). Identification of gifted minority students: A national problem, needed changes, and a promising solution. *Gifted Child Quarterly, 40*, 41–50.

Maller, S. J. (2000). Item invariance in four subtests of the Universal Nonverbal Intelligence Test (UNIT) across groups of deaf and hearing children. *Journal of Psychoeducational Assessment, 18*, 240–254.

McCallum, R. S., & Bracken, B. A. (2007). *Gifted Screening Scales.* Itasca, IL: Riverside.

McCallum, R. S., Bracken, B. A., & Wasserman, J. (2001). *Essentials of nonverbal assessment.* New York: Wiley.

Naglieri, J. A. (1996). *Naglieri Nonverbal Ability Test.* San Antonio, TX: The Psychological Corporation.

Naglieri, J. A., LeBuffe, P. A., & Pfeiffer, S. I. (1994). *Devereux Scales of Mental Disorder.* San Antonio, TX: The Psychological Corporation.

Olszewski-Kubilius, P. (1995). A summary of research regarding early entrance to college. *Roeper Review, 18*, 121–126.

Pasko, J. R. (1994). Chicago—Don't miss it. *Communique, 23*(4), 2.

Passow, A. (1991). Urban schools a second (?) or third (?) time around: Priorities for curricular and instructional reform. *Education and Urban Society, 23*, 243–255.

Pfeiffer, S. I. (2003). Challenges and opportunities for students who are gifted: What the experts say. *Gifted Child Quarterly, 47*, 161–169.

Pfeiffer, S. I., & Jarosewich, T. (2003). *Gifted Rating Scales.* San Antonio, TX: The Psychological Corporation.

Renzulli, J. S., Smith, L. H., White, A. J., Callahan, C. M., & Hartman, R. K. (1976). *Scales for Rating the Behavioral Characteristics of Superior Students.* Mansfield Center, CT: Creative Learning Press.

Reynolds, C. R., & Kamphaus, R. (1992). *Behavior Assessment System for Children.* Circle Pines, MN: American Guidance Service.

Reynolds, C. R., & Kamphaus, R. W. (2005). *Reynolds Intellectual Assessment System.* Lutz, FL: Psychological Assessment Resources.

Rohrer, J. C. (1995). Primary teacher conceptions of giftedness: Image, evidence, and nonevidence. *Journal for the Education of the Gifted, 18*, 269–283.

Rycraft, J. R. (1990). Behind the walls of poverty: Economically disadvantaged gifted and talented children. *Early Child Development and Care, 63*, 139–147.

Sarouphim, K. M. (1999). Discovering multiple intelligences through a performance-based assessment: Consistency with independent ratings. *Exceptional Children, 65*, 151–161.

Seguin, E. (1907). *Idiocy and its treatment by the physiological method.* New York: Teachers College.

Ulik, C. (1997, January 6). Civil rights officials check Tempe schools; limited-English programs studied. *The Arizona Republic/The Phoenix Gazette, Tempe Community Section*, p. 1.

U.S. Bureau of the Census. (2000). *U.S. Summary: 2000*. Washington, DC: Author.

Wasserman, J. D., & Bracken, B. A. (2002). Selecting appropriate tests: Psychometric and pragmatic considerations. In J. F. Carlson & B. B. Waterman (Eds.), *Social and personal assessment of school-aged children: Developing interventions for educational and clinical settings* (pp. 18–43). Needham Heights, MA: Allyn & Bacon.

Nonverbal Test Scores as One Component of an Identification System: Integrating Ability, Achievement, and Teacher Ratings

David F. Lohman & Joni Lakin

> There is always an easy solution to every
> human problem—neat, plausible, and wrong.
> H. L. Mencken (1949, p. 443)

Poor and minority students are underrepresented in programs that serve academically advanced and talented students (Donovan & Cross, 2002). Because of this, program administrators have searched for alternative procedures for identifying academic talent that would increase the ethnic, linguistic, and socioeconomic diversity of children in their programs. Nonverbal ability tests can help educators achieve these goals. Indeed, the best individual and group-administered ability tests long have incorporated nonverbal subtests (e.g., Lorge & Thorndike, 1954; Wechsler, 1949). But, exactly how should nonverbal tests be used? Can they be used as the primary tool for screening students for participation in a program for the gifted? Are they culture-fair? Do they eliminate differences between different ethnic or language groups? Do they predict academic success about as well as tests that have verbal content?

Although some researchers have answered yes to all of these questions, others have taken the opposite stance on several of these points. These critics note that the nonverbal score generally has been viewed as a supplementary measure of ability for examinees who are native speakers of the language in which the test is administered and as a surrogate measure of ability for those who are disabled or who are not native speakers of that language. These critics point out that nonverbal tests are not simply verbal tests shorn of language. Rather, they say, the constructs that nonverbal tests measure underrepresent the construct of intelligence. In their view, language is a particularly powerful vehicle for representing abstract and nuanced relationships that cannot be captured in the well-structured geometric shapes used on figural reasoning tests. The bottom line for the critics, then, is that eliminating language also eliminates much of what we mean by intelligent thinking.

In this chapter, we attempt to address both the claims made by advocates of nonverbal tests and the cautions and counterarguments offered by their critics. Although our presentation is not technical, we occasionally will give reference to supporting research. If the research is new and not widely available, then we sometimes give a brief summary of it. However, our main goal is to describe an approach for identifying academically talented students from all backgrounds that incorporates nonverbal tests as one part of a more comprehensive talent identification system.

Six principles guide the approach that we describe. First, to identify the right students, one must assess those aptitudes needed to succeed in the learning context. The development of different kinds of expertise requires different aptitudes. Therefore, one must specify the kind of competence that one hopes that students will develop and the demands that educational systems that develop competence place on the students. Second, nonverbal tests can be used to supplement verbal and quantitative measures, but are not interchangeable with those tests, especially for program decision making. Third, different inferences from test scores require different comparison or norm groups. Common norms and standards are appropriate for inferences about a student's level of development in a domain. However, inferences about aptitude require comparisons to others who have had similar opportunities to acquire the knowledge and skills measured by a test. Using common norms to estimate the abilities of all students—regardless of their opportunities to learn—leads either to the use of tests that are inferior measures of academic aptitude or to the identification of very few minority students. Fourth, students of the same age who are inferred to have particular academic talents often have markedly different instructional needs. An undifferentiated label such as *gifted* does not usefully guide decisions about the kind of instruction students need, especially as they mature. Fifth, the label *gifted* implies a permanent superiority that misleads. The majority of primary-level children who obtain high scores on an ability or achievement test generally do not retain their status for more than a year or two. Each year, new children excel. Others whose accomplishments were unusual at one age may show less precocity a few years later (Lohman & Korb, 2006; Mills & Jackson, 1990). Therefore, identification of unusual talent and accomplishment should be an ongoing activity. Finally, the best procedures for identifying academically talented students combine different sources of information—such as ability test scores, achievement test scores, and teacher ratings—in a principled way that is guided by research. We present several methods for doing this in the final section of the chapter.

Measure the Right Aptitudes

For many years, the late Richard Snow tried to convince educational researchers of the importance of the concept of aptitude.[1] He defined the concept of aptitude much more broadly than most people would define it. As he used the term, *aptitude* implies a readiness to learn or to perform well in a particular situation. This means that the person not only is capable of performing well in the situation, but actually is in tune with it. There is a beneficial match between what the situation demands or makes possible and what the person brings to it. The attainment of a high level of competence in any domain requires many different kinds of personal resources—some

---

1   For a summary of Snow's contributions and a more in-depth discussion of the concept of aptitude, see Corno et al., 2002).

cognitive (e.g., reasoning abilities, prior knowledge, and skill), some affective (e.g., motivation, interest), and some conative (e.g., persistence). The particular mix of aptitudes required for success varies across disciplines and within a discipline as the learner gains competence. Students' particular combinations of cognitive and noncognitive skills make them better suited for learning in some disciplines and better served by some kinds of instruction. Indeed, one of the most important features of an aptitude perspective is that it goes beyond simplistic talent identification systems that ignore interest, motivation, perseverance, anxiety, or even accumulated knowledge and skill in a domain. *Aptitude* is thus a word that is similar to—but much broader than—the word *talent*. As such, it meshes better with programs that aim to identify and develop specific talents rather than those programs that first identify those who are "gifted" and only secondarily seek to discover what those gifts might be and how to address them.

Aptitude cannot be understood apart from either the kind of learning that must occur or the instructional contexts in which it must take place. An aptitude perspective begins not with the person but with the kind of expertise that is to be developed. Is the goal to become a writer? A research chemist? A mathematician? Each requires not only the ability to learn different kinds of knowledge and skills, but a high level of interest in the domain and willingness to persist in the pursuit of excellence in it. Next, one must understand the demands and affordances of the educational systems that students must negotiate if they are to develop this competence. Thriving in classes that require much independent learning requires different personal resources than thriving in more structured classes. Being the youngest person, the only female, or the only Black student in the class requires other personal resources. Changing the demands of the learning situation (e.g., from discovery to didactic teaching) also changes the likelihood that a student will succeed.

Most talent identification systems are far more restrictive in the model of readiness that guides their identification procedures and therefore more restrictive in the kinds of information that they collect. Some do collect a variety of information on each student, but have no empirically substantiated way of combining it to identify those students who are most likely to someday attain expertise. This turns out to be critical for the identification of academically talented minority students. Multiple sources of information about students must be combined and considered in a way that not only increases the inclusiveness of a program, but also successfully identifies the most academically talented students in all ethnic groups. Methods that achieve the first goal often do not achieve the second goal.

Should we use different procedures for identifying talented minority students? Does talent manifest itself in different ways in minority students than in nonminority students? Although this is surely true to some degree, on the whole there is much more commonality than difference. Many researchers (e.g., Keith, 1999; Lohman, 2005; Willingham, Lewis, Morgan, & Ramsit, 1990) have investigated the predictors of academic success in different ethnic groups. They take large datasets and extract the test scores for all of the Black, Hispanic, or Asian American children. They then look at the ability variables that predict academic success for each group of children. All of these researchers have found that the ability and achievement variables that best predict academic success for minority students are the same as those that best predict academic success in nonminority children. In academic domains, these predictive variables are prior learning or achievement in the domain, the ability to reason in the symbol systems (language, numbers, music notation, etc.) used to communicate new knowledge, interest in the domain, and the ability to persist in striving for excellence in it. This means that if the goal is to identify those minority students most likely to excel in mathematics, then one should find the minority students who currently display the best mathematics achievement, who score the highest on tests of quantitative and nonverbal reasoning, who express an interest in mathematics, and who teachers rate as being motivated and persistent. For success in verbal domains, the best predictors are current achievement in those domains—verbal reasoning abilities in the language(s) of instruction, interest, and motivation.

However, some schools do not measure the characteristics that are most logically and psychologically related to academic success in particular domains. Instead, they rely exclusively or primarily on nonverbal tests. Many who do this believe that eliminating language from the test eliminates the unfair advantage on the test for native speakers of that language while measuring the cognitive ability of students. But, does this in fact occur? Are nonverbal tests culture-fair? Are differences between English Language Learners (ELL) and non–ELL children eliminated—or at least drastically reduced on nonverbal measures? And, what about differences between other ethnic groups (such as Black or Asian American students) on such measures?

Nonverbal Tests as the Panacea?

Novices in any field tend to judge things by their appearances. This holds true for judgments about what tests measure. Figural reasoning tests appear to measure something that is less the product of experience than, say, a series completion task that uses numbers or letters of the alphabet. These in turn would be judged as less influenced by experience than a vocabulary test that required a clear understanding of the meanings of commonly used words. But, appearances can be misleading. The relative contributions of heredity and environment are the same for all three. Indeed, it is the figural reasoning test that is most subject to practice effects and that has shown the greatest increase in scores over the past 50 years (Flynn, 1999)[2].

There are no truly culture-free or culture-fair tests (Anastasi & Urbina, 1997; Scarr, 1994). However, this is not the message educators want to hear. Good people want to believe that if we could just get it right, we could, in fact, eliminate bias and then measure innate ability in a way uncluttered by experience or education. But, we cannot measure innate ability any more than we can measure innate physical fitness. All ability tests measure

---

2   Most people are unaware of the extent to which norms on ability and achievement tests have changed over the past generation. IQ scores have increased at the rate of approximately 3 points per decade. Changes have been even larger on nonverbal reasoning tests, making these norms prone to overestimating the ability of test takers (Flynn, 1999).

developed abilities; they are really just special kinds of achievement tests. This does not mean that individual differences in abilities or achievements can be attributed solely to environmental factors. Indeed, among those who have had supportive environments, genetic factors explain most of the variation in both general ability and overall academic achievement. But, this is only because individuals have had roughly similar opportunities to develop the abilities that are assessed. If environmental opportunities for students vary, then the importance of genetic factors declines accordingly.

The belief that one should be able to measure innate ability has caused considerable difficulty in the field of gifted education. As anyone who works in education knows, differences between underrepresented minority and majority students on both achievement and ability tests are substantial—typically in the range of a half to a full standard deviation. On tests with an IQ-like scale, this would be a difference of 7 to 16 points.

The belief that nonverbal tests might be the silver bullet that would solve the problem of disproportionate representation of minority students was given a significant boost several years ago. Researchers reported that the Naglieri Nonverbal Ability Test (NNAT; Naglieri, 1997) identified equal proportions of high-scoring White, Black, and Hispanic children in a large sample of students who participated in standardization of the test (Naglieri & Ford, 2003). However, no one has been able to replicate this finding with other samples of Black or Hispanic children. Nor have questions of other researchers about the integrity of the data analysis been answered.[3] Indeed, in an independent analysis of standardization data for this test, George (2001) found a median difference of 11 points on an IQ-like scale between scores of White and Black students and a median difference of 6 points between the scores of White and Hispanic students. Even small group differences at the mean generally result in much larger group differences at the tails of the score distribution. Therefore,

---

[3]   See Lohman (2005). For Black students, see studies by Shaunessy, Karnes, and Cobb (2004) and by Stephens, Kiger, Karnes, and Whorton (1999). For Hispanic students, see the study by Lewis (2001). The only way that this result could have been obtained was by reweighting the data so that they would show these effects. For an explanation of how this was done, see Lohman (2006b).

differences of 11 and 6 points at the mean cannot be reconciled with the original report of equal proportions of high-scoring White, Black, and Hispanic children.

These differences between ethnic groups are of similar magnitude to those observed on other nonverbal tests. This was shown in a large, carefully conducted study by Laing, Castellano, and Buss (2006)[4]. This research team administered the NNAT, the Standard Progressive Matrices (SPM; Raven, Court, & Raven, 1983), and Form 6 of the Cognitive Abilities Test (CogAT; Lohman & Hagen, 2001a) to more than 2,000 students (with approximately half being ELL students) in grades K–6. Tests were administered in a counterbalanced order by trained examiners. Directions were given in English or Spanish, as appropriate.

When scores for the three nonverbal tests were placed on a common scale, ELL students in grades K–6 scored 10 points lower than non-ELL students on the NNAT, 9 points lower on the CogAT Nonverbal Battery, and 8 points lower on the SPM (Lohman et al., 2007). However, these differences in means capture only a small part of the picture. For example, across all students the average score on the SPM was 10 points higher than the average score on the NNAT or the CogAT-Nonverbal. The SPM scores also were inconsistent with students' average scores on a recently normed achievement test. Because the norms were too "easy," the SPM vastly overidentified the number of gifted students—especially in the non-ELL group. This is shown in the rightmost panel of Figure 3.1. On the other hand, ELL children in grades 1 and 2 had significantly lower scores on the NNAT than on the CogAT-Nonverbal. The preponderance of low scores for ELL students on the NNAT across all grades is shown in the leftmost panel of Figure 3.1. In fact, the most common score on the NNAT for ELL children in grade 1 was a stanine score of 1. Only CogAT-Nonverbal scores (middle panel) showed the expected normal distributions for both ELL and non-ELL children. These and

---

4   Drs. Naglieri and Lohman were contributing partners to this study, and both were given the data to analyze. The results reported here were performed by Lohman, Korb, & Lakin, 2007.

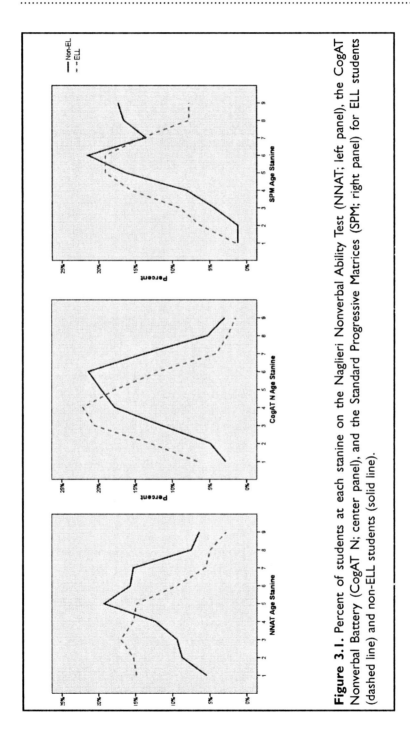

Figure 3.1. Percent of students at each stanine on the Naglieri Nonverbal Ability Test (NNAT; left panel), the CogAT Nonverbal Battery (CogAT N; center panel), and the Standard Progressive Matrices (SPM; right panel) for ELL students (dashed line) and non-ELL students (solid line).

other differences in the distributions of scores showed that the three nonverbal tests were not interchangeable, even though the differences between the mean scores of ELL and non–ELL children on the three tests were, on average, quite similar.

Nevertheless, differences between ELL and non–ELL students were much smaller on the three nonverbal tests (SPM, NNAT, and CogAT-Nonverbal) than on the Verbal and Quantitative batteries of CogAT. Across grades, the average difference between ELL and non–ELL students was 16.6 SAS points on the CogAT Verbal battery and 13.2 points on the Quantitative battery. Thus, the differences between ELL and non–ELL students were exactly twice as large on the CogAT Verbal battery (16.6 points) as on the CogAT Nonverbal battery (8.3 points). As this study and many others show, nonverbal tests reduce, but by no means eliminate, differences between ELL students and native speakers of the English language. But, does this mean that the nonverbal test is a better measure of academic talent?

Construct–Relevant and Construct-Irrelevant Score Variation

An important source of test score invalidity is the presence of unwanted sources of difficulty. These introduce what psychologists call *construct–irrelevant* variation into the scores. On a test of mathematical skills, for example, the ability to understand the directions written in English is generally unrelated to the construct of interest (i.e., the ability to solve math problems). By reducing or eliminating this source of difficulty, one can better assess math skills and compare the scores of all children to the same set of norms or standards (Abedi & Lord, 2001). However, the ability to understand the English language also can be an important aspect of the construct one hopes to measure. In this case, the variation would be construct-relevant rather than construct-irrelevant. For example, how well an ELL child understands ideas that are communicated in English can be a critical aptitude for success in a class where English is the language of instruction. More generally, eliminating verbal content may

reduce the extent to which the test measures important constructs of interest for all children. Language is required not
only to understand a teacher or a textbook, but also for private
reflection and reasoning. Indeed, the ability to reason depends
critically on what we know and on how well we regulate our
thinking. Both are rooted in language. Eliminating language
(and numbers or other symbols) results in a test that captures
only a part of our ability to think. Reasoning with spatial figures
is tied to a figural symbol system, just as verbal reasoning is tied
to a linguistic symbol system. The important question, then, is
"What is the construct that we hope to measure with this ability test?"

We have long known that one of the most important aptitudes for academic learning is the ability construct Spearman
(1923) called g. Spearman believed that virtually all cognitive
tasks required g to one degree or another. One of the most per-
vasive misunderstandings in the field is the belief that all measures of general ability (or g) are more or less interchangeable.
If one cannot administer a Stanford–Binet or Wechsler test,
then the Raven will measure the same thing. But, this is not
true. Even though nonverbal, figural reasoning tests such as the
Progressive Matrices (Raven et al., 1983) are good measures of g,
they are not interchangeable with selection tests that use verbal
and quantitative content any more than weight and height are
interchangeable measures of general physical growth. Indeed,
only about half of the variation in scores on the best verbal and
nonverbal ability tests can be attributed to g. The remaining half
reflects the influence of other cognitive factors, things that are
specific to the test and its format and to errors of measurement.
*This means that differences between students' scores on a nonverbal test
are as likely to be caused by factors other than g as by g.*

Second, as in the example of height and weight, whether
these other factors help or hurt predictions of success depends
on what one wants to predict. To weigh more could be helpful
in football; to be taller could be more advantageous in basket-
ball. Both common sense and careful study show that children's
success in school depends heavily on their ability to understand
what other people say and to communicate their own thoughts

in words. Verbal reasoning abilities are thus critical for success in school in any culture. Indeed, the bilingual child's ability to reason with words in the English language is an excellent predictor of how well he or she will do in schools in which English is the primary language of instruction. Anyone who has struggled to understand another language knows that the ability to make good inferences about the meaning of unfamiliar words is a constant—not an occasional—activity. When possible, then, these abilities should be measured.

On the other hand, figural reasoning ability is a less direct predictor of success in academic learning for all ethnic groups— White, Black, Hispanic, and Asian American. For example, the CogAT Nonverbal score correlates about $r = .6$ with reading achievement on the Iowa Tests of Basic Skills (ITBS; Hoover, Dunbar, & Frisbie, 2001). However, the CogAT Verbal score correlates about $r = .8$ with reading achievement (Lohman & Hagen, 2002). Although this may not seem like a very large difference, it actually makes the verbal reasoning score a much better predictor of success in reading. For example, when looking at the most able students (e.g., top 3%), a correlation between tests of $r = .6$ means that the predictor test correctly identifies the top students only half as often as when the correlation between tests is $r = .8$. Therefore, even a small difference in correlation can have a large impact on the accuracy of the identification of able students. Given the typical correlations between nonverbal tests and achievement, only about a quarter to a third of those who obtain the top 3% of scores on the nonverbal test within their ethnic group are those who currently obtain similarly high scores on achievement tests in mathematics, science, reading, or any other academic domain when compared with other students in that ethnic group. Selecting students on the basis of their nonverbal test scores thus eliminates the majority of high-achieving students in all ethnic groups.

Finally, once one has accounted for the *g* variation in figural reasoning tests, the specific part often shows a *negative* relationship with success in school—especially in those domains that depend heavily on verbal abilities (Case, 1977; Lohman et al., 2007). In fact, students whose nonverbal reasoning scores are significantly higher than their verbal and quantitative reasoning scores actually do *less* well in school than students who show a relative weakness on figural reasoning tests (Lohman & Hagen, 2001b).[5] In other words, two students with equally high scores on a nonverbal test can have dramatically different aptitudes for schooling as it is presently structured. But, this cannot be known unless the students' verbal and quantitative reasoning abilities also are measured.

The Importance of Multiple Perspectives

Nonnative speakers of English can be disadvantaged on tests that use English. Nonverbal tests reduce (but do not eliminate) the influence of language and therefore increase the number of bilingual and ELL students who are included in the program. Because of this, even those who recognize the importance of assessing verbal and quantitative reasoning often resort to nonverbal tests. The unstated assumption is that all children must be compared to all other children in the nation who are exactly the same age or who are in the same grade in school. This is neither necessary nor desirable.

The appropriateness of the norm or reference group depends on the inference that one wants to make. Inferences about aptitude often require different norm groups than inferences about level of accomplishment. The surest indicator of aptitude for anything is the observation that the person learns in a few trials what it takes other people many trials to learn. This means that inferences about aptitude are defensible only when one has controlled for opportunity to learn.

On ability tests, opportunity to learn is approximated by the child's age. We estimate the intellectual ability of a 6-year-old child by how well she performs compared to other children who have been living in the culture for 6 years. Changing this reference group by 6 months changes our estimate of the child's

5   The pattern of higher verbal and quantitative scores than nonverbal scores is particularly common among Black students (Lohman, 2005). This means that screening students on the basis of their nonverbal test scores not only will eliminate many of the most academically capable Black students, it also will include even more students who seem to find conventional schooling particularly uncongenial to their preferred ways of thinking. This applies not only to the CogAT Nonverbal battery, but also to the Standard Progressive Matrices (Raven et al., 1983) and the NNAT (Naglieri, 1997).

learning ability. The score that gives an average IQ for 6-year-old children gives a below-average IQ for children 6 years and 6 months old. However, age-mates are an inappropriate reference group if the child has not lived in the culture for as long as the other children in the reference group. For example, the current level of competence of a bilingual child in using the English language might be a year or two behind that of native speakers of the language. But, if she has had much less opportunity to learn English than the other children, this could indicate a remarkable aptitude for learning English. The only way to know this would be to compare her performance to that of other bilingual children who have had roughly similar learning opportunities. A rough grouping such as ELL versus non-ELL students goes a long way to solving the problem. The tradeoff here is between making precise statements about a student's rank within the wrong norm group and less precise statements about her rank within the right—or at least a better—norm group.

Consider once again the ELL students in the Laing et al. (2006) study. Recall that, across grades, their standard age scores (SAS) on the CogAT Nonverbal battery were much higher than their SAS scores on the other two CogAT test batteries—particularly the Verbal battery. But, SAS scores show how the child's performance on the test compared to all other children of the same age in the normative sample. There are many other norm groups that could be used. For example, on achievement tests it is common practice to estimate the grade level that corresponds with the raw score on the test. For these ELL students who were just learning the English language, their grade-equivalent scores were approximately one year behind their non-ELL classmates on the Quantitative battery and approximately 2 years behind on the Verbal battery.

The point of this exercise is to demonstrate that the performance of ELL students on a test appears unusually low only when they are compared to students of the same chronological age. If their scores were to be compared with children one year younger (for Quantitative reasoning) or 2 years younger (for Verbal reasoning), then their percentile ranks (and the SAS scores associated with each percentile rank) would be in the same range as their current SAS scores on the Nonverbal battery. The problem is not that the verbal test measures the wrong abilities. On the contrary, verbal reasoning abilities in the English language are the single most important aptitude for academic learning when English is the language of instruction. Rather, the problem is that the scores that the child obtains on the test are routinely compared to the wrong norm group. Instead of all children in the nation who are in third grade or who are 9 years old, the ELL child's scores should also be compared to those of other ELL children who are in third grade or who are 9 years old. Such comparisons take "opportunity to learn" factors into consideration while still measuring the most important academic skills.

Why is this not done more routinely? There are several reasons. First, those who come from a tradition in which each child is assessed individually have no easy way of creating test norms for the local population or opportunity-to-learn subgroups within that population (e.g., other ELL second graders in the school district). This is not the case for group-administered tests. If all of the children in a particular grade in a school district are administered a test, one can easily look not only at the child's rank on national norms, but also at her rank compared to a local population and even to subgroups within the local population. Second, many people erroneously believe that ability tests measure—or ought to measure—innate ability. This makes irrelevant any discussion of opportunity to learn. Third, it is administratively convenient to use a single norm group.

A caution or clarification: Knowing that a child is doing well when compared to others who also have had limited opportunities is important for making inferences about aptitude but is much less helpful when making inferences about the child's current educational needs. To know what instruction is appropriate for a student, we also need to know her level of achievement when compared to others in the classes in which she will participate. These inferences typically require common norms or standards. The most sensible policy is to get *multiple perspectives* on the child by comparing the child's test score to several different norm groups: the nation, the local population (e.g., the district or school), and the opportunity-to-learn subgroup (e.g., ELL versus native speakers in the class). Procedures for doing this are outlined below.

Two Procedures for Identifying Academically Talented Minority Students

We have argued that the best way to identify students who are likely to excel in particular domains is to measure the aptitudes that are most needed for successful learning in those domains under particular instructional arrangements. In this section, we show how this can be done. We also show how scores on nonverbal tests can contribute to the identification process.

We describe two procedures. The first procedure shows how to determine a child's standing on any score (or combination of scores) in three norm groups: the nation, the local population, and opportunity-to-learn subgroups within that population. The procedure works best when all students in a particular grade in the local population (i.e., school or district) are administered the screening test. It also requires that one know the basics of using a spreadsheet application such as Microsoft Excel.

The second procedure is simpler. It shows how to combine information from a nationally (or locally) normed ability test with teacher ratings of only those students who are likely to be included in the gifted program. It can be used to help make decisions about which students are most likely to profit from some form of acceleration and which might be served best by enrichment or additional instruction at grade level.

These procedures were developed using the CogAT Form 6 (Lohman & Hagen, 2001a), the Iowa Tests of Basic Skills (ITBS; Hoover et al., 2001), and the Scales for Rating the Behavioral Characteristics of Superior Students (SRBCSS; Renzulli et al., 2002). Decisions about educational programming—especially whole-grade acceleration—would require additional information, such as some measure of the student's interests, social skills, anxiety, and other characteristics that would be expected to influence the probability of successful learning in the different educational placement options under consideration (Assouline, Colangelo, Lupkowski-Shoplik, Lipscomb, & Forstadt, 2003).

The Cognitive Abilities Test

Because the procedures here are based on the CogAT, it is important to understand something about this test. The CogAT is a group-administered series of reasoning tests that are organized into three different batteries that measure verbal reasoning, quantitative reasoning, and nonverbal reasoning. These correspond with the (verbal) sequential reasoning, quantitative reasoning, and (figural) inductive reasoning abilities that Carroll (1993) identified as the three main constituents of the general fluid ability (Gf) factor. On the Primary Edition of the test (grades K–2), each battery has two untimed tests. On the Multilevel Edition (grades 3–12), each battery has three tests. Using two or three different tests to measure each of the three reasoning abilities reduces the confounding effects of test format that occur when all items follow the same format, thereby increasing both the construct validity and reliability of the three reasoning scores. In addition to the scores for each of the three batteries, an overall composite score is routinely reported, as well. Partial composite scores (e.g., a Quantitative-Nonverbal or QN Composite) are also available from the publisher (or can be computed by test users). As will be seen, the QN partial composite is an important component of one of the identification procedures that we describe. The overall composite score is not used and generally should not be used in the identification of gifted children (Lohman & Hagen, 2001b, 2001c; Thorndike & Hagen, 1978, 1987, 1993).

There are several features of CogAT that can assist users in avoiding misuses of test scores. For example, the pattern of each student's responses is analyzed to detect inconsistencies. A warning is printed if a student misses many easy items but answers difficult items correctly, or if she performs much better on one subtest than on the other two subtests in a battery. This can happen, for example, if the student skips one row on the answer sheet or misunderstands the directions for one of the subtests.[6] Extensive interpretive manuals—both print and online—provide explicit guidance on how to interpret each student's score profile. Importantly, only about 30–40% of the students at all score levels obtain scores on the three batteries that do not differ significantly. This means that the majority of students are not well described by their overall composite or g scores. In fact, profiles that show a markedly lower score on one of the three batteries are much more common among the most able students than among average ability students (see Lohman & Hagen, 2001c).

How best to combine scores from the three CogAT batteries when predicting academic success is well documented in the research literature. Importantly, the weights that should be applied to each test battery in making these predictions are the same for all ethnic groups that have been studied (Lohman, 2005). Competence in a broad range of verbal domains (e.g., reading comprehension and literary skills) is best predicted by the CogAT Verbal standard age score. On the other hand, success in mathematics and domains of study that demand quantitative thinking is best predicted by a combination of the CogAT Quantitative and Nonverbal Reasoning batteries. Therefore, we recommend using the Verbal battery score and the Quantitative-Nonverbal (QN) Composite score to guide admissions decisions.[7] Students—especially those who take the multilevel battery—should be considered for admission if they obtain either a high Verbal standard age score (SAS) or a high QN Composite SAS.

---

6   In fact, these procedures were developed after reviewing the case of a gifted boy in Seattle who made this mistake in using the test answer sheet. See the case study of Maxwell in Lohman and Hagen (2001b).

7   This composite score can be obtained from the publisher when requesting score reports or computed by averaging scale scores for the Quantitative battery and the Nonverbal battery and then looking up the corresponding SAS and percentile rank scores. Note that simply averaging SAS or percentile ranks on the separate batteries will not give the proper composite score. Further, the QN composite works best on the Form 6 Multilevel battery. For the Form 6 Primary battery, the best split is between the VQ Composite and the Nonverbal score.

Procedure 1: Multiple Norm Groups

Detailed directions for using this method are provided in Lohman (2006a) and in the sample data set that accompanies that monograph (see http://faculty.education.uiowa.edu/dlohman). Examples in the sample data set that is available on the Web site show how to combine ability and achievement test scores. This is important because identification procedures that average ability and achievement scores for particular domains better identify not only those who currently excel, but also those who most likely will continue to excel (see Lohman & Korb, 2006).

First, get the required data into a spreadsheet. For each student, this would include an opportunity-to-learn index (such as ELL status) and national percentile ranks or standard age scores. Second, sort the data by percentile ranks (or SAS). This will provide local ranks.[8] Those with the highest scores will be at the top of the list. Local score distributions generally provide a better way to determine which students are most likely to be mismatched with the instruction they are receiving than do national norms. They also make it much easier to identify a relatively consistent number of students across years.

Third, sort the data again by opportunity to learn (as the first sorting variable in Excel) and then percentile rank or SAS (as the second sorting variable in Excel). For example, if two opportunity-to-learn groups are used (e.g., ELL versus native speakers), then the most talented ELL students will be those with the highest ranks within the first group and the most talented native-speaking students will be those with the highest ranks in the second group. What kind of enrichment or acceleration to suggest for each depends on the students' levels of achievement and on other factors (such as interest, motivation, and the availability of different educational programs).

---

8   Note that ranks are not the same as the percentile ranks provided in norm tables. However, for most purposes, a simple rank order of the scores is all that is needed. Other scores (e.g., Standard Age Scores) provide additional information on the size of the score gaps between students with different ranks.

Procedure 2: Using Ability Test Scores and Teacher Ratings

This procedure uses scores from all three CogAT batteries and the Learning Ability, Motivation, and Creativity scales from the Scales for Rating the Behavioral Characteristics of Superior Students (SRBCSS; Renzulli et al., 2002). For additional details and examples, see Lohman and Renzulli (2007). The procedure assumes that CogAT Verbal and Quantitative-Nonverbal composite scores are available for all students, and that those students who score above the 80th percentile rank have been rated by their teachers. Although either local or national percentile ranks can be used, we and others (e.g., Renzulli, 2005) recommend using local norms for local talent searches. Both local and national percentile ranks for the CogAT Verbal and the Quantitative-Nonverbal composite can be requested from the test publisher when tests are scored and can output from the online version of the SRBCSS. We recommend local norms because the need for special services depends primarily on the disparity between children's cognitive and academic development and that of the other children in the classes that they attend, not all other children in the nation at the time that the test was normed.[9]

Information is combined using the identification scheme shown in Figure 3.2. The vertical dimension distinguishes children who exhibit superior reasoning abilities in *either* the verbal domain *or* in the quantitative-nonverbal domain from those who exhibit strong but less stellar reasoning abilities in these domains. We have arbitrarily set two cut-scores to distinguish these groups: the 96th and 80th percentile ranks on *either* verbal reasoning *or* quantitative-nonverbal reasoning.

The horizontal dimension of the matrix distinguishes between children who, when compared to other children who might be included in the program, obtain above-average teacher ratings from students who obtain below-average teacher ratings on any one of the three SRBCSS scales. Of course, schools can

---

9   If the QN composite was not obtained, then a simple approximation is to assign point values to percentile ranks (national or local) for the separate Quantitative and Nonverbal test scores using the tables in Lohman and Renzulli (2007). The point system transforms percentile scores to a common metric so that they can be combined.

Teacher Ratings on Learning Ability, Motivation, or Creativity			
		All teacher ratings below average	One or more above average teacher ratings
CogAT Verbal OR Quantitative-Nonverbal Reasoning	≥ 96th percentile rank	II	I
	80th–95th percentile rank	IV	III

Figure 3.2. A method for combining ability test scores on two dimensions (Verbal or Quantitative-Nonverbal partial composite score) and teacher ratings on three scales (Learning Ability, Motivation, and Creativity).

Note. National or local percentile ranks are used for ability test scores. However, teacher ratings are obtained only on those students who are nominated for the program.

implement a rule that is either more stringent or more lenient than above (or below) average.

Combining these two criteria gives four categories of assessment results.

- Children in Category I exhibit superior reasoning abilities on CogAT and are rated as highly capable, motivated, or creative by their teachers. These are easy cases.
- Children in Category II also exhibit superior reasoning abilities but, when compared to other children who were nominated, are not rated as highly by their teachers on any one of the three major scales of the SRBCSS. Most programs would also accept children in Category II. However, the progress of children in Category II should be monitored more closely. For example, once they are available, achievement test scores should be considered, as well.
- Children in Category III exhibit somewhat lower but strong reasoning abilities (80th to 95th percentile rank) on CogAT, and are rated as highly capable, motivated,

or creative by their teachers. These children would be included in schoolwide enrichment programs that aim to serve a broader range of children than are served by traditional gifted programs (Renzulli, 2005). Schools that serve minority children would find that many of their most talented minority students would fall in this category. Combining test scores and ratings in this way would enable these schools to identify the students most likely to benefit from curriculum compacting or enrichment programs, including instruction at a higher level than that received by most other students in the school.

- Finally, children in Category IV exhibit good but not exceptional reasoning abilities (80th and 95th percentile rank), and are not rated as unusually capable, motivated, or creative by their teachers. Although good students, these children would generally not be provided with special programming on the basis of either their CogAT scores or teacher ratings. However, they should be reconsidered when information on achievement is available. Indeed, given the inevitability of regression to the mean in all status scores (e.g., percentile ranks and teacher ratings; Lohman & Korb, 2006), the level of participation of all children in the program should be routinely reevaluated (Renzulli, 2005). This can be made more palatable if children (and their parents) are told that they are being identified for participation in a talent development program in a particular domain rather than being identified as "gifted."

These procedures can be a helpful first step in creating a talent pool (Renzulli, 2005). They show how to make effective use of some of the most important information that should be gathered. But, they do not show how to incorporate all of the other information that can usefully inform how best to assist students in developing their talents. For example, student interests should always be assessed and used to help students direct their choice of educational activities.

Conclusion

Those students who, when compared to the proper norm group, reason best in the symbol systems used to communicate new knowledge in a domain and who show the best current achievement in it are the ones most likely to achieve at a higher level later. This applies to students from all ethnic, social class, and language groups. Therefore, high nonverbal scores are most informative when accompanied by (a) evidence of reasonably high accomplishment in the academic domain in which accelerated instruction or enrichment is offered and (b) evidence that the student's verbal or quantitative reasoning abilities are also high *relative to other children who have had similar opportunities to develop these abilities.* Most schools have this evidence for achievement, and those that administer ability tests such as CogAT that appraise verbal and quantitative reasoning in addition to nonverbal reasoning have the corresponding evidence for ability, as well. For these schools, combining evidence of current achievement, reasoning abilities, and teacher ratings can help increase the diversity of gifted programs while also identifying the students in all ethnic groups most likely to benefit from special instruction.

References

Abedi, J., & Lord, C. (2001). The language factor in mathematics tests. *Applied Measurement in Education, 14,* 219–234.

Anastasi, A., & Urbina, S. (1997). *Psychological testing* (7th ed.). Upper Saddle River, NJ: Prentice Hall.

Assouline, S., Colangelo, N., Lupkowski-Shoplik, A., Lipscomb, J., & Forstadt, L. (2003). *Iowa Acceleration Scale* (2nd ed.). Scottsdale, AZ: Great Potential Press.

Carroll, J. B. (1993). *Human cognitive abilities: A survey of factor-analytic studies.* Cambridge, England: Cambridge University Press.

Case, M. E. (1977). *A validation study of the nonverbal battery of the Cognitive Abilities Test at grades 3, 4, and 6.* Unpublished doctoral dissertation, University of Illinois at Urbana-Champaign.

Corno, L., Cronbach, L. J., Kupermintz, H., Lohman, D. F., Mandinach, E. B., Porteus, A. W., et al. (2002). *Remaking the con-*

cept of aptitude: Extending the legacy of Richard E. Snow. Hillsdale, NJ: Lawrence Erlbaum.

Donovan, M. S., & Cross, C. T. (Eds.). (2002). *Minority students in special and gifted education*. Washington, DC: National Academy Press.

Flynn, J. R. (1999). Searching for justice: The discovery of IQ gains over time. *American Psychologist, 54,* 5–20.

George, C. E. (2001). *The Naglieri Nonverbal Ability Test: Assessment of cross-cultural validity, reliability, and differential item functioning*. Unpublished doctoral dissertation, Fordham University.

Hoover, H. D., Dunbar, S. B., & Frisbie, D. A. (2001). *Iowa Tests of Basic Skills: Form A*. Itasca, IL: Riverside.

Keith, T. Z. (1999). Effects of general and specific abilities on student achievement: Similarities and differences across ethnic groups. *School Psychology Quarterly, 14,* 239–262.

Laing, P., Castellano, J., & Buss, R. (2006). *Project Bright Horizon*. Phoenix, AZ: Washington Elementary School District.

Lewis, J. D. (2001, March). *Language isn't needed: Nonverbal assessments and gifted learners. Proceedings of the Growing Partnerships for Rural Special Education Conference*. San Diego, CA: American Council on Rural Special Education. (ERIC Document Reproduction Service No. ED453026)

Lohman, D. F. (2005). The role of nonverbal ability tests in the identification of academically gifted students: An aptitude perspective. *Gifted Child Quarterly, 49,* 111–138.

Lohman, D. F. (2006a). *Identifying academically talented minority students* (RM05216). Storrs: National Research Center on the Gifted and Talented, University of Connecticut.

Lohman, D. F. (2006b, May). *Identifying academically gifted children in a linguistically and culturally diverse society*. Keynote Presentation at the Eighth Biennial Henry B. & Jocelyn Wallace National Research Symposium on Talent Development, Iowa City, IA. Retrieved July 1, 2007, from http://faculty.education.uiowa.edu

Lohman, D. F., & Hagen, E. P. (2001a). *Cognitive Abilities Test (Form 6)*. Itasca, IL: Riverside.

Lohman, D. F., & Hagen, E. P. (2001b). *Cognitive Abilities Test (Form 6): Interpretive guide for teachers and counselors*. Itasca, IL: Riverside.

Lohman, D. F., & Hagen, E. P. (2001c). *Cognitive Abilities Test (Form 6): Interpretive guide for school administrators*. Itasca, IL: Riverside.

Lohman, D. F., & Hagen, E. P. (2002). *Cognitive Abilities Test (Form 6): Research handbook*. Itasca, IL: Riverside.

Lohman, D. F., & Korb, K. A. (2006). Gifted today but not tomorrow? Longitudinal changes in ITBS and CogAT scores during elementary school. *Journal for the Education of the Gifted, 29*, 451–484.

Lohman, D. F., Korb, K., & Lakin, J. (2007, April). *Identifying academically gifted English language learners using nonverbal tests: A comparison of the Raven, NNAT, and CogAT.* Paper presented at the annual meeting of the American Education Research Association, Chicago. Retrieved July 1, 2007, from http://faculty.education.uiowa.edu/dlohman

Lohman, D. F., & Renzulli, J. (2007). *A simple procedure for combining ability test scores, achievement test scores, and teacher ratings to identify academically talented children.* Retrieved July 1, 2007, from http://faculty.education.uiowa.edu/dlohman/pdf/Lohman_Renzulli_ID_system.pdf

Lorge, I., & Thorndike, R. L. (1954). *The Lorge-Thorndike Intelligence Tests.* Boston: Houghton-Mifflin.

Mencken, H. L. (1949). The divine afflatus. In H. L. Mencken (Ed.), *A Mencken chrestomathy* (pp. 442–448). New York: Knopf.

Mills, J. R., & Jackson, N. E. (1990). Predictive significance of early giftedness: The case of precocious reading. *Journal of Educational Psychology, 82*, 410–419.

Naglieri, J. A. (1997). *Naglieri Nonverbal Ability Test: Multilevel technical manual.* San Antonio, TX: Harcourt Brace.

Naglieri, J. A., & Ford, D. Y. (2003). Addressing underrepresentation of gifted minority children using the Naglieri Nonverbal Ability Test (NNAT). *Gifted Child Quarterly, 47,* 155–160.

Raven, J. C., Court, J. H., & Raven, J. (1983). *Manual for Raven's Progressive Matrices and Vocabulary Scales, section 3: Standard Progressive Matrices.* London: H. K. Lewis.

Renzulli, J. S. (2005). *Equity, excellence, and economy in a system for identifying students in gifted education: A guidebook* (RM05208). Storrs: National Research Center on the Gifted and Talented, University of Connecticut.

Renzulli, J. S., Smith, L. H., White, A. J., Callahan, C. M., Hartman, R. K., & Westberg, K. L. (2002). *Scales for Rating the Behavioral Characteristics of Superior Students.* Mansfield Center, CT: Creative Learning Press.

Scarr, S. (1994). Culture-fair and culture-free tests. In R. J. Sternberg (Ed.), *Encyclopedia of human intelligence* (pp. 322–328). New York: Macmillan.

Shaunessy, E., Karnes, F. A., & Cobb, Y. (2004). Assessing potentially gifted students from lower socioeconomic status with nonverbal measures of intelligence. *Perceptual and Motor Skills, 98,* 1129–1138.

Spearman, C. E. (1923). *The nature of intelligence and the principles of cognition.* London: Macmillan.

Stephens, K., Kiger, L., Karnes, F. A., & Whorton, J. E. (1999). Use of nonverbal measures of intelligence in identification of culturally diverse gifted students in rural areas. *Perceptual and Motor Skills, 88,* 793–796.

Thorndike, R. L., & Hagen, E. P. (1978). *Cognitive Abilities Test (Form 3).* New York: Houghton Mifflin.

Thorndike, R. L., & Hagen, E. P. (1987). *Cognitive Abilities Test (Form 4).* Chicago: Riverside.

Thorndike, R. L., & Hagen, E. P. (1993). *Cognitive Abilities Test (Form 5).* Chicago: Riverside.

Willingham, W. W., Lewis, C., Morgan, R., & Ramsit, L. (1990). *Predicting college grades: An analysis of institutional trends over two decades.* New York: The College Board.

Wechsler, D. (1949). *Wechsler Intelligence Scale for Children.* New York: The Psychological Corporation.

Traditional IQ: 100 Years of Misconception and Its Relationship to Minority Representation in Gifted Programs

Jack A. Naglieri

Introduction

The underrepresentation of minority children in classes for the gifted has been and continues to be one of the most important problems facing educators of gifted students (Ford, 1998; Naglieri & Ford, 2005). The severity of the problem was made obvious in the United States Department of Education's recent report that Black, Hispanic, and Native American students are underrepresented by 50–70% in gifted education programs (Naglieri & Ford, 2003). Efforts to address this situation include, for example, use of multiple criteria for inclusion, refinement of the referral procedures, and reexamination of the very definition of the term *gifted*. Some have argued that the content of the ability tests used and procedures followed fail to take into consideration the characteristics of culturally, ethnically, and linguistically diverse populations (Frazier et al., 1995; Naglieri & Ford, 2005).

The concept of intelligence has been defined by the tests used to measure this construct since the early 1900s. Traditional intelligence tests have had the now familiar verbal, quantitative, and nonverbal format since Binet and Simon (1905) and Wechsler (1939) published their influential tests. The division of items by content was not based on a theory of verbal, quantitative, and nonverbal intelligences. In fact, the division was a practical one as noted by Yoakum and Yerkes when they wrote that the Army Beta (nonverbal) tests were used because it was known that a person could fail the Army Alpha (verbal and quantitative) tests because of limited skills in English. To avoid "injustice by reason of relative unfamiliarity with English" (1920, p. 19), these persons were then tested with the nonverbal tests. It is important to note that there is no mention of the need to measure different types of intelligence even though verbal, nonverbal, and quantitative tests were all used to measure general ability.

Content of Traditional IQ Tests

Traditional IQ tests measure *general ability* through questions that are verbal (e.g., vocabulary or word analogies), spatial (e.g., arranging blocks to match a simple design or assembling puzzles to make a common object), or quantitative (e.g., math word problems or math calculation). The spatial tests have been described as *nonverbal*, because it is an easier concept to understand, not because of any intention to measure nonverbal ability. In fact, this lack of theoretical basis was noted by Pintner (1923) when he wrote "we did not start with a clear definition of general intelligence . . . [but] borrowed from every-day life a vague term implying all-round ability and . . . we [are] still attempting to define it more sharply and endow it with a stricter scientific connotation" (p. 53). The use of a vague definition of intelligence leaves unspecified the differences between a test of intelligence and a test of achievement. The result has been that our tests have been used to define the theory of intelligence the test is intended to measure.

Traditionally, IQ has been measured using verbal, quantitative, and nonverbal tests since the tests were initially formulated in 1905 with the publication of the Stanford-Binet (Binet & Simon, 1905) and in 1939 with the publication of the Wechsler-Bellevue Scales (Wechsler, 1939). These tests made a significant and long-lasting contribution to our understanding of how to measure and conceptualize intelligence. The results obtained from these tests have influenced the lives of countless children and adults in the United States and around the world. Although intelligence tests represent one of the most influential contributions made by psychology to society in general (Anastasi & Urbina, 1997), they also have become engrained in our culture as *the* way to measure ability.

There is considerable experimental support for the concept of general intelligence as measured by tests such as the Wechsler and Binet (see Jensen, 1998, for a review). Among the most important sources of validity evidence for IQ tests is the fact that the scores the tests yield are a good prediction of school achievement (Naglieri & Bornstein, 2003; Ramsey & Reynolds, 2004). It made sense in the early 1900s, as it does today, however, that limited academic skills interfere with the measurement of general ability when verbal tests are used. For example, in the immigration museum at Ellis Island there is a story about a young woman whose verbal skills suggested she may have been mentally retarded. Once a nonverbal test was administered, which she completed easily, it became clear that it was a mistake to think she was not smart, even though she did not know English. The issue is no different today, but compounded when verbal and quantitative tests are more closely examined and their similarity to tests used to measure achievement become more apparent.

If a student has not had the chance to acquire verbal and quantitative skills due to limited opportunity to learn, or a disability, verbal and quantitative tests designed to measure general ability may be a good predictor of current academic performance but not a good reflection of his or her ability to learn after having had ample instruction. For example, typical Native American Navajo children living on a reservation in northern Arizona earn low scores on the Verbal but average scores on the Performance scale of the Wechsler (Naglieri & Yazzie, 1983) because they speak English as a second language and have had insufficient exposure to the language of a typical American child. Suzuki and Valencia (1997) argued that verbal and quantitative questions found on most traditional IQ tests interfere with accurate assessment of minority children. Importantly, the similarity in knowledge and skills required to complete IQ and achievement tests is becoming more apparent. To illustrate, the similarities of the verbal and quantitative questions included in tests of intelligence that include verbal, nonverbal, and quantitative components and tests of achievement will be explored.

The oldest intelligence test in use today is the Stanford–Binet 5 (SB-5; Roid, 2003). This test has Quantitative Reasoning items that, for example, require the student to calculate the total number of circles on a page (e.g., two circles in one box plus three in a second box plus one in a third box). The same type of question appears on the Wechsler Intelligence Scale for Children–Fourth Edition (WISC-IV; Wechsler, 2003a) Arithmetic subtest (now a supplemental subtest), which requires the child to count, for example, the number of birds pictured on a page. Very similar items appear on the Wechsler Individual Achievement Test (WIAT-II, Wechsler, 2001). On that test of knowledge, for example, a Numerical Operations subtest item requires the child to determine the total number of balls shown (e.g., 3 plus 5). Similarly, a Woodcock-Johnson Tests of Achievement (WJ-III ACH; Woodcock, McGrew, & Mather, 2001a) Applied Problems subtest item asks the child to count the number of pencils pictured (e.g., 4). Moreover, a SB-5 Quantitative Reasoning item requires the child to complete a simple math problem (e.g., $4 + 2 = ?$) just as the WJ-III ACH Math Fluency (e.g., $7 + 2 = ?$) and the WIAT-II Numerical Operations (e.g., $3 + 2 = ?$) tests do. This also is found on the Cognitive Abilities Test's (CogAT; Lohman & Hagen, 2001) Quantitative battery and the Iowa Tests of Basic Skills' (ITBS; Hoover, Dunbar, & Frisbie, 2001) mathematics tests. The CogAT Equation Building Test, for example, demands basic math skills to determine how numbers and symbols can be combined to yield a specific numerical value (e.g., $8 \times 3 = ?$ and $12 + 4 - 6 + 2 = ?$) and the ITBS Mathematics tests include one test in particular (Math Concepts) that also involves understanding equations. In that test, the student is shown a math problem and asked to select which of four possible equations answers the question. Thus, knowledge of equations is used to test *ability* in the CogAT and *achievement* in the ITBS. Although it seems reasonable that math skills should be part of a test of achievement, it does not seem reasonable that math skills should be used to measure ability because acquired skills are influenced by both instruction and ability. The same issue applies to verbal tests.

Verbal questions are found on both traditional IQ tests and measures of achievement. For example, all traditional IQ tests include a measure of word knowledge and, amazingly sometimes use the same words on both types of tests. For example, students are required to define a word like *bat* on subtests included in the SB-5 or WISC-IV intelligence tests and the WJ-III ACH. The WJ-III Tests of Cognitive Abilities (WJ-III COG; Woodcock, McGrew, & Mather, 2001b) battery contains a Verbal Comprehension subtest that has an item similar to "Tell me another word for *small*," and the WJ-III ACH contains a Reading Vocabulary question like "Tell me another word for *little*." In addition, an item on the WJ-III ACH Reading Vocabulary test is something like "Tell me another word for (examiner points to the word *big*)," and in the WJ-III COG, the examiner asks something like "Tell me another word for *tiny*." Additionally, the WJ-III COG Verbal Comprehension test contains 23 Picture Vocabulary items and the WJ-III ACH includes 44 Picture Vocabulary items, some of which are the same between the tests. The CogAT Verbal battery also contains tests that demand knowledge of words. The Verbal Classification items require the child to determine how words such as "red, green, and yellow" are alike by choosing from options such as "color, crayon, blue, and marker." Similarly, the reading portion of the ITBS includes a Vocabulary test. A word is presented in a short phrase or sentence, and the student is required to select the answer that has the same meaning as the target word. For example, the child reads the phrase "To *look* in the room" and chooses a corresponding word from among this list: push, sit, fix, peek. These items also require reading skills that sometimes exceed the reading level of those students for whom the test is intended (Naglieri & Ford, 2005).

Naglieri and Ford (2005) evaluated the reading levels required for the items for the CogAT Form 6 Level D Sentence Completion test. This test is intended for children of average ability in grades 5 and 6. They calculated the readability of the items using the Flesch-Kincaid Grade Level method (Flesch, 1948), which is among the most widely used methods of evaluating reading requirements of text (Chall & Dale, 1995). The Sentence Completion test readability grade level was 6.1 and the readabilities of the individual items ranged from grade 3.7 to 10.4. These findings indicate that children with poor reading skills potentially due to a learning disability, language difference, or limited exposure to English will be at a disadvantage when tested with the CogAT Sentence Completion test because of the achievement demands of this measure of ability.

Acquisition of reading, math, and language skills is a fundamental goal of any formal educational system and in addition, often encouraged, if not explicitly taught, in the home environment. The quality of the educational system and the level of enrichment at home play an important role in the knowledge and skills the child attains. For some children this means that there may be more or less opportunity. For example, Hispanics ages 25 and older are less likely to have a high school diploma (57%) than Whites (88.7%). Importantly, 27% of Hispanics have less than a ninth-grade education compared with only 4% of Whites and only 14.2% of Hispanics are in managerial or professional occupations compared with 35.1% of Whites (Ramirez & de la Cruz, 2002). In order to equitably evaluate the level of ability for a population such as this, or any others with limited opportunity to learn, tests that do not gauge intelligence on the basis of verbal and quantitative skills are necessary.

Practitioners need to understand that the conceptualization of general intelligence that has dominated the field for more than 100 years and which most professionals in education and psychology readily accept as what intelligence is needs to be reexamined. The notion that verbal, quantitative, and nonverbal intelligences are real must be understood within a more accurate historical perspective. The methods used by the U.S. military in the early 1900s (Yoakum & Yerkes, 1920) had utility, but the results must be interpreted differently when applied to those who have limited English skills and learning experiences.

Perhaps most importantly, practitioners need to understand that the originators of these tests did *not* think that the content of the tests represented separate constructs of intelligence; but rather, the different content was used to more fairly assess a wide variety of individuals, many of whom did not have requisite language and math skills.

Wechsler's Influence

Wechsler's view of intelligence was that verbal and nonverbal were *not* two different types of intelligence; despite the fact that for years his tests yielded both Verbal and Performance (nonverbal) IQ scores. He argued that nonverbal tests help to

> minimize the over-diagnosing of feeble-mindness that was, he believed, caused by intelligence tests that were too verbal in content . . . and he viewed verbal and performance tests as equally valid measures of intelligence and criticized the labeling of performance [nonverbal] tests as measures of special abilities (Boake, 2002, p. 396).

There has been widespread acceptance of the inclusion of verbal, quantitative, and nonverbal tests in both ability and achievement tests even though their similarity is obvious. There has been obvious failure to differentiate these constructs, apparent in the descriptions of the tests themselves provided by the authors. Interestingly, the ITBS Vocabulary test is described as "a useful indicator of overall verbal *ability* [emphasis added]" on the publisher's Web page (http://riverpub.com/products/itbs/details.html). Identification of a score from a test of *achievement* as a measure of *ability* does not seem defensible. Nonverbal measures of general ability can be used as a way to circumvent this problem. Using a score from a test of achievement as a measure of ability is illogical because achievement and ability tests should be measuring different constructs—acquired knowledge and skills in contrast to intelligence, respectively. Nonverbal measures of general ability can be used as a way to circumvent this problem.

General Ability Measured Using Nonverbal Tests

The essence of a nonverbal test of general ability is that it does not contain verbal and quantitative test questions, although it may involve verbal solutions to the problem. For example, Figure 4.1 shows a simple nonverbal test question that could be included in a test described as a progressive matrix. The matrix varies across the horizontal and vertical dimensions. The difference between the top and bottom rows is that the shape inside that square changes (a circle appears on the top row and a triangle on the bottom row). The difference between the first and second column included in the top row is the addition of shading to the circle. The child needs to understand the interrelationships among these variables (shape and shading across the columns and rows) to arrive at the correct answer (option 3). The child may, or may not, use a verbal description (in any language) of the matrix as just described or the child may simply look at the shapes and understand which option is the answer with minimal verbal analysis.

Tests that measure general ability nonverbally may have different types of nonverbal questions, but the essential aspect of these tests is measuring ability nonverbally. Although there is consistency across nonverbal tests in terms of the content of the questions, there are some differences in views about the directions. For example, nonverbal test directions for administration may be spoken as in the Naglieri Nonverbal Ability Test (NNAT; Naglieri, 1997). Another method is to use pictorial directions as found in the Wechsler Nonverbal Scale of Ability (WNV; Wechsler & Naglieri, 2006), and some authors argue that the entire test must be administered using pantomime, which is perhaps best illustrated by the Universal Nonverbal Intelligence Test (UNIT; Bracken & McCallum, 1998). The slight variation in administration format notwithstanding, the goal is the same: to measure general ability nonverbally. Two examples of tests are provided in the section that follows.

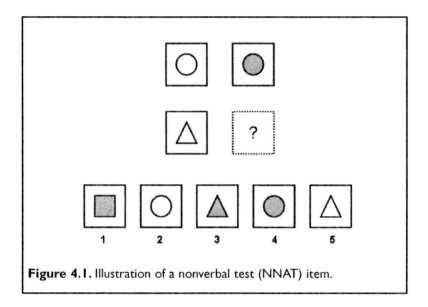

Figure 4.1. Illustration of a nonverbal test (NNAT) item.

Group and Individual Nonverbal Measures of Ability

The NNAT

The Naglieri Nonverbal Ability Test (NNAT; Naglieri, 1997) is a group-administered nonverbal test of general ability organized into multiple levels of items composed of diagrams as illustrated in Figure 4.1.

The NNAT consists of seven separate booklets organized into levels, each of which is comprised of 38 items presented in the colors blue, white, and yellow, because these colors are least influenced by color-impaired vision. The seven levels and corresponding grades for which they are intended are as follows: Level A: Kindergarten; Level B: Grade 1; Level C: Grade 2; Level D: Grades 3–4; Level E: Grades 5–6; Level F: Grades 7–9; Level G: Grades 10–12. Each level contains items shared from both the adjacent higher and lower levels, as well as exclusive items. The shared items were used to develop a continuous scaled score across the entire standardization sample. These items yield a total raw score that is converted to a Nonverbal Ability Index standard score set at a mean of 100 with a standard deviation of 15 through an intermediate Rasch value called a scaled score. Thus, each child's raw score is converted to a scaled score (Rasch value) based upon the NNAT level administered, and then the scaled score is converted to a standard score based upon the age of the child. For more information see Naglieri (1997).

The NNAT was standardized on a nationally representative sample of 89,600 children in grades K–12 (ages 5–18 years). The sample included 22,600 children tested in the fall of 1995 and 67,000 children tested in the spring of 1996. The final complete sample used to create the NNAT norms tables closely matches the U.S. population on the basis of geographic region, socioeconomic status, urbanicity, ethnicity, and school setting (private and parochial). The sample included children in special educational settings such as those with emotional disturbance, learning disabilities, hearing and visual impairment, and those who were mentally handicapped. Children with limited English proficiency also were included in the standardization sample. This standardization procedure also involved concurrent administration of the Stanford Achievement Test–Ninth Edition (SAT-9; 1995). More details may be obtained from the NNAT Technical Manual (Naglieri, 1997). It is important to note that as of the time of this writing, the NNAT is being revised and a second edition of the test, as well as an online version, is expected to be published at the end of 2007.

Summary of NNAT Research

The validity of the NNAT that has particular relevance to the assessment of gifted minority children has been examined in a series of published research papers and will be briefly described here. This will include the examination of White and minority populations, bilingual children, gender differences, and relationships to achievement.

Naglieri and Ronning (2000a, 2000b) studied mean score differences and correlations to achievement for matched samples of White (n = 2,306) and Black (n = 2,306); White (n = 1,176) and Hispanic (n = 1,176); and White (n = 466) and Asian American (n = 466) students in grades K–12. The three pairs of groups were carefully selected from a larger sample included in the NNAT standardization sample and matched on the demographic characteristics of the U.S. population, including geographical region, socioeconomic status, ethnicity, and type of school setting (public or private). Only small differences were found between the NNAT scores for the White and Black samples (Cohen's d-ratio = .25 or about 4 standard score points). Minimal differences between the White and Hispanic (d-ratio = .17 or about 3 standard score points), as well as White and Asian American (d-ratio = .02 or less than one standard score point) groups also were reported. Additionally, the correlations between NNAT and academic achievement were strong and consistent across grades K–12. Importantly, the NNAT correlated similarly for the White, Black, and Hispanic samples. The small mean score differences and the strong correlations strongly suggest that the NNAT has utility for fair assessment of White and minority children and that the scores the test yields are good for statistical prediction of academic achievement.

Naglieri, Booth, and Winsler (2004) examined the performance of Hispanic children with limited English–language skills. They studied the differences between Hispanic children with (n = 148) and without (n = 148) limited English proficiency who were administered the NNAT (Naglieri, 1997) and the SAT-9 (1995). The two groups of Hispanic children were selected from 22,620 children included in the NNAT standardization sample and matched on geographical region, gender, socioeconomic status, urbanicity, and ethnicity. The results showed that there was only a small difference (d-ratio = 0.1) between the NNAT standard scores for the Hispanic children with limited English proficiency (mean = 98.0) and those without limited English proficiency (mean = 96.7). In addition, the NNAT correlated similarly with achievement for the Hispanic children with and without limited English proficiency. The results suggested that the NNAT scores have use for assessment of Hispanic children with and without limited English proficiency and that these children earned scores that were close to average.

Perhaps one of the most important studies of the NNAT and racial/ethnic differences that suggested that the NNAT may be particularly useful as a fair measure of general ability for gifted minority children was reported by Naglieri and Ford (2003). They studied the practical question—if the NNAT yields small mean score differences between minority and majority groups, would it identify similar percentages of White, Black, and Hispanic children as gifted? Of course, the NNAT would be one part of the larger assessment process used to determine placement in classes for the gifted, albeit an important part. If children would be similarly identified as gifted using the NNAT scores, then the numbers of minority children who may have the opportunity to be selected for gifted programs might increase. To study this question, Naglieri and Ford (2003) used a sample of 20,270 children from the NNAT standardization sample tested during the fall of 1995. These students were representative of the national school population according to socioeconomic status, urban background, and ethnicity and the characteristics of the separate Black, Hispanic, and White groups were also similar in composition. The question addressed by Naglieri and Ford (2003) was: Are the percentages of children who earned NNAT standard scores from 120 to 140 comparable by racial and ethnic groups? To answer this question, standard score frequency distributions were compared to obtain the percentage of each group that would meet the intellectual ability criteria based upon a standard score of 120, as well as 125, 130, 135, and 140 or above (corresponding to the 91st, 95th, 98th, 99th, and 99.6th percentile ranks).

Naglieri and Ford (2003) found that 5.6% of the White (n = 14,141), 5.1% of the Black (n = 2,863), and 4.4% of the Hispanic (n = 1,991) children earned an NNAT standard score of 125 (95th percentile rank) or higher and 2.5% of White, 2.6% of Black, and 2.3% of Hispanic children earned NNAT standard scores of 130 or higher (98th percentile). The identification rates at each 5-point interval from 120 to 140 are shown in Figure 4.2.

These data suggest that the percentages of children that would be identified if the NNAT was used are similar across race

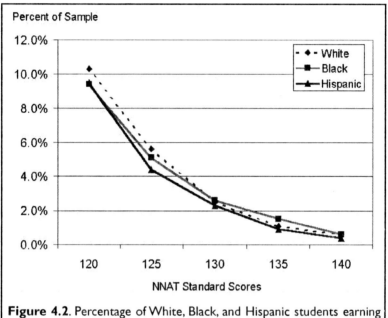

Figure 4.2. Percentage of White, Black, and Hispanic students earning various NNAT standard scores.

and ethnic groups and that the NNAT was effective at identifying diverse students at levels appropriate for gifted education services. The results also suggest that the use of this instrument may help address the persistent problem of the underrepresentation of diverse students in gifted education.

Rojahn and Naglieri (2006) examined gender differences on the NNAT for the entire standardization sample. They found that the NNAT scores for children ages 6–9 (14,468 males and 14,668 females) did not differ (100.2 for both genders). Males (*n* = 14,273) and females (*n* = 14,443) ages 10–13 scored the same on the NNAT (100.0 and 100.2, respectively). Finally, males (*n* = 5,681) and females (*n* = 5,940) ages 15–17 also scored the same on the NNAT (99.1 for both genders). Scores for this sample by NNAT level then yielded the same results, indicating that on average, males and females earn the same scores on this nonverbal measure of ability.

Wechsler Nonverbal Scale of Ability

Sometimes an individually administered nonverbal measure of general ability is desired and in this case a test like
the Wechsler Nonverbal Scale of Ability (WNV; Wechsler &
Naglieri, 2006) could be considered. The test yields a standard
score (mean of 100 and SD of 15) based on the combination of
either two or four subtests scaled using a T-score metric (mean
of 50 and SD of 10). The WNV is comprised of subtests that
were either adapted from other Wechsler tests, are new, or are
modeled after the Naglieri Nonverbal Ability Tests (Naglieri,
1997, 2003). The WNV consists of six subtests—Matrices,
Coding, Object Assembly, Recognition, Spatial Span, and
Picture Arrangement—carefully selected to take into consideration developmental differences between the ages of 4 years, 0
months, and 21 years, 11 months (4:0–21:11). For this reason,
the age range was divided into two age bands, ages 4:0–7:11,
and ages 8:0–21:11, with each age band having different combinations of subtests comprising both a two- and four-subtest battery. This test was standardized on a large representative sample
of children ages 4–21 who closely represented the U.S. population on a number of important demographic variables. The
WNV was also standardized on a large representative sample
of Canadian children ages 4–21 who closely represented the
characteristics of that country (for more details see Wechsler &
Naglieri, 2006).

The WNV uses a new method for informing the examinee of the demands of the subtest called Pictorial Directions,
designed to provide a nonverbal and engaging method of communicating the task requirements to the examinee. Students are
shown a series of pictures that illustrate what is required along
with gestures by the examiner that draw attention to the correspondence between the pictured directions and the stimuli in
front of the subject.

Pictorial directions are supplemented by simple verbal
directions in English, French, Spanish, Chinese, German, and
Dutch. The translated verbal directions are used only as needed
and by a professional who is able to perform the testing in the

examinee's preferred language. If the use of the pictorial directions and supplemental verbal directions proves ineffective for explaining the demands of the subtest, examiners are instructed to provide additional help as needed. That is, the examiner may interact with the examinee (e.g., refer back to pictorial directions, gesture, demonstrate, and say or sign additional words) to ensure that he or she understands the task requirements. The amount of assistance offered is based on professional judgment, reactions of the examinee, and the particular subtest.

The composition of the WNV reflects the authors' recognition of the value of measuring general ability and the particular advantage of using nonverbal tests to do so. The WNV is like other Wechsler tests in that it uses subtests that vary in content and specific requirements, but different from other Wechsler tests because it was designed to measure general ability using tests that do not have verbal content. The advantage of using nonverbal tasks to measure general ability is that the need for language skills is minimized, and requirements that the examinee have spoken or written language, as well as mathematical, skills are greatly reduced. Although the nonverbal tests on the WNV are all alike in that they do not require language or arithmetic skills, they are diverse in their specific requirements. For example, some of the subtests have a strong visual–spatial requirement, others demand paper-and-pencil skills, and others require the recall of the sequence of information. This multidimensionality of task requirements distinguishes the WNV from tests that use one type of task requirement, such as the NNAT (Naglieri, 1997). Despite the variability of subtest content and task demands, the WNV, like other nonverbal tests have essentially the same goal of measuring general ability nonverbally.

Summary of WNV Research

Due to the recent publication of the WNV, there are comparatively fewer studies on it than on the NNAT, but there are important preliminary findings that bear on the assessment of gifted children that will be briefly described here (see the test manual for more details).

The WNV is strongly correlated with other Wechsler tests (see Wechsler & Naglieri, 2006) but more importantly it is an effective tool for measuring general ability for diverse populations. Gifted children earn high scores on the WNV and the test yields Full Scale scores as high as 170 for both the two- and four-subtest versions. Importantly, the WNV Manual provides a study of English Language Learners. The sample included students whose native language was not English, the primary language they spoke was not English, a language other than English was spoken at home, and/or their parents had resided in the United States fewer than 6 years. The 55 students ages 8–21 were administered the WNV and compared to a group matched on basic demographics. The results showed that the students learning English earned essentially the same score (mean = 101.7) as the matched control of English-speaking students group (mean = 102.1). These results indicate that the WNV measures general ability effectively and fairly for those with limited English language skills.

General Ability and Gifted Children

There is considerable need to carefully examine the tests used to help identify children who are gifted and to select those tests that provide all children an equal opportunity to perform. Bracken and Naglieri (2003) argue that traditional tests of intelligence with their verbal, nonverbal, and quantitative tests are best described as measures of general ability. They go on to state that "general intelligence tests with verbal content and nonverbal content measure essentially the same construct as general ability tests that are entirely nonverbal" (p. 247). Both types of tests measure general ability, but one test measures general ability with varying content (verbal, quantitative, and nonverbal); and the other takes an exclusively nonverbal approach. It is important to recognize that the term *nonverbal assessment* describes the methods used to measure the construct of general intelligence, not a theoretical construct of nonverbal ability (Bracken & McCallum, 1998). That is, there is no assumption that nonverbal, as opposed to verbal or quantitative, *abilities* are being measured. Instead, general ability is measured using non-verbal tests so that a wide variety of individuals may be assessed, using the same set of questions.

The importance of excluding tests with obvious achievement content from a test of ability is particularly salient for children with limited English language skills or those from lower socioeconomic levels where enrichment in the home is limited. It is well-known that high poverty is correlated with low test scores because of issues associated with educational enrichment at home and at school. Many students who live in poverty receive low test scores because of limited opportunity to learn. These students, who may be from all racial and cultural backgrounds, are sometimes penalized on traditional tests of intelligence and subsequently denied access to gifted education programs and services.

Nonverbal measures of general ability are less influenced by limited English language and quantitative skills, making them more appropriate for assessment of culturally and linguistically diverse children (Hayes, 1999; Naglieri & Ford, 2005; Naglieri & Yazzie, 1983; Suzuki & Valencia, 1997). For this and other reasons, nonverbal tests of ability are considered appropriate for a wide variety of persons, especially those with limited English language skills and academic failure (Bracken & McCallum, 1998; Zurcher, 1998). Nonverbal tests can help identify children with high ability who may lack verbal and quantitative skills. The identification method, therefore, has considerable influence on who is served.

There is no consensus about how gifted children should be identified. Although standardized tests often are used as part of the identification process, there is considerable variability as to which tests should be used and what other information should be gathered. Some (e.g., Lohman, 2005) argue that verbal, quantitative, and nonverbal tests are absolutely necessary to identify academically talented students but others (e.g., Naglieri & Ford, 2003, 2005) argue that limiting the definition of gifted to those who demonstrate high achievement and excluding children with high nonverbal scores but lower academic scores perpetuates the problem of underrepresentation of minority children in gifted programs. They suggest that nonverbal tests are advantageous to provide a more equitable way of evaluating a wide variety of children and give greater opportunity for those from culturally and linguistically diverse populations to participate in gifted programs.

More Inclusive Screening

The identification of gifted children who may not excel in academic skills despite high ability poses an important dilemma to those working in the field of gifted education. The implications for our understanding of what a gifted child is, as well as how he or she should be instructed, are considerable. What the use of a nonverbal test of general ability provides is a way to identify children who might otherwise have been excluded, including children with high ability but lower academic skills. The high nonverbal score suggests that the child can acquire the information, and when combined with an understanding of the child's background, provides a more complete picture of what could be expected. Current academic achievement does predict later academic achievement in most children, but not everyone. Using a nonverbal test of general ability allows us to identify those children who have great potential for academic attainment because of high ability and to give more children the opportunity to get additional educational services.

It is important to stress that a high score on a nonverbal test of ability does not mean that instruction should be nonverbal. The term *nonverbal* describes the method of testing, not the type of ability or thinking. Children identified as gifted on a nonverbal test have the intellectual ability to succeed, and they have the ability to understand and learn at a fast pace. They see the big picture and can understand the detail, but their communication and knowledge base may limit the extent to which they can demonstrate their ability. Their curriculum should provide delivery of academic skills at their level and at a pace that is consistent with their fast rate of learning. Performance is, of course, the desired outcome of many variables, not just ability. Importantly, the interaction of ability with knowledge, motivation, emotional status, and the classroom, school, and home environments plays an important role. Smart children who earn very high scores on a nonverbal test of ability but whose achievement skills are not at the same high level should be viable candidates for gifted programming and provided the opportunity to raise their academic skills to a level commensurate with their ability.

Conclusions

The need to identify more minority children who are gifted is clear. How to achieve this goal is complicated. In this chapter, I have outlined one dimension of the problem. That is, ability tests that are achievement-laden can become a barrier to smart children who do not have adequate academic skills. Nonverbal measures of ability are, therefore, more appropriate for identification of gifted minority children, especially those who come from disadvantaged homes (Naglieri & Ford, 2003, 2005). Any apparent psychometric advantage verbal and quantitative tests have over nonverbal tests for prediction of achievement is due to the similar skills needed to solve the items included in the verbal and quantitative portions of ability tests and verbal and quantitative portions of achievement tests. The disadvantage of such tests outweighs any advantages, and the failure to include diverse populations because of limited academic skills can be described as a social injustice.

There is a well-documented achievement gap between minority students and those from low-income homes, in contrast to middle and upper socioeconomic and White students, and documented underrepresentation of minority children in programs for the gifted (Bemak & Chung, 2005; Naglieri & Ford, 2003). The methods that have been used and the assumptions about who is gifted have influenced who has been selected to receive additional academic instruction. There is a need for administrators of gifted programs and teachers of the gifted to reduce the achievement gap and foster social justice and equity for minority students who have high ability, yet lower academic skills. We must, therefore, carefully consider the implications of the test choices we make in addition to the other methods we use for the identification of gifted children.

References

Anastasi, A., & Urbina, S. (1997). *Psychological testing.* Upper Saddle River, NJ: Prentice Hall.

Binet, A., & Simon, T. (1905). New methods for the diagnosis of the intellectual level of subnormals. *L'Année Psychologique, 11,* 191–244.

Bemak, F., & Chung, R. (2005). Advocacy as a critical role for urban school counselors: Working toward equity and social justice. *Professional School Counseling, 8,* 196.

Boake, C. (2002). From the Binet-Simon to the Wechsler-Bellevue: Tracing the history of intelligence testing. *Journal of Clinical & Experimental Neuropsychology, 24,* 383–405.

Bracken, B. A., & McCallum, R. S. (1998). *Universal Nonverbal Intelligence Test.* Itasca, IL: Riverside.

Bracken, B. A., & Naglieri, J. A. (2003). Assessing diverse populations with nonverbal tests of general intelligence. In C. R. Reynolds & R. W. Kamphaus (Eds.), *Handbook of psychological and educational assessment of children* (pp. 243–273). New York: Guilford.

Chall, J. S., & Dale, E. (1995). *Readability revisited: The new Dale-Chall readability formula.* Cambridge, MA: Brookline Books.

Flesch, R. (1948). A new readability yardstick. *Journal of Applied Psychology, 32,* 221–233.

Ford, D. Y. (1998). The underrepresentation of minority students in gifted education: Problems and promises in recruitment and retention. *Journal of Special Education, 32,* 4–14.

Frazier, M. M., Martin, D., Garcia, J., Finley, V. S., Frank, E., Krisel, T, et al. (1995). *A new window for looking at gifted children.* Storrs: National Research Center on the Gifted and Talented, University of Connecticut.

Hayes, S. C. (1999). Comparison of the Kaufman Brief Intelligence Test and the Matrix Analogies Test-Short Form in an adolescent forensic population. *Psychological Assessment, 11,* 108–110.

Hoover, H. D., Dunbar, S. B., & Frisbie, D. A. (2001). *Iowa Tests of Basic Skills.* Itasca, IL: Riverside.

Jensen, A. R. (1998). *The 'g' factor: The science of mental ability.* Westport, CT: Praeger.

Lohman, D. F. (2005). Review of Naglieri and Ford (2003): Does the Naglieri Nonverbal Ability Test identify equal proportions of high-scoring White, Black, and Hispanic students? *Gifted Child Quarterly, 49,* 19–28.

Lohman, D. F., & Hagen, E. P. (2001). *Cognitive Abilities Test.* Itasca, IL: Riverside.

Naglieri, J. A. (1997). *Naglieri Nonverbal Ability Test multilevel form.* San Antonio, TX: The Psychological Corporation.

Naglieri, J. A. (2003). *Naglieri Nonverbal Ability Test individual form.* San Antonio, TX: The Psychological Corporation.

Naglieri, J. A., Booth, A., & Winsler, A. (2004). Comparison of Hispanic children with and without limited English proficiency on the Naglieri Nonverbal Ability Test. *Psychological Assessment, 16,* 81–84.

Naglieri, J. A., & Bornstein, B. T. (2003). Intelligence and achievement: Just how correlated are they? *Journal of Psychoeducational Assessment, 21,* 244–260.

Naglieri, J. A., & Ford, D. Y. (2003). Addressing under-representation of gifted minority children using the Naglieri Nonverbal Ability Test (NNAT). *Gifted Child Quarterly, 47,* 155–160.

Naglieri, J. A., & Ford, D. Y. (2005). Increasing minority children's participation in gifted classes using the NNAT: A response to Lohman. *Gifted Child Quarterly, 49,* 29–36.

Naglieri, J. A., & Ronning, M. E. (2000a). Comparison of White, African-American, Hispanic, and Asian Children on the Naglieri Nonverbal Ability Test. *Psychological Assessment, 12,* 328–334.

Naglieri, J. A., & Ronning, M. E. (2000b). The relationships between general ability using the NNAT and SAT reading achievement. *Journal of Psychoeducational Assessment, 18,* 230–239.

Naglieri, J. A., & Yazzie, C. (1983). Comparison of the WISC-R and PPVT-R with Navajo children. *Journal of Clinical Psychology, 39,* 598–600.

Pintner, R. (1923). *Intelligence testing.* New York: Henry Holt.

Ramirez, R. R., & de la Cruz, G. (2002). *The Hispanic population in the United States: March 2002* (Current Population Reports, 20-545). Washington, DC: U.S. Census Bureau.

Ramsey, M. C., & Reynolds, C. R. (2004). Relations between intelligence and achievement tests. In G. Goldstein & S. Beers (Eds.), *Comprehensive handbook of psychological assessment* (pp. 25–50). New York: John Wiley.

Rojahn, J., & Naglieri, J. A. (2006). Developmental gender differences on the Naglieri Nonverbal Ability Test in a nationally normed sample of 5–17 year olds. *Intelligence, 34*, 253–260.

Roid, G. (2003). *Stanford-Binet Intelligence Scale* (5th ed.). Itasca, IL: Riverside.

Stanford Achievement Test (9th ed.). (1995). San Antonio, TX: The Psychological Corporation.

Suzuki, L. A., & Valencia, R. R. (1997). Race–ethnicity and measured intelligence. *American Psychologist, 52*, 1103–1114.

Wechsler, D. (1939) *Wechsler-Bellevue Intelligence Scale.* New York: The Psychological Corporation.

Wechsler, D. (2001). *Wechsler Individual Achievement Test* (2nd ed.). San Antonio, TX: The Psychological Corporation.

Wechsler, D. (2003a). *Wechsler Intelligence Scale for Children* (4th ed.). San Antonio, TX: The Psychological Corporation.

Wechsler, D., & Naglieri, J. A. (2006). *Wechsler Nonverbal Scale of Ability.* San Antonio, TX: Harcourt Assessment.

Woodcock, R. W., McGrew, K. S., & Mather, N. (2001a). *Woodcock Johnson III Tests of Achievement.* Itasca, IL: Riverside.

Woodcock, R. W., McGrew, K. S., & Mather, N. (2001b). *Woodcock-Johnson III Tests of Cognitive Abilities.* Itasca, IL: Riverside.

Yoakum, C. S., & Yerkes, R. M. (1920). *Army mental tests.* New York: Henry Holt & Company.

Zurcher, R. (1998). Issues and trends in culture-fair assessment. *Intervention in School and Clinic, 34*, 103–106.

Using Off-Level Testing and Assessment for Gifted and Talented Students

Paula Olszewski-Kubilius & Marilynn J. Kulieke

The identification and programming for students who are significantly beyond grade level is a current challenge facing many educators. Even with a desire to educate highly gifted students to their potential, measuring the nature and extent of achievement, aptitude, and cognitive abilities is complex. Additionally, difficulties determining student progress as a result of specific programmatic options for such students, given the limitations of typically used tests, often thwarts a school's efforts to appropriately meet their needs.

One strategy that can be used to measure the performance of students beyond grade level is called *off-level* or *above-grade-level testing*. This involves administering an assessment that was designed for use with students at a higher grade level with younger students for a specific purpose. These purposes might include:

- measuring the extent of exceptional achievement, aptitude, or cognitive abilities;
- analyzing a student's knowledge about a topic before instruction; and
- evaluating growth and progress after a programmatic intervention (e.g., a gifted program).

Off-level testing as an assessment practice within gifted education is not widely used by educators, particularly to analyze a student's knowledge before instruction or to evaluate growth as a result of a program or intervention. It is, however, the basis of a nationwide program aimed at identifying talented students, namely the talent search programs conducted by several universities across the United States.

Talent search programs have been in existence for more than 25 years and have successfully assisted hundreds of thousands of students by identifying their abilities, nurturing their talents through educational programs, and connecting schools and families to appropriate resources, services, and programs (VanTassel-Baska, 1998). As documented in numerous publications (e.g., Assouline & Lupkowski-Shoplik, 1997; Benbow, 1992a, 1992b; Brody, 1998; Jarosewich & Stocking, 2003; Olszewski-Kubilius, 1998a), the talent search was initiated in the early 1970s by Dr. Julian Stanley at Johns Hopkins University as part of the Study of Mathematically Precocious Youth (SMPY). Its primary goal at that time was to identify mathematically talented pre-high school aged students using the Scholastic Aptitude Test-Math (SAT-M). Talent searches currently include several off-level tests that assess both mathematical and verbal areas in elementary and middle school aged children.

Talent search is predicated on the belief that gifted children need to be assessed with tests commensurate with their abilities, developmental rates, and preexisting knowledge and skills, not their chronological age or grade. Several major university-based gifted institutes, such as the Center for Talent Development at Northwestern University, the Talent Identification Program at Duke University, the Center for Talented Youth at Johns Hopkins University, and the Rocky Mountain Talent Search at the University of Denver, conduct talent search programs annually in order to provide students in grades 3–9 who score at the 95th percentile or above on nationally normed tests with more accurate information about their academic abilities.

Talent search programs include the following major components: the diagnosis and evaluation of the area and level of students' abilities via off-level tests such as ACT, SAT, or EXPLORE; educational placement for individual students based on test scores; access to further talent development opportunities such as weekend programs, summer programs, and distance education programs; and guidance and expert advice via newsletters, magazines, and conferences (Olszewski-Kubilius, 1998a, 2004).

Talent search programs have become a major force within gifted education and are the key provider of out-of-school specialized programming. Based on data from 2004, almost a quarter of a million students in grades 3–9 participated in off-level testing offered by talent search programs. Of these, almost 34,000 subsequently participated in an educational program sponsored by a talent search in 2004. Almost half of the program participants were in summer programs and another 10,000 students were involved in Saturday and weekend programs, 7,500 in distance learning courses, and 460 in leadership programs. Although these programs serve many gifted students, it should be noted that males participate at slightly higher rates than females (55% versus 45%) and minority students are underrepresented, particularly in educational programs and less so in off-level testing (Lee, Matthews, & Olszewski-Kubilius, in press).

There is a comprehensive body of research about talent search and talent search participants—literally hundreds of published research studies produced by the talent search programs. These studies document the validity of using the ACT and SAT with middle school students by showing that students' performance on these tests is similar to the average college-bound senior (Bartkovich & Mezynski, 1981; Benbow, 1992a; Olszewski-Kubilius, 1998b; Olszewski-Kubilius & Lee, in press); the predictive validity of talent search scores for later school achievement and career success (Barnett & Durden, 1993; Benbow, 1992a, 1992b; Benbow & Arjmand, 1990; Burton, 1988; Lubinski, Webb, Morelock, & Benbow, 2001; Webb, Lubinski, & Benbow, 2002); and the predictive validity of talent search scores within the gifted population by discriminating different patterns of achievement into adulthood for students scoring at the top versus bottom quartile of the top 1% (Benbow, 1992b; Wai, Lubinski, & Benbow, 2005).

Off-level testing can be approached in a number of different ways. It could involve using classroom assessments developed for higher grade levels to assess learning or existing knowledge, using standardized tests designed for higher grade levels to assess ability, using final examinations that cover coursework beyond the grade-level curriculum, or using a performance/product that is judged using above-grade-level benchmarks. Any of these approaches is useful and appropriate depending upon the purpose of the assessment. The focus of this chapter is specifically on the use of standardized test measures for determining off-level or above–grade-level performance. It is a strategy that has high credibility for both educators and parents in making decisions about students and their intervention needs.

This chapter provides information on:
- determining purposeful measures for off-level testing,
- interpreting scores from off-level tests, and
- using off-level testing (a case study).

Determining Purposeful Measures for Off-Level Testing

Off-level tests are generally used when a student's performance is expected to be two to four grade levels above his or her age-mates. An off-level test is like a high-powered microscope. It allows educators to see detail that is useful for diagnosis and intervention. "What are we diagnosing?" and "How are we intervening?" become very important questions for choosing appropriate off-level measures.

Understanding the "what" of diagnosis begins with a classification of measures into achievement, aptitude, and intelligence/cognitive abilities. Educators are most familiar with *achievement tests*—or tests that measure specific knowledge and skills that are appropriate for specific content areas. *Aptitude tests* measure a student's natural talents or special abilities for doing or learning to do certain kinds of things. *Intelligence* or *cognitive abilities tests* measure analytic skills that are "content blind" and represent a student's ability to reason and think.

Table 5.1

Distinguishing Characteristics of Achievement, Aptitude, and Intelligence Measures

	Achievement	Aptitude	Intelligence or Cognitive Abilities
Purpose	• Measure student's academic performance	• Measure student's talents or abilities to perform academically	• Measure student's analytic skills to perform complex tasks
Content	• Content-area knowledge and skills	• Talents or special abilities for doing or learning certain knowledge and skills	• Content "blind" analytical skills
Example	• EXPLORE/ PLAN/ACT • SAT II • Stanford Achievement Tests	• Test of English as a Foreign Language (TOEFL) • Graduate Record Exam (GRE)	• Naglieri Cognitive Assessment System • Test of Cognitive Skills

Table 5.1 lists some general features of achievement, aptitude, and intelligence/cognitive abilities tests. It is important to consider these distinctions in determining purposeful off-level measures.

The type of off-level measure needed to diagnose student performance is inextricably tied to the potential program interventions. For example, it is not very helpful to identify a 6th-grade student as having 10th-grade achievement in mathematics if there are no advanced mathematics interventions available for the student. And, it becomes further complicated if a student accelerated in mathematics has no other program options when he or she reaches 12th grade. The interaction between type of measure and programmatic intervention must be considered as a part of an off-level testing strategy.

Another consideration in using an off-level testing strategy is the standardization of the administration. Most test scores that are used by educators are based on tests that are administered under standard conditions (e.g., a certain amount of time and in a similar way). The more variation there is in an administration, the more difficulty in interpreting a test score. Lack of reliability or high degrees of variation in scores from one test administration to the next, in particular, becomes a problem in measuring the extent to which a student's achievement, aptitude, or cognitive ability is significantly beyond grade level.

The choice of a specific standardized test form two to four levels higher than the student's grade level is the first step in using an off-level testing strategy. The next is interpreting the meaning of the results. The following section provides a framework for interpreting off-level test scores.

Interpreting Scores From Off-Level Tests

Figure 5.1 illustrates a model for transforming standardized test data into meaningful information about gifted students. Although these steps are commonly followed in interpreting test results, the specific concerns facing educators who are using an off-level testing strategy with gifted students will be addressed.

Raw Scores

The score that educators are most familiar with is a raw score. This is the number of test items that a student has answered correctly. The perennial problem with raw scores is that they are difficult to interpret, especially if the number of items changes from one test to another. For example, teachers may include raw scores from their classroom tests in their grade books, but

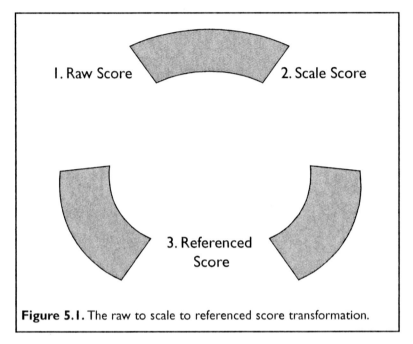

Figure 5.1. The raw to scale to referenced score transformation.

they often transform a raw score to a scale score (percent correct), which makes the scores more comparable and meaningful across tests. Because tests and subtests differ in length, content, and difficulty, raw scores are not easily usable in an off-level testing situation.

Raw scores are specifically problematic for gifted students who are expected to be significantly above grade level. Students who get all the items correct or "hit the ceiling" do not have the opportunity to show how much more they know or are able to do. The use of an off-level test provides more difficult items that should present students with more challenge, which ultimately means that they can be compared to their academic peers.

Scale Scores

A scale score (SS) is one that shows the results of a test on a single common scale. A scale score often is used as the basis of calculating other scores across different test forms. Have you ever

Table 5.2
Examples of Different Scale Scores and Score Ranges

Test	Type of Score	Score Range
Classroom Test	Percent Correct	0 to 100
Scholastic Aptitude Test (SAT I)	Scale Score	200 to 800
ACT Test	Scale Score	1 to 36
Map Tests	RIT Score	Infinite, but most scores between 140 to 300

wondered why an ACT score *always* ranges from 1 to 36 or an SAT score always ranges from 200 to 800? Neither score matches the number of items on the test. Scale scores are based on the difficulty of item content and the distributions of the test-taking group (e.g., college-bound students for the ACT and SAT [see Table 5.2 for comparisons of scale score models]).

Scale scores have been created to provide stability across years and subtests. Educators will always know the range of the scores in the scale used for a particular test. Virtually all standardized tests, including tests such as the Stanford 10 and the California Achievement tests, have an underlying scale score that can be used to compare scores from one test level to another or in a particular subject area over time.

Using scale scores is one of the easiest ways to evaluate gifted student growth and progress after a programmatic intervention. Scale scores are always equal interval scores, which means that they can be added, subtracted, multiplied, and divided. They are not always easily interpretable but their functionality in examining off-level student growth is good.

Referenced Scores

The final step in creating meaningful scores that can be used to measure gifted student performance is referencing. Referencing provides the basic rationale for off-level testing— that gifted students should not be compared to their age-mates at a particular grade level but to their academic peers who may include older students and students at a higher grade level. By making this comparison, educators can better understand the level of students' abilities and match them with programmatic interventions to meet their needs.

This is the most difficult of the transformations because it not only requires an understanding of the meaning of a referenced score, but also what student the score is referenced to. There are predominantly two types of referencing—norm and criterion referencing. There are many excellent books on the topic of referencing and this section will only summarize the characteristics of these two models in relationship to off-level testing.

Norm-Referenced Scores

A norm-referenced score is one that only is meaningful in terms of its relative position with respect to other scores on the same test. The goal of a norm-referenced score is to discriminate between students. In order to accomplish this, about 40% to 60% of the students in a particular grade level national group should be able to answer each item correctly on a leveled test.

The most commonly used norm-referenced score is the National Percentile Rank. This score indicates a student's score in reference to a normal distribution of grade level test takers nationwide and ranges from 1–99. A student's percentile rank score of 99 means that 99% of the scores in the normal distribution are below this student's score. There never can be a percentile rank of 100, because 100% of the scores could never be below a student's score.

Figure 5.2 shows the distribution of the percentile rank scores. Notice that they are not equal interval scores, which means that they can't be added, subtracted, multiplied, or divided.

Norm-referenced scores on on-level tests are not very useful to educators in providing new information about a gifted student who has already been identified as academically talented—or even determining whether or not there has been any growth—because we already know that these students typically

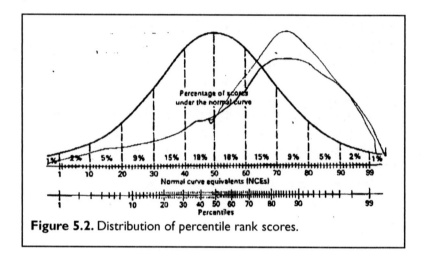

Figure 5.2. Distribution of percentile rank scores.

rank at the top. Figure 5.3 shows an example of how off-level tests (e.g., ACT, SAT, EXPLORE) can provide very useful information about students who score between the 95th and 99th percentile ranks on an on-level reading achievement test. The figure demonstrates that in the use of on-level tests, students are indistinguishable from each other—all scoring at the ceiling of the on-level test. But, with the use of an off-level test, further discriminations can be made regarding the abilities of students. Some students score at the low end of the off-level test and some score at the high end. Students who might be treated the same in terms of their educational provisions on the basis of scores on the on-level tests are really very different in terms of learning ability on the basis of their scores on the off-level tests. These students have very different educational needs, which would go undetermined if we relied on scores from the on-level test only.

The issue of a "measurement ceiling" is essential to understanding the need for off-level tests. Measurement ceiling occurs when a test has inadequate items to discriminate between test scorers. How do you know when a student has hit the ceiling of a test? The easiest way is to determine whether or not a student's score will go up if another item is answered correctly. If the score does not change, then the "ceiling" has been attained.

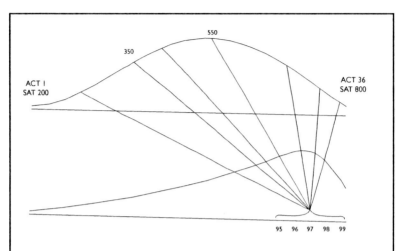

Figure 5.3. Comparison of on-level reading percentile ranks compared to off-level average scale scores.

Note. From "Talent Search: Purposes, Rationale and Role in Gifted Education," by P. Olszewski-Kubilius, 1998a, *Journal of Secondary Gifted Education, 9*, p. 108. Copyright © 1998 Prufrock Press. Reprinted with permission.

The problem with most on–level tests for bright students is that they easily will hit the ceiling on them, and the nature of their true abilities cannot be measured adequately. It is akin to using a yardstick to measure the height of a group of adults. All you can say is that the adults are all at least 3 feet tall. Your measuring instrument is unable to detect further differences in height. And, these unmeasured differences in height have tremendous implications for, say, pant size. If you ordered pants for the group of adults just on the basis of the measurement of the yardstick, you would get them all the same size, which in reality, would fit very few of them adequately. Relying on on-level tests to measure gifted students' abilities or achievements often has a one-size-fits-all result.

Criterion-Referenced Scores

Criterion-referenced scores are those that are interpreted by comparing a student's performance to a determined standard. The goal of criterion-referenced testing is to determine the extent to which a student has mastered specific knowledge and skills. These types of tests are usually developed at a particular grade level and often are used to determine the extent to which a student has mastered the in-grade curriculum.

The ACT provides a good example of a scale score that is criterion-referenced. The ACT originally was designed to discriminate between those students who had the knowledge, skills, or abilities to succeed in college. Universities throughout the United States and the world depend on the fact that a student who receives a certain ACT score has a better chance of being successful at his or her university. The criterion referencing the ACT employs makes a test like this very appropriate for off-level testing. Meaning has been created for certain scores and that meaning is recognized throughout the world. ACT's College Readiness Standards further provide students with additional information on their specific knowledge and skills.

There are many examples of norm- and criterion-referenced scores that are meaningful in measuring the true achievement, aptitude, and cognitive ability of gifted students. Choosing an appropriate standardized test that has an apt reference group provides students with the opportunity to demonstrate what they really know and are able to do in relation to the standard for success in a particular learning context.

Using Off-Level Testing: A Case Study

The Midwest Academic Talent Search (MATS), sponsored by the Center for Talent Development at Northwestern University, was one of the pioneers in the use of off-level testing. Started in the early 1980s, the Center for Talent Development has been testing students in the third through ninth grade who have recognized talent—predominantly identified through a student's norm-referenced test score at the 95th percentile or above.

The Center for Talent Development has chosen three achievement tests to use as off-level tests. Table 5.3 shows the levels (both off-level and on-level) for the tests utilized in the MATS program.

Table 5.3
Overview of MATS Off-Level Tests

Test Name	Off-Level (On-Level)	Achievement Areas
SAT Developed by College Board	Grades 7–9 (11–12)	Mathematics, reading, writing
ACT Developed by the American College Testing Service	Grades 7–9 (11–12)	English, mathematics, reading, science reasoning, writing
EXPLORE Developed by the American College Testing Service	Grades 4–6 (8)	English, mathematics, reading, science reasoning, writing

The scale scores achieved by many off-level test takers on the SAT, ACT, and EXPLORE tests have demonstrated the ceiling effect described in Figures 5.4 and 5.5. In examining the ACT, EXPLORE, and SAT scale scores achieved by off-level test takers in comparison to the older students who typically take these tests and for whom the tests were originally designed, the following results were found in 2004–2005. As can be seen from these tables, a sizeable proportion of the younger students score at or above the averages for the older students, indicating that these off-level tests are not too difficult for younger students.

The Center for Talent Development suggests that there are a variety of interventions that may be appropriate for students within different scale score ranges (see Table 5.4). These include:

1. within-class interventions (e.g., enrichment, acceleration, individualization, differentiation);
2. resource room/pull-out (e.g., independent projects or studies);
3. homogeneous or full class (e.g., acceleration one or more years above grade levels);

	EXPLORE: Percent Above Eighth Graders (SS = 13.9)	ACT: Percent Above College Bound (SS = 21.3)	SAT: Percent Above College Bound (SS = 504)
Grade 3	18%		
Grade 4	37%		
Grade 5	54%		
Grade 6	73%	19%	11%
Grade 7		31%	22%
Grade 8		48%	39%

Figure 5.4. Percent of younger students scoring above mean for older students: Reading/Verbal 2005–2006.

Note. Data taken from "Midwest Academic Talent Search Statistical Summary," by Center for Talent Development, Northwestern University, 2006, Evanston, IL: Author. Copyright © 2006 Center for Talent Development. Adapted with permission.

	EXPLORE: Percent Above Eighth Graders (SS = 14.4)	ACT: Percent Above College Bound (SS = 20.7)	SAT: Percent Above College Bound (SS = 516)
Grade 3	13%		
Grade 4	34%		
Grade 5	60%		
Grade 6	85%	4%	17%
Grade 7		10%	25%
Grade 8		28%	43%

Figure 5.5. Percent of younger students scoring above mean for older students: Mathematics 2005–2006.

Note: The Center for Talent Development has divided test scores into three ranges to help parents and staff determine the most needed types of programming for each scoring level. The scale scores denoting each score range were based on best practices for different levels of gifted learners. Data taken from "Midwest Academic Talent Search Statistical Summary," by Center for Talent Development, Northwestern University, 2006, Evanston, IL: Author. Copyright © 2006 Center for Talent Development. Adapted with permission.

4. accelerative strategies and options (e.g., grade placement from one to four grade levels in areas of strengths, AP, IB, dual enrollment, summer programs); and
5. extracurricular options (e.g., clubs, contests, mentorships, internships, and career counseling).

The match between referenced scores and programmatic interventions is an important aspect of the CTD program. Without the means for identifying high-performing students and the means of providing programs for students at various levels, an important opportunity is missed.

Conclusions

The question that often is asked by parents and educators alike is "Why should a student participate in off-level testing? We already know that he is gifted." There are a number of benefits to participating in off-level testing. First, off-level testing provides more accurate measurement for high-achieving or high-ability students due to the higher ceiling of grade-level tests. It also yields information that can be useful for grade placement, subject area placement, acceleration, or grouping of students. Finally, because of the higher ceiling, the test can measure growth or progress from year to year.

However, off-level testing is not a panacea for gifted students. Problems that are faced by educators include the fact that norm-referenced test scores such as percentile ranks and stanines are quite common. When a student takes an off-level test, it is more difficult to interpret the results. It also may create some uneasiness among students and parents who fear a more difficult test. Finally, scores may be disconcerting to parents who are used to and expect high test scores and an excellent percentile rank.

Overall, off-level testing provides a good strategy for identifying and determining appropriate programming interventions for gifted students who are two or more grade levels above their age-mates in achievement, aptitude, or ability. Programs internationally have shown the applicability of this model for providing an appropriate education for the most gifted and talented students in our midst.

Table 5.4
Three Ranges of Scale Scores (A, B, C) for Differentiated Gifted Programming 2005–2006

Ranges	EXPLORE Reading SS	ACT Reading SS	SAT Reading/ Verbal SS	Intervention
Reading "A" Range	1–13★	1–21★★	230–470	Enrichment in home/school settings in reading
Reading "B" Range	14–18★	22–27★★	480–580	Advanced classes in language arts, writing, etc.
Reading "C" Range	19 and above★	28 and above ★★	Above 580	Accelerated learning through advanced coursework at university talent searches
Math "A" Range	1–14★	1–17	200–510	Enrichment in mathematics
Math "B" Range	15–18★	18–23	520–600	Advanced classes in mathematics
Math "C" Range	19 and above★	24 and above	Above 600	Accelerated study in university in talent search mathematics classes

Note. Data from *Recommended Planning and Resource Guide for ACT and SAT Test-Takers*, by Center for Talent Development, Northwestern University, 2007, Evanston, IL: Author. Copyright ©2007 Center for Talent Development. Adapted with permission.
★These scores are recommended for fifth and sixth graders and would be slightly lower for fourth graders.
★★English scale scores may be considered in determining the range of scores appropriate for different interventions.

References

Assouline, S., & Lupkowski-Shoplik, A. (1997). Talent searches: A model for the discovery and development of academic talent. In N. Colangelo & G. A. Davis (Eds.), *Handbook of gifted education* (2nd ed., pp. 170–179). Needham Heights, MA: Allyn & Bacon.

Barnett, L. B., & Durden, W. G. (1993). Education patterns of academically talented youth. *Gifted Child Quarterly, 37*, 161–168.

Bartkovich, K. G., & Mezynski, K. (1981). Fast-paced precalculus mathematics for talented junior-high students: Two recent SMPY programs. *Gifted Child Quarterly, 25*, 73–80.

Benbow, C. P. (1992a). Mathematical talent: Its nature and consequences. In N. Colangelo, S. G. Assouline, & D. L. Ambroson (Eds.), *Talent development: Proceedings from the 1991 Henry B. and Jocelyn Wallace National Research Symposium on Talent Development* (pp. 95–123). New York: Trillium.

Benbow, C. P. (1992b). Academic achievement in mathematics and science of students between ages 13 and 23: Are there differences among students in the top one percent of mathematical ability? *Journal of Educational Psychology, 84*, 51–61.

Benbow, C. P., & Arjmand, O. (1990). Predictors of high academic achievement in mathematics and science by mathematically talented students: A longitudinal study. *Journal of Educational Psychology, 82*, 430–441.

Brody, L. E. (1998). The talent searches: A catalyst for change in higher education. *Journal of Secondary Gifted Education, 9*, 124–133.

Burton, N. W. (1988). *Survey II: Test-taking history for 1980–81 young SAT-takers* (Report No. 88-1). New York: College Entrance Examination Board.

Center for Talent Development, Northwestern University. (2006). *Midwest Academic Talent Search statistical summary*. Evanston, IL: Author.

Center for Talent Development, Northwestern University. (2007). *Recommended planning and resource guide for ACT and SAT test-takers.* Evanston, IL: Author.

Jarosewich, T., & Stocking, V. B. (2003). Talent search: Student and parent perceptions of out-of-level testing. *Journal of Secondary Gifted Education, 14*, 137–150.

Lee, S.-Y., Matthews, M. S., & Olszewski-Kubilius, P. (in press). A national picture of talent search and talent search educational programs. *Gifted Child Quarterly.*

Lubinski, D., Webb, R. M., Morelock, M. J., & Benbow, C. P. (2001). Top 1 in 20,000: A 10 year follow-up of the profoundly gifted. *Journal of Applied Psychology, 85*, 718–729.

Olszewski-Kubilius, P. (1998a). Talent search: Purposes, rationale and role in gifted education. *Journal of Secondary Gifted Education, 9*, 106–114.

Olszewski-Kubilius, P. (1998b). Research evidence regarding the validity and effects of talent search educational programs. *Journal of Secondary Gifted Education, 9*, 134–138.

Olszewski-Kubilius, P. (2004). Talent searches and accelerated programming for gifted students. In N. Colangelo, S. G. Assouline, & M. U. M. Gross (Eds.), *A nation deceived: How schools hold back America's brightest students* (Vol. 2, pp. 69–76). Iowa City, IA: The Connie Belin & Jacqueline N. Blank International Center for Gifted Education and Talent Development.

Olszewski-Kubilius, P., & Lee, S.-Y. (in press). Specialized programs serving the gifted. In F. A. Karnes & K. R. Stephens (Eds.), *Gifted education*. Columbus, OH: Pearson.

Wai, J., Lubinski, D., & Benbow, C. P. (2005). Creativity and occupational accomplishments among intellectually precocious youths: An age 13 to age 33 longitudinal study. *Journal of Educational Psychology, 97*, 484–492.

Webb, R. M., Lubinski, D., & Benbow, C. P. (2002). Mathematically facile adolescents with math-science aspirations: New perspectives on their educational and vocational development. *Journal of Educational Psychology, 94*, 785–794.

VanTassel-Baska, J. (1998). Key issues and problems in secondary programming. In J. VanTassel-Baska (Ed.), *Excellence in educating gifted and talented learners* (3rd ed., pp. 241–259). Denver: Love.

Intelligence Testing and Cultural Diversity: The Need for Alternative Instruments, Policies, and Procedures

Donna Y. Ford

There is great deal of concern and debate about the low performance of racially and linguistically diverse students—those of Black, Hispanic, and Native American descent—on standardized tests. Nowhere are the debates and controversies surrounding intelligence testing more prevalent than in gifted education and special education. These two educational fields rely extensively on tests to make educational and placement decisions. In gifted education, low test scores often prevent diverse students from being identified as gifted and receiving services; in special education, low test scores often result in the identification of these students as learning disabled, developmentally delayed, and so forth.

Racially and linguistically diverse students (Black, Hispanic, and Native American students) are underrepresented in gifted education and overrepresented in special education (see Council of State Directors of Programs for the Gifted and National Association for Gifted Children, 2003; U.S. Department of Education [USDE], 2003). Ford (1998) and Frasier, García, and Passow (1995) reported that Black, Hispanic, and Native American students always have been underrepresented in gifted education programs. In 1993, the U.S. Department of Education noted that Black and Hispanic students were underrepresented by 50% in gifted programs, and Native American students were underrepresented by 70%. More recent data (USDE, 1998) indicate that, in 1997, Black students' under-representation *increased* to 60%.

There are two persistent perspectives surrounding minority students' intelligence test performance. In one camp, scholars argue that the low test performance of minority students can be attributed to cultural deprivation or disadvantage(s); con-notatively, this refers to the notion of diverse students being inferior to other students (see Rushton, 2003). Unfortunately, deficit-thinking orientations are present even today (e.g., Ford, Harris, Tyson, & Frazier Trotman, 2002). For instance, Frasier, García, et al. (1995), Frasier and Passow (1994), and Harmon (2002) argued that teachers tend not to refer racially and cultur-ally diverse students to gifted programs because of their defi-cit thinking and stereotypes about diverse students. When the focus is on what diverse students cannot do rather than what they can do, then they are not likely even to be referred for gifted education services.

Offering a different perspective, other scholars argue that minority students are culturally different, but not culturally dis-advantaged or deficient (e.g., Boykin, 1986; Delpit, 1995; Hale, 2001; Nieto, 1999; Rodriguez & Bellanca, 1996; Shade, Kelly, & Oberg, 1997). These individuals acknowledge that culture impacts test performance, but they do not equate or associate low performance with inferiority.

There also are equally spirited and rigorous debates about the use of standardized tests with diverse groups, with the greatest attention to issues of test bias (Armour-Thomas, 1992; Helms, 1992). Publications on test bias seem to have waned in the last decade although *The Bell Curve* (Herrnstein & Murray, 1994) generated renewed debates and controversy. Many test developers have gone to great length to decrease or eliminate (if this is possible) culturally biased (or culturally loaded) test items (Johnsen, 2004). Accordingly, some scholars contend that test bias no longer exists (e.g., Jensen, 1980, 1998, 2000; Rushton, 2003; also see discussion by Fancher, 1985). Others contend that tests can be reduced culturally so that bias can be decreased; still others contend that tests never can be bias-free or culturally neutral because they are manmade instruments, reflecting the culture of the test developer. Absolute fairness to every examinee is impossible to attain for no other reason than that tests have imperfect reliability, and validity can vary by context and degree (American Educational Research Association, American Psychological Association, & National Council on Measurement in Education, hereafter referred to as "Joint Standards," 1999, p. 73).

In sum, there is little consensus in education (or psychology) about the reasons diverse students score lower on standardized tests of intelligence than do mainstream students. Further, there is little consensus regarding the definition of intelligence, the definition of test bias, the existence of test bias, the types of test biases, the impact of test bias on diverse students, and the nature and extent of test bias in contemporary or newly renormed tests.

With so many unanswered questions and controversies regarding intelligence, testing in general, and testing diverse students in particular, what can educators in gifted education do to ensure that these students have access to and are represented in gifted education programs and services?

Testing and Diverse Populations: Beyond Historical Issues

There is a long-standing and persistent debate regarding the equitable use of tests and assessment strategies with diverse populations. This debate and related concerns especially are prevalent in cases of high-stakes testing, where tests are used to make important and long-term educational decisions about students. As Lam (1993) observed, once test scores become numbers in students' files, they provide the basis for high-stakes decisions concerning selection, placement, certification, and promotion that are made without consideration of the inequities surrounding testing.

Psychological and psychoeducational assessment is an area that has been heavily subjected to complaints about the differential treatment of diverse groups. Hilliard (1991), Korchin (1980), Olmedo (1981), and others contend that standardized tests have contributed to the perpetuation of social, economic, and political barriers confronting diverse groups (Padilla & Medina, 1996; Suzuki, Meller, & Ponterotto, 1996). Specifically, questions have been raised regarding whether standardized intelligence tests are biased. Tests can be biased in terms of impact (e.g., how they are used), as well as the kinds of items they contain. Tests can be biased if they treat groups unfairly or discriminate against diverse groups by, for example, "underestimating their potential or over-pathologizing their symptoms" (Suzuki, Meller, et al., 1996, p. xiii). This concept is referred to as *disparate impact* (Office for Civil Rights [OCR], 2000) and may not be associated with statistical biases, defined next. The Joint Standards (1999) defined statistical bias as a systematic error in a test score. In discussing test fairness, statistical bias may refer to construct underrepresentation or construct-irrelevant components of test scores that differentially affect the performance of different groups of test takers (pp. 76, 77, 172). Thus, it is important to note that when tests are used for selecting and screening, the potential for denying diverse groups access to advanced educational opportunities, such as gifted education programs, is great.

The consequences of misinterpretation of tests are grave. For instance, because many school districts rely on a single test score to place students in gifted education programs and, given the lower performance of diverse groups on tests, this practice serves as an effective gate-keeping mechanism. Interpreting test performance—high or low—based on one test or measure must be avoided due to the limited data provided from a single score. The National Association for Gifted Children (1997), OCR (2000), and Joint Standards (1999) have noted the serious limitations and negative consequences (e.g., disparate impact) of using one test score to identify students as gifted and to determine their need for placement in gifted education programs. In other words:

Tests are not perfect. Test questions are a sample of possible questions that could be asked in a given area. Moreover, a test score is not an exact measure of a student's knowledge or skills. A student's scores can be expected to vary across different versions of a test— within a margin of error determined by the reliability of the test, and as a function of the particular sample of questions asked and/or transitory factors, such as the student's health on the day of the tests. Thus, no single test score can be considered a definitive measure of a student's knowledge. (OCR, 2000, p. 14)

Test scores can mislead just as easily as they can lead (Kaufman, 1994, p. 13). For many reasons, students get high test scores (e.g., coaching, tutoring, practice effects) and for many reasons, students get low scores (e.g., poor test-taking skills, test anxiety, poor listening skills, poor reading skills, poor attention span). Thus, if an interpretive approach relies strictly on one view of the world, no matter how theoretically or psychometrically defensible that view may be, it is doomed to fail for some children (Kaufman, 1994, p. 23). According to the most recent report by the Council of State Directors of Programs for the Gifted and the National Association for Gifted Children (2003), in 2001–2002, only 24 states mandated nondiscriminatory testing in their gifted education policies and procedures while 18 reported no such mandate (pp. 53–54). Further, several states reported using only one score to make placement decisions (e.g., Arizona, Oregon, Ohio).

Our basic obligation as educators is to meet the needs of students as they come to us—with their different learning styles, economic backgrounds, cultural backgrounds, and academic skills. In *Larry P. v. Riles* (1979), the court argued:

If tests predict that a person is going to be a poor employee, the employer can legitimately deny the person the job, but if tests suggest that a young child is probably going to be a poor student, a school cannot on that basis alone deny that child the opportunity to improve and develop the academic skills necessary to succeed in our society.

Stated differently, gifted education must not only teach gifted students who demonstrate their gifts and talents, they also must address student potential and, thus, create talent development models (Callahan & McIntyre, 1994; USDE, 1993, 1998).

The Influence of Culture on Test Performance: Black Students as a Case in Point

Culture can be defined as the collective beliefs, attitudes, traditions, customs, and behaviors that serve as a filter through which a group of people view and respond to the world (Ford & Harris, 1999; Ford et al., 2002; Hall, 1959, 1976). Culture is a way of life, a way of looking at and interpreting life, and a way of responding to life. This definition becomes more clear when one thinks of the "terrible twos," the teen or adolescent culture, the culture of poverty, and so forth. Members of these groups have common beliefs, attitudes, traditions, customs, and behaviors (e.g., Storti, 1998).

In a thoughtful and compelling monograph entitled *A New Window for Looking at Gifted Children,* Frasier, Martin, and colleagues (1995) stated, "Manifestation of characteristics associated with giftedness may be different in minority children, yet educators are seldom trained in identifying those behaviors in ways other than the way they are observed in the majority culture" (p. 33). This statement was confirmed in a study that included teachers' perceptions of giftedness among diverse students (Frasier, Hunsaker, et al., 1995).

Helms (1992) provided another thoughtful, conceptual treatise on the issue of how culture impacts test performance and, thereby, raises questions about the validity of tests when used with diverse groups (for other definitions of culture and the impact of culture on test performance, see Groth-Marnat, 1997, 2003; Miller, 1996; Sattler, 1992; Sternberg, 1982). Helms (1992) maintained that the notion of cultural or functional equivalence must be considered when diverse students are being tested or assessed. Using Boykin's (1986) research on the modal characteristics of Blacks, Helms (1992) hypothesized how these Afrocentric cultural dimensions or characteristics can and do influence the test performance of Black students (see Figure 6.1). The Afrocentric styles gleaned from Boykin's research include: spirituality, harmony, verve and movement, affect, communalism, expressiveness, orality, and social time perspective[10]. They are explained as follows:

- *Spirituality* is a belief that nonmaterial forces have governing powers in one's everyday affairs. It is a conviction that all of life is governed by a power greater than oneself.
- *Harmony* is seeing oneself as one with environmental surroundings; the aim is to blend in with the setting, to be a member of the setting; harmony also is an enhanced ability to read the environment and to read nonverbal behaviors well.
- *Verve* is a propensity for high levels of energy and stimulation; it denotes a disdain for routine and doing things in a rigid, sequential fashion. Verve entails a preference for doing things simultaneously and instantaneously.
- *Movement* is a preference for being active, mobile, and physically engaged or involved; it is a rhythmic orientation to life, as seen in music and dance, and an ability to express oneself nonverbally.
- *Affect* involves a propensity to be feeling-oriented, to engage in or avoid activities and people for whom one has strong positive or negative feelings, respectively. Students strong in affect can be impulsive and very sensitive or emotional. Like harmony, affect also includes a keen ability to read the emotional cues of others.
- *Communalism* refers to social interdependence and connectedness; this is a social orientation that is often accompanied by a strong need for affiliation; group affiliation is important as denoted by an "other-centeredness" rather than

---

10   Boykin's (1994) data-based model of Afrocentric cultural styles has been examined and discussed in hundreds of publications; for a discussion of the cultural styles of Blacks, Hispanics, Asian Americans, and Native Americans, see, for example, Baldwin and Vialle (1999); Banks and Banks (2004); Callahan and McIntyre (1994); Castellano (2003); Cline and Schwartz (1999); Maker and Schiever (1989); Shade et al. (1997); Storti (1998); and USDE (1998).

Dimension	General Description	Influence on Test Responses
Spirituality	Greater validity of the power of immaterial forces in everyday life over linear and factual thinking.	It may be difficult to separate relevant aspects of the test stimuli from factors caused by luck or circumstances.
Harmony	The self and one's surroundings are interconnected; individual reads environment and nonverbal and body language well.	The ambience in which one takes the test may influence one's responses; the test taker may be distracted by events taking place during the test.
Movement and Verve	Personal conduct is organized through movement. Students are spontaneous, active, energetic, and lively.	Active test-taking strategies may result in better performance than sedentary ones; test taker may have difficulty sitting through and concentrating during lengthy tests.
Affect	Integration of feelings with thoughts and actions; sensitive and emotional.	Feelings may facilitate or hinder test performance; test taker may find it difficult to "understand" persons in test stimuli who act without feeling.
Communalism	Valuing of one's group(s) more than outsiders or other individuals; social; interdependent.	Performance may be influenced when test taker is anxious about the test scores being reflective of his or her cultural group and having negative consequences for the group.
Expressiveness	Unique personality is expressed through one's behavioral styles; creative, risk taker; spontaneous.	Test taker may choose the more imaginative response alternative; may be impulsive in choosing responses.
Orality (oral tradition)	Knowledge may be gained and transmitted orally and aurally; a preference to talk and explain verbally.	Test performance may differ when the test taker is tested orally and aurally; test taker may be frustrated by paper-and-pencil tests.
Social Time (polychronicity)	Time is measured by socially meaningful events and customs; person is able to do more than one thing simultaneously.	The belief that obtaining a "good" answer is more important than finishing on time may lead the test taker to "waste" or mismanage time; he or she may not begin responding immediately to the test.

Figure 6.1. African cultural components in cognitive ability testing: Hypothesized effects of African-centered values and beliefs.

Note. Adapted from "Why Is There No Study of Equivalence in Standardized Cognitive-Ability Testing?" by J. Helms, 1992, *American Psychologist, 47,* p. 1096; also see Boykin (1986).

self-centeredness. Students with this orientation prefer to work in groups and make group decisions rather than work independently or alone.

- *Expressiveness* (also known as *expressive individualism*) refers to an orientation of being creative and a risk taker. There is concern about style, being spontaneous, and original in dress, music, speech, and other forms of expression. Life is approached in artistic and creative ways.

- *Orality* (also referred to as *oral tradition*) refers to the emphasis and preference placed on communicating by word of mouth; it is a special sensitivity to aural modes of communication, and an ability to use words to convey meaning and feelings in expressive ways. To speak is to perform, which also entails playing with words and language (e.g., being blunt, and using humor, puns, riddles, proverbs). To speak is to affirm, as denoted by the "call-and-response" mode of communicating.

- *Social time perspective* (also called *polychronicity*) indicates that time is social and circular; time is not a limited commodity so there is plenty of it; time is to be spent having fun and enjoying others, not worrying about appointments, deadlines, the future, and so forth. Social time perspective is also the realization that nothing in life is guaranteed, so enjoy the moment, the here and now.

Figure 6.1 examines these dimensions in respect to the hypothetical testing responses of Black students.

These dimensions affect students' communication styles, learning styles, thinking styles, and test-taking styles and skills (Ford & Harris, 1999; Helms, 1992). For instance, students for whom movement and verve are strong dimensions of their being will be spontaneous, active, and energetic; they may have a difficult time sitting through lengthy tests. Students for whom orality is strong may prefer to explain their answers or write essays rather than respond to multiple-choice items; students for whom time perspective is predominant may have difficulty managing their time when taking tests. When students have a communal orientation, they may prefer to work in groups rather than alone; this preference may be interpreted as imma-turity, laziness, or cheating by educators who are unfamiliar with cultural diversity (Delgado–Galtan & Trueba, 1985).

The dimensions described by Boykin (1986) are research-based, and they describe many, but not all, Black students. The point here is that culture matters not only when students are learning, but also when they are taking tests; this reality should not be ignored, negated, or minimized with examining the test scores of diverse students. Accordingly, Helms (1992) asks:

1. Is there evidence that the culturally conditioned intel-lectual skills used by Blacks and Whites generally differ and that these differences have been equivalently incor-porated into the measurement procedures?

2. Do Blacks and Whites use the same test-taking strategies when ostensibly responding to the same material, and do these strategies have equivalent meaning?

3. If different strategies are used by different racial groups, to what extent are these differences an aspect of test prediction and criteria?

4. How does one measure the cultural characteristics of intelligence tests? (p. 1097)

The implications of these questions for educators is that, when differences in performance on intelligence tests are attributed to racial or ethnic differences, educators must recognize this explanation for the non sequitur that it is. Instead of continu-ing to use such measures until something better comes along, educators must challenge the scientists on whose work their test usage is based to find culturally defined psychological explana-tions (e.g., culture-specific attitudes, feelings, and behaviors) for why such racial and ethnic differences exist (Helms, 1992, p. 1097).

Sattler (1992) negated the influence of culture on test perfor-mance; he stated: "Items on intelligence tests represent impor-tant aspects of competence in the *common* culture" (p. 568). This statement begs the question: Items on intelligence tests represent important aspects of competence common in *whose* culture? Relative to socioeconomic status, children in poverty live in a different culture than children in middle-class families. One has only to look at the enriched educational experiences— mainly due to economic opportunity and higher educational backgrounds—that middle-class families provide their children compared to families that live in poverty. Further, children who are limited English proficient may not be able to respond to the questions if they do not understand the vocabulary words, if they use the vocabulary words in different ways, and if the word does not exist or does not translate into their language. Zigler and Butterfield (1968) concluded: "Although ethnic minority children may have an adequate storage and retrieval system to answer questions correctly, they may fail in practice because they have not been exposed to the material" (as cited in Sattler, 1992).

Lam (1993) discussed five assumptions that summarize the many concerns that persist relative to the intelligence testing of diverse groups:

1. Test developers assume that test takers have no linguistic barriers (or differences) that inhibit their performance on tests.
2. Test developers assume that the content of the test at any particular level is suitable and of nearly equal difficulty for test takers.
3. Test developers assume that test takers are familiar with or have the test sophistication for taking standardized tests.
4. Test developers assume that test takers are properly motivated to do well on the test.
5. Test developers assume that test takers do not have strong negative psychological reactions to testing.

Although not discussed by Lam (1993) and Gregory (2004), another erroneous but prominent assumption among laypersons and those not familiar with standardized tests is that intelligence tests measure innate ability, and that the tests are not measuring achievement and the impact of educational experiences and exposure (Fagan & Holland, 2002; Groth-Marnat, 1997; Sternberg, 1982), including instructional quality.

Promising Practices and Considerations

In this section, promising practices and considerations are discussed, including culturally sensitive assumptions, diversity training for professionals, test interpretation considerations, and comprehensive data collection.

Culturally Sensitive Assumptions

The accuracy and appropriateness of the intellectual assessment process is based on a number of assumptions, a few of which were discussed earlier. Kaufman (1990, 1994) suggested alternative assumptions worthy of adoption because they offer promise in making testing more culturally sensitive:

1. *The focus on an assessment is the person being assessed, not the test* (Kaufman, 1990, p. 24). Stated differently, professionals should not become preoccupied with the IQ scores to the detriment of the individual being assessed. An individual is not best represented by a sum of scores (Suzuki, Vraniak, & Kugler, 1996). Thus, useful information for interpreting and using test scores can be gained when professionals observe students during the assessment process.

2. *The goal of any examiner is to be better than the tests he or she uses* (Kaufman, 1990, p. 25). It requires knowledge, skills, and cultural competence to make a complete and comprehensive assessment of students from diverse groups. Professionals should be familiar with the culturally diverse individuals being assessed, be sensitive to cultural diversity, and incorporate this information into the selection of tests and the interpretation of the scores and assessment information.

3. *Intelligence tests measure what the individual has learned* (Kaufman, 1990, p. 25). The content of all tasks, whether verbal or nonverbal, is learned within a culture (Miller, 1996). Therefore, all tests are culturally loaded. Individuals bring learning from home, school, and the community to the test-taking situation. When interpreting test

scores, educators and decision makers must consider the influence of educational background and opportunity to learn the content.

4. *The tasks composing intelligence tests are illustrative samples of behavior and are not meant to be exhaustive* (Kaufman, 1990, p. 26). Collateral information (e.g., learning styles, motivation, interests, health) must be collected to develop a profile of an individual's strengths and weaknesses in order to develop educational interventions and opportunities.

5. *Intelligence tests measure mental functioning under fixed experimental conditions* (Kaufman, 1990, p. 26). As such, how individuals will demonstrate their intelligence in other settings cannot be accurately predicted without gathering extensive information—test data and other types of data—on individuals in other settings. Essentially, test scores simply assist educators in making conditional probability statements on the basis of the particular test (Frisby, 1998).

6. *IQ tests must be interpreted on an individual basis by a "shrewd and flexible detective"* (Kaufman, 1990, p. 27). Professionals must investigate all information collected on students in order to provide a comprehensive picture of the individual in his or her cultural context.

7. *Intelligence tests are best used to generate hypotheses of potential help to the person; they are misused when the results lead to harmful outcomes* (Kaufman, 1990, p. 27). Too often, data obtained from intelligence tests have been used to indicate the inferiority of culturally diverse groups (see lengthy discussions on this topic by Gould, 1995, and Fancher, 1995). Professionals need to move beyond deficit thinking when assessing diverse populations (Ford et al., 2002; Samuda, 1998). Such thinking is counterproductive, seldom offering constructive information that can be used to guide educational and instructional interventions.

Test Interpretation

Sandoval, Frisby, Geisinger, Scheuneman, and Grenier (1998) offered the following recommendations relative to promoting equitable assessments with diverse groups; these recommendations primarily focus on ways to improve interpretations of diverse students' scores.

- *Identify preconceptions*—Self-awareness is the first step in gaining the capacity to understand others. Professionals must identify their conceptions and viewpoints—negative and positive—about diverse groups, and recognize that these perceptions influence their assessment of diverse groups.
- *Develop complex schemas or conceptions of groups*—A major problem with interpreting the test scores of diverse groups is that results are examined with little regard to the many factors that affect the lives and performance of these groups. Simplistic interpretations of scores are insufficient when complex factors affect test performance.
- *Actively search for disconfirmatory evidence*—When using and interpreting test scores, especially low test scores of individuals from diverse groups, professionals must constantly search for alternative explanations. For example, central questions might be: "Did the individual have the opportunity to learn the information or to express it on the test?" "How does the individual's culture affect his or her test performance?"
- *Resist a rush to judgment*—Professionals must be reflective, thoughtful, and inquisitive in their practice of interpreting and using test scores with individuals from diverse groups. In order to avoid rushing to judgment, Kaufman (1994) recommended that professionals spend time interacting in the neighborhoods that are serviced by their schools as a firsthand means of learning local cultural values, traditions, and customs.

Summary: Guiding Principles for Equitable and Culturally Responsive Assessment

Regardless of whether one is using traditional intelligence tests or tests considered to be less culturally loaded, testing, assessment, test interpretation, and test use must be guided by sound, defensible, and equitable principles and practices. Based on the issues raised in this chapter, the following guiding principles are offered for consideration:

1. Every school system must be committed to equity in finding potentially gifted students; this goal is nonnegotiable (Frasier, Martin, et al., 1995, p. 23).
2. Although there are arguments to be made for a purely technical definition of bias and validity, there are strong arguments to be made for the inclusion of politics, values, and culture in considering the full context of test interpretation and test use in which test bias arises (Messick, 1989, as cited in Padilla & Medina, 1996, p. 7). No discussion of test bias is complete when it only focuses on technical bias.
3. In addition to examining test bias, we must examine test fairness (Gregory, 2004). We must not become complacent in the belief that finding a test to be unbiased means that the test is fair—an unbiased test can still be unfair (Gregory, 2004). Test bias *and* test fairness should be explored.
4. The effects of threats to a test's validity and reliability must be examined and considered when interpreting and using test scores (Joint Standards, 1999).
5. A given pattern of test performances represents a cross-sectional view of the individual being assessed within a particular context (i.e., ethnic, cultural, familial, social; Joint Standards, 1999, p. 134).
6. There is no test score that can tell, ex post facto, the native potential that a student may have had at birth (Samuda, 1998, p. iii). Do not overvalue IQs or treat them as a magical manifestation of a child's inborn

potential (Kaufman, 1994, p. 24); do not overinterpret test scores by assigning them undue power.

7. Test scores should not be allowed to override other sources of evidence about test takers (Joint Standards, 1999).

8. In educational settings, a decision or characterization that will have major impact on a student should not be made on the basis of a single test score (National Association for Gifted Children, 1997). Other relevant information should be taken into account if it will enhance the overall validity of the decision (Joint Standards, 1999, p. 146).

9. Comprehensive assessment, the gathering of a wide range of information about test takers, helps to place test scores into a sociocultural context by considering how an examinee's performance is influenced by acculturation, language proficiency, socioeconomic background, and ethnic/racial identity (Samuda, Feuerstein, Kaufman, Lewis, & Sternberg, 1998, p. 230).

10. In educational settings, reports of group differences in test scores should be accompanied by relevant contextual information, where possible, to enable meaningful interpretation of these differences. When appropriate contextual information is not available, users should be cautioned against misinterpretation (Joint Standards, 1999, p. 148).

11. It is the responsibility of those who mandate the use of tests to identify and monitor their impact and to minimize potential negative consequences (Joint Standards, 1999, p. 168).

12. In cases where a language–oriented test is inappropriate due to the test takers' limited proficiency in that language, a nonverbal test may be a suitable alternative (Joint Standards, 1999, p. 91). Thus, both verbal and nonverbal tests can provide balanced and important information about diverse students (Samuda et al., 1998).

13. When interpreting test scores, the examiner or tester must take into account that many traditional tests have

not been normed adequately with various cultural groups (Samuda et al., 1998, p. 239).

14. Validation of the test is the joint responsibility of the test developer and test user (Joint Standards, 1999, p. 11).

15. The ultimate responsibility for appropriate test use and interpretation lies predominantly with test users (Joint Standards, 1999, p. 112); they must gain experience in working with culturally diverse groups in order to improve their ability to interpret and effectively use test scores (Kaufman, 1994).

16. Tests selected should be suitable for the characteristics and background of the test taker (Joint Standards, 1999). Test scores must not be interpreted and used in a color-blind or culture-blind fashion (Ford, 1996).

17. Every effort must be made to eliminate prejudice, racism, and inequities and to provide accurate and meaning-ful scores linked to appropriate intervention strategies (Samuda et al., 1998). Essentially, test scores should be used to help students, not to hurt them. Tests can be helpful to diverse students if they do not serve as the sole gatekeeper for selection into gifted education classes.

Conclusion

Culturally and linguistically diverse students are consis-tently underrepresented in gifted programs. In this chapter, it was argued that underrepresentation exists primarily because of diverse students' performance on traditional intelligence tests. These tests have served as gatekeepers for diverse students. Accordingly, this chapter focused strongly on intelligence tests because of the assumptions, perceptions, and misperceptions about the origins of intelligence and the debates surrounding test fairness and appropriateness of using IQ data with diverse groups. Yet, selecting, interpreting, and using tests are compli-cated endeavors. When one adds student differences, including cultural diversity, to the situation, the complexity increases.

Wiggins (1989) stated that when an educational problem persists despite the well-intentioned efforts of many people to solve it, it's a safe bet that the problem hasn't been properly framed. Given the array of unresolved assessment issues regarding the identification of talent potential among minority students, the probability is raised that the questions being asked need reframing (Frasier, García, et al., 1995, p. 12).

Professionals must be vigilant about finding and solving factors that hinder the test performance of diverse students. Tests are tools. The ultimate responsibility for equitable assessment rests with those who develop, administer, interpret, and use tests. Tests in and of themselves are harmless; they become harmful when misunderstood and misused. Historically, diverse students have been harmed educationally by test misuse. What better time than today to be more responsible in eliminating barriers to the representation of diverse students in gifted education?

References

American Educational Research Association, American Psychological Association, & National Council on Measurement in Education. (1999). *Standards for educational and psychological testing*. Washington, DC: Author.

Armour-Thomas, E. (1992). Intellectual assessment of children from culturally diverse backgrounds. *School Psychology Review, 21*, 552–565.

Baldwin, A. Y., & Vialle, W. (1999). *The many faces of giftedness: Lifting the masks*. Belmont, CA: Wadsworth.

Banks, J. A., & Banks, C. A. M. (Eds.). (2004). *Multicultural education: Issues and perspectives*. Hoboken, NJ: John Wiley and Sons.

Boykin, A. W. (1986). The triple quandary and the schooling of Afro-American children. In U. Neisser (Ed.), *The school achievement of minority children* (pp. 57–91). Hillsdale, NJ: Lawrence Erlbaum.

Boykin, A. W. (1994). Afro-cultural expression and its implications for schooling. In E. Hollins, J. King, & W. Hayman (Eds.), *Teaching diverse populations: Formulating a knowledge base* (pp. 225–273). Albany, NY: State University of New York Press.

Callahan, C. M., & McIntyre, J. A. (1994). *Identifying outstanding talent in American Indian and Alaska Native students*. Washington, DC: U.S. Department of Education.

Castellano, J. A. (2003). *Special populations in gifted education: Working with diverse gifted learners.* Boston: Allyn & Bacon.

Cline, S., & Schwartz, D. (Eds.). (1999). *Diverse populations of gifted children: Meeting their needs in the regular classroom and beyond.* Columbus, OH: Merrill/Prentice Hall.

Council of State Directors of Programs for the Gifted, & National Association for Gifted Children. (2003). *State of the states gifted and talented education report, 2001–2002.* Washington, DC: National Association for Gifted Children.

Delgado-Galtan, C., & Trueba, H. T. (1985). Ethnographic study of the participant structures in task completion: Reinterpretation of "handicaps" in Mexican children. *Learning Disability Quarterly, 8,* 67–75.

Delpit, L. (1995). *Other people's children: Cultural conflict in the classroom.* New York: The New Press.

Fagan, J. F., & Holland, C. R. (2002). Equal opportunity and racial differences in IQ. *Intelligence, 30,* 361–387.

Fancher, R. E. (1985). *The intelligence men: Makers of the IQ controversy.* New York: W. W. Norton.

Ford, D. Y. (1996). *Reversing underachievement among gifted Black students: Promising practices and programs.* New York: Teachers College Press.

Ford, D. Y. (1998). The under-representation of minority students in gifted education: Problems and promises in recruitment and retention. *Journal of Special Education, 32,* 4–14.

Ford, D. Y., & Harris, J. J., III. (1999). *Multicultural gifted education.* New York: Teachers College Press.

Ford, D. Y., Harris, J. J., III, Tyson, C. A., & Frazier Trotman, M. (2002). Beyond deficit thinking: Providing access for gifted African American students. *Roeper Review, 24,* 52–58.

Frasier, M. M., García, J. H., & Passow, A. H. (1995). *A review of assessment issues in gifted education and their implications for identifying gifted minority students* (RM95204). Storrs: National Research Center on the Gifted and Talented, University of Connecticut.

Frasier, M. M., Hunsaker, S. L., Lee, J., Finley, V. S., Frank, E., García, J. H., et al. (1995). *Educators' perceptions of barriers to the identification of gifted children from economically disadvantaged and limited English proficient backgrounds* (RM95216). Storrs: National Research Center on the Gifted and Talented, University of Connecticut.

Frasier, M. M., Martin, D., García, J. H., Finley, V. S., Frank, E., Krisel, S., et al. (1995). *A new window for looking at gifted children*

(RM95222). Storrs: National Research Center on the Gifted and Talented, University of Connecticut.

Frasier, M. M., & Passow, A. H. (1994). *Toward a new paradigm for identifying talent potential* (RM94112). Storrs: National Research Center on the Gifted and Talented, University of Connecticut.

Frisby, C. L. (1998). Culture and cultural differences. In J. Sandoval, C. L. Frisby, F. K. Geisinger, J. D. Scheuneman, & J. R. Grenier (Eds.), *Test interpretation and diversity: Achieving equity in assessment* (pp. 51–73). Washington, DC: American Psychological Association.

Gould, S. J. (1995). *The mismeasure of man.* New York: Norton.

Gregory, R. J. (2004). *Psychological testing: History, principles and applications* (3rd ed.). Boston: Allyn & Bacon.

Groth-Marnat, G. (1997). *Handbook of psychological assessment* (3rd ed.). New York: John Wiley & Sons.

Groth-Marnat, G. (2003). *Handbook of psychological assessment* (4th ed.). New York: John Wiley & Sons.

Hale, J. E. (2001). *Learning while Black: Creating educational excellence for African American children.* Baltimore: Johns Hopkins.

Hall, E. T. (1959). *The silent language.* New York: Doubleday.

Hall, E. T. (1976). *Beyond culture.* New York: Doubleday.

Harmon, D. (2002). They won't teach me: The voices of gifted African American inner-city students. *Roeper Review, 24,* 68–75.

Helms, J. (1992). Why is there no study of equivalence in standardized cognitive-ability testing? *American Psychologist, 47,* 1083–1101.

Herrnstein, R. J., & Murray, C. (1994). *The bell curve: Intelligence and class structure in American life.* New York: Free Press.

Hilliard, A. G., III. (Ed.). (1991). *Testing African American students.* Morristown, NJ: Aaron Press.

Jensen, A. R. (1980). *Bias in mental testing.* New York: Free Press.

Jensen, A. R. (1998). *The g factor.* Westport, CT: Praeger.

Jensen, A. R. (2000). Testing: the dilemma of group differences. *Psychology, Public Policy, and Law, 6,* 121–127.

Johnsen, S. K. (2004). *Identifying gifted students: A practical guide.* Waco, TX: Prufrock Press.

Kaufman, A. S. (1990). *Assessing adolescent and adult intelligence.* Needham Heights, MA: Allyn & Bacon.

Kaufman, A. S. (1994). *Intelligent testing with the WISC-III.* New York: John Wiley & Sons.

Korchin, S. J. (1980). Clinical psychology and minority populations. *American Psychologist, 35,* 262–269.

Lam, T. C. M. (1993). Testability: A critical issue in testing language minority students with standardized achievement tests. *Measurement and Evaluation in Counseling and Development, 26*, 179–191.

Larry P. v. Riles (1979, October). NO. C-712270 RFP (N. C. Cal.).

Maker, J., & Schiever, S. W. (Eds.). (1989). *Critical issues in gifted education: Defensible programs for cultural and ethnic minorities* (Vol. II). Austin, TX: Pro-Ed.

Miller, J. G. (1996). A cultural-psychological perspective on intelligence. In R. J. Sternberg & E. L. Grigorenko (Eds.), *Intelligence, heredity, and environment* (pp. 269–302). New York: Cambridge University Press.

National Association for Gifted Children. (1997). *Position paper on testing.* Washington, DC: Author.

Nieto, S. (Ed.). (1999). *The light in their eyes: Creating multicultural learning communities.* New York: Teachers College Press.

Office for Civil Rights. (2000). *The use of tests as part of high-stakes decision-making for students: A resource guide for educators and policy-makers.* Washington, DC: Author.

Olmedo, E. L. (1981). Testing linguistic minorities. *American Psychologist, 36*, 1078–1085.

Padilla, A. M., & Medina, A. (1996). Cross-cultural sensitivity in assessment: Using tests in culturally appropriate ways. In L. A. Suzuki, J. P. Meller, & J. G. Ponterotto (Eds.), *Handbook of multicultural assessment: Clinical, psychological, and educational applications* (pp. 3–28). San Francisco: Jossey-Bass.

Rodriguez, E. R., & Bellanca, J. (1996). *What is it about me you can't teach?: An instructional guide for the urban educator.* Arlington Heights, IL: SkyLight.

Rushton, J. P. (2003). Brain size, IQ and racial-group differences: Evidence from musculoskeletal traits. *Intelligence, 31*, 139–155.

Samuda, R. J. (1998). *Psychological testing of American minorities: Issues and consequences* (2nd ed.). Thousand Oaks, CA: Sage.

Samuda, R. J., Feuerstein, R., Kaufman, A. S., Lewis, J. E., & Sternberg, R. J. (1998). *Advances in cross-cultural assessment.* Thousand Oaks, CA: Sage.

Sandoval, J., Frisby, C. L., Geisinger, K. F., Scheuneman, J. D., & Grenier, J. R. (Eds.). (1998). *Test interpretation and diversity: Achieving equity in assessment.* Washington, DC: American Psychological Association.

Sattler, J. M. (1992). *Assessment of children* (Rev. ed.). San Diego, CA: Author.

Shade, B., Kelly, C., & Oberg, M. (1997). *Creating culturally respon-sive classrooms.* Washington, DC: American Psychological Association.

Sternberg, R. J. (1982). *Handbook of human intelligence.* New York: Cambridge University Press.

Storti, C. (1998). *The art of crossing cultures.* Yarmouth, MN: Intercultural Press.

Suzuki, L. A., Meller, P. J., & Ponterotto, J. G. (Eds.). (1996). *Handbook of multicultural assessment: Clinical, psychological, and educational applica-tions.* San Francisco: Jossey-Bass.

Suzuki, L. A., Vraniak, D. A., & Kugler, J. F. (1996). Intellectual assessment across cultures. In L. A. Suzuki, P. J. Meller, & J. G. Ponterotto (Eds.), *Handbook of multicultural assessment: Clinical, psy-chological, and educational applications* (pp. 141–177). San Francisco: Jossey-Bass.

U.S. Department of Education. (1993). *National excellence: A case for developing America's talent.* Washington, DC: Author.

U.S. Department of Education. (1998). *Elementary and secondary schools civil rights survey.* Washington, DC: Author.

U.S. Department of Education, National Center for Education Statistics. (2003). *Status and trends in the education of Blacks.* Washington, DC: Author.

Wiggins, G. (1989). A true test: Toward more authentic and equitable assessment. *Phi Delta Kappan, 70,* 703–713.

Author Note

This chapter is based on the following monograph: Ford, D. Y. (2004). *Intelligence testing and cultural diversity: Concerns, cautions, and considerations* (RM04204). Storrs: National Research Center on the Gifted and Talented, University of Connecticut.

Identifying Low-Income and Minority Students for Gifted Programs: Academic and Affective Impact of Performance-Based Assessment

Annie Xuemei Feng & Joyce VanTassel-Baska

Many in the field of gifted education have suggested that new conceptions of giftedness and a new paradigm for identifying and selecting students will help low socioeconomic (SES) and minority students become more represented in gifted programs (Ford, 1996; VanTassel-Baska, Patton, & Prillaman, 1991). This new paradigm of identification would recognize the different ways in which students display giftedness and would call for more varied and authentic assessments.

Based on our current understanding of the problem of underrepresentation of low-income and minority students in gifted programs and preliminary studies, the use of performance-based assessment as a nontraditional tool for enhancing the possibility of greater representation of such students in these programs appears to be a promising development (VanTassel-Baska, Johnson, & Avery, 2002).

An important facet in the development of an instrument for use in identification is its predictive value; in other words, how well does the instrument identify students it intends to identify? Subsequently, the consequential validity of the instrument becomes the concern of both researchers and stakeholders. One cannot help asking if the consequences of using the instrument are responsive to educational goals. Given the broader access to gifted program services through alternative identification, how well did alternatively identified students fare in the gifted program academically and social-emotionally?

This chapter examines the academic and social-emotional impact of performance task assessment, utilizing data from a follow-up study of gifted students' identification and achievement profiles over 6 years (VanTassel-Baska, Feng, & de Brux, in press) and vignette analyses of students of special prototypes in terms of socioeconomic status, ethnic membership, and ability profiles (VanTassel-Baska, Feng, Chandler, Quek, & Swanson, 2005).

Research on the Use of Alternative Assessment

Research literature on nontraditional assessment suggests that alternative assessment has its theoretical assumptions in the belief that abilities are malleable and developmental, in contrast to the conservative assumptions that view abilities as relatively stable. Critics of traditional assessment tools suggest that ability measures often are embedded in a cultural context in which nonmainstream students (e.g., students from poverty, minority students) often are placed in a disadvantaged position. Dynamic or alternative assessment is nontraditional in that it focuses on tapping fluid rather than crystallized abilities. Such an approach is used to assess cognitive abilities that frequently are not apparent when most forms of traditional standardized tests are used. This type of assessment usually consists of a test-intervention-retest format, with the focus on the improvement students make after an intervention, specifically based on their learning cognitive strategies related to mastery of the testing task (Feuerstein, 1986; Kirschenbaum, 1998).

Performance task assessment is one type of such assessment (VanTassel-Baska et al., 2002). Performance assessments focus on challenging open-ended problems that require high-level thinking and problem solving, and put an emphasis on the process the student uses to come to an answer rather than on whether or not the student can quickly find the right answer. In 1998, the State Department of Education in South Carolina contracted with The

Center for Gifted Education at The College of William and Mary to develop performance task protocols as a pilot project to assess their efficacy in identifying low-SES and Black students within the state. Based on pilot, field test, and statewide implementation data from the project, the performance tasks proved to be useful tools toward this end, finding in the range of 12–18% more underrepresented students (VanTassel-Baska et al., 2002).

Based on the success of these performance tasks in locating more underrepresented students for gifted programs, they were officially adopted as a third dimension of the state identification system (Dimension C) in 1999. Therefore, a statewide implementation of performance task assessment, in addition to a traditional ability and achievement identification method, was institutionalized in the state of South Carolina.

Now, students in South Carolina may be admitted to gifted programs through meeting specified criteria on a group or an individual ability measure (Dimension A), a group achievement measure in the verbal or mathematical domain (Dimension B), and/or verbal or nonverbal performance tasks (Dimension C). Verbal performance-based assessments refer to verbal reasoning tasks that require written responses or correct manipulation of words. Nonverbal performance-based assessments refer to mathematical and spatial tasks. All of the performance-based assessment tasks are verbally mediated and assisted through a preteaching process on the test item prototype.

"Traditionally identified gifted students" refers to students who qualified either (1) through reaching the 96th percentile or above on an ability test or (2) through meeting the criteria of a combination of 90th percentile or higher on an ability test and 94th percentile or higher on an achievement measure. "Performance task-identified students" were defined as gifted students who qualified (1) through meeting the criteria of 80% correct rate on verbal or nonverbal performance tasks and (2) through meeting the standard of the 90th percentile on an ability test or the 94th percentile on an achievement test but not on both. Table 7.1 illustrates these three dimensions of assessment and qualification criteria for gifted program services under current regulations in the state.

Table 7.1

Identification Test Dimensions and Threshold Criteria

	Traditionally-Identified Gifted Students		Performance Task-Identified Gifted Students	
Dimension[1]	A	A & B	A & C	B & C
Types of Tests	Aptitude	Aptitude & Achievement	Aptitude & Performance Tasks	Achievement & Performance Task
Criteria Threshold	A ≥ 96th percentile	A ≥ 90th percentile & B > 94th percentile	A ≥ 90th percentile & C ≥ 80th percentile	B ≥ 94th percentile & C ≥ 80th percentile

[1] In the state where this study was conducted, a student can qualify for gifted program services by passing the threshold on two assessment dimensions, namely, an ability or aptitude test (Dimension A), an achievement test (Dimension B), and/or performance tasks (Dimension C). If the aptitude test score is at or above 96th percentile, this criterion alone allows the student to participate.

Note. From "A Study of Identification and Achievement Profiles of Performance Task-Identified Gifted Students Over 6 Years," by J. VanTassel-Baska, A. X. Feng, and E. de Brux, 2007, *Journal for the Education of the Gifted, 31*, p. 13. Copyright © 2007 Prufrock Press. Adapted with permission.

Advantages of Performance Tasks in Locating Underrepresented Gifted Students

Since the inception of statewide use of performance assessments for identification of gifted students in the 1999–2000 school year, all school districts in South Carolina have participated in the testing. In a follow-up study of statewide gifted student identification profiles over 6 years (2000–2005), VanTassel-Baska et al. (in press) found that performance task protocols consistently identified higher percentages of low-income (23%) and Black students (14%) than traditional identification tools (18% and 11%, respectively). Despite the fact that a great majority of gifted students came from middle class or higher income family backgrounds regardless of the identification method employed (81.4% traditional method vs. 77% performance tasks), performance task protocols demonstrated important advantages in identifying more underrepresented populations.

Higher Probability of Uneven Verbal-Nonverbal Students Among Performance Task-Identified Students

Except for students who qualified for gifted services through a 96th percentile or above score on an ability measure, the current gifted regulations allowed students to be identified through the combination of either a verbal or a nonverbal score (i.e., mathematical, quantitative, or spatial) from any two types of assessment, namely, ability (A), achievement (B), or performance tasks (C).

The 6-year trend analysis findings suggested that a higher percentage of performance task-identified students (40.5%) than traditionally identified students (20.8%) fell into the category of being identified in one content domain only by meeting the criteria for achievement and performance-based assessment, suggesting a higher proportion of unbalanced identification profiles (verbal or nonverbal only) among performance task-identified students, and doubling what was found among traditionally identified students. Moreover, a large majority of both groups of gifted students, regardless of identification approaches, qualified for the program through the nonverbal area (quantitative, mathematical, or spatial).

The finding that there was a higher proportion of uneven identification profiles among performance task-identified students in comparison to their counterparts identified through traditional methods suggests that flexible instructional accommodations are necessary for performance task-identified students. Therefore, a relatively unique group of gifted learners with more demands for accommodations have created challenging tasks for gifted classroom teachers to meet the needs of a more diversified group of gifted learners.

Academic Outcomes of Performance Task-Identified Students

How well did performance task-identified students fare in gifted programs in terms of academic outcomes? Their performances on the English and mathematics portion of the state standardized test (PACT) were examined in comparison to those of traditionally identified students over 4 years (2001–2004).

The data sources used for this statewide analysis of PACT performances of gifted students originated from the GIFT data. The South Carolina GIFT Data Set is a database created for recording gifted students' identification information. It is composed of 169 fields from basic demographics, to the qualifying dimensions, types of tests taken, qualifying test scores, and date and grade level when the students were tested and placed into gifted programs. Each school district in South Carolina was provided the GIFT data template and requested to record their current gifted students' information accordingly. The follow-up study constitutes the analysis of an assembled data set from 20 school districts in the state; students' performance on the PACT from 2001 to 2004 in the areas of English and mathematics were merged into the GIFT data set for the study of gifted students' achievement profiles on mathematics and English on the state tests for 4 years.

A three-way (identification route x gender x ethnicity) multivariate analysis of variance (MANOVA) was conducted to investigate the extent of difference on academic performance in relationship to dimensions through which students were identified, and their gender and ethnicity. The eight standard scores of PACT English and mathematics (2001–2004) were the dependent variables; and gifted identification qualification route, gender, and ethnicity were independent variables (or between-subject factors) of the multivariate test.

The multivariate tests showed that there were overall performance differences on the English and mathematics components of PACT 2001 to PACT 2004 between students who were identified through alternative methods ($F = 3.32, p = .000$, $\eta^2 = .008$), among students who were of different ethnicities ($F = 3.99$, $p = .000$, $\eta^2 = .01$), and between male and female students ($F = 4.53, p = .000, \eta^2 = .011$). The performance mean differences among students identified through different dimensional combinations ranged from 3–9 points in English and 3–11 points in mathematics across 4 years (2001–2004), translating into a .2 to .6 difference on Cohen's d effect size index.

There seemed to be a range of variability in terms of practical importance of the differences reflected in gifted students' PACT performance.

Statistically significant mean differences were found between students under each of the two identification approaches in PACT English across 4 years (p <.001), with students identified under Dimension A performing the best, on average, followed by students who were identified under Dimensions A and B, Dimensions B and C, and Dimensions A and C. Similar descending order was found in PACT mathematics except that no statistically significant differences were found between students identified under Dimensions B and C and Dimensions A and C across 4 years (p > .05).

The magnitude of performance differences as indexed by effect sizes (i.e., Cohen's d) between each two groups of students varied. Students' performance in English ranged from .4–.6 between the A and A & C groups, to .06 between the A & B and B & C groups; the between-group effect size differences in PACT mathematics ranged from .67–.80 between the A and A & C groups, to .1–.2 between the A & B and B & C groups. These data suggest that the PACT performance differences were fairly large between traditionally identified students who qualified through the 96th percentile on an ability test and performance task–identified students who qualified in combination with an ability test. By contrast, performance task–identified students who qualified in combination with an achievement test performed closely to traditionally identified students qualifying through the combination of an ability and an achievement measure.

It is not surprising that traditionally identified gifted students performed better than alternatively identified students on PACT English and mathematics, given that the latter group already started at a lower ability threshold (below 90th percentile) or achievement score (below 94th percentile). The larger magnitude of differences that occurred on the PACT assessments appeared to parallel the ability and/or achievement level obtained during identification.

Achievement gaps by ethnicity still appear to exist in the gifted population in South Carolina, favoring White and Asian Americans on both the English and math portions of the state standardized test (p <.01). However, the lack of educationally significant differences on multiyear standardized state tests, particularly on the PACT English test (d = .12–.26) across ethnicity groups seems to suggest a shrinking achievement gap by ethnicity membership in the South Carolina gifted population.

Female gifted students demonstrated significantly better performance on PACT English 2001–2004 (p = .011–.018; d = .24–.33); male students performed significantly better than their female counterparts on PACT math in 2004 (p = .033; d = .06). Such gender differences on math and English seem to be consistent with the literature, although gender differences in mathematics and verbal performance may vary by age and type of testing items (Campbell, Hombo, & Mazzeo, 2000; Hyde, Fennema, & Lamon, 1990).

PACT Performance by Strength Area

Because the performance-based protocol was used to identify students in one domain only, the distribution of PACT performance among performance task-identified students was compared with those who were identified in the verbal domain and those who were identified through the nonverbal domain. MANOVAs were conducted to examine South Carolina gifted students' PACT performance by verbal or nonverbal areas of strength. The results showed that there were statistically significant performance differences on PACT English language arts (2001–2004) between verbally identified and nonverbally identified students, favoring students with verbal strength. The magnitude of difference was moderate (d = .4)

In the area of mathematics, there was an overall statistically significant performance difference, favoring nonverbally identified students. However, the magnitude of difference was small (d =.06–.2). By the year 2004, there was no statistically significant difference on PACT mathematics between verbally and nonverbally identified gifted students.

The results of this statewide follow-up study suggest that the performance-based protocols used in South Carolina are consistent across time in locating a higher percentage of students from a number of underrepresented categories; yet identification and program placement appeared not to demonstrate a strong effect on their academic outcomes reflected in the state standardized tests.

Social-Emotional Impact of the Alternative Identification: Interview Results

However, the other side of the same question is how well did these alternatively identified gifted students adjust in the gifted program? Particular populations of interest are those underrepresented groups including students from low-income and/or minority families, students with twice-exceptionality, and students who possessed uneven verbal/nonverbal profiles. How did students perceive themselves and their gifted program opportunities? What pattern of changes, if any, did their teachers and parents notice in class and out of school? How are alternatively identified students under these prototypes similar or different from those identified through traditional methods?

In a parallel in-depth study of the learning characteristics of performance task-identified students who were classified into special prototypes based on socioeconomic status, ethnicity, verbal-nonverbal strength, and twice-exceptionality, we also examined the social-emotional outcomes of the alternative identification. Using a structured interview format, participants comprised 37 seventh or eighth graders who were identified as gifted learners in 2000, when a broader implementation of performance tasks were promulgated at the state level. These students were selected from each of four participating school districts, based on the prespecified selection criteria. Parent(s)/guardian(s) and the gifted class and regular science teachers of each sampled student also were selected for interviews. Traditionally identified students under the same prototype also were sampled to form a comparison group.

The interview questions probed the learning opportunities gifted programs provided, parental support, students' social-emotional adjustment to the program, developmental milestones, and creative outlets, as well as other cognitive and affective factors that were related to students' learning. Thirty-seven vignettes were developed from triangular perspectives of the student, teachers, and parents to portray the individual profiles of each student in terms of cognitive, academic, and social-emotional profiles (VanTassel-Baska et al., 2005).

Student Perceptions of Gifted Program Benefits

A salient theme that occurred throughout the student interviews was the advanced learning opportunities received through gifted program participation. It echoed again and again in the interviews that these students, many from a disadvantaged family background, were very much appreciative of the learning opportunities, challenge, fast pace, high expectations, and "prestige" that a gifted class student was afforded. They appeared to be well aware of the pressure of studying with a group of similar caliber students, articulating that they were willing to work harder in a gifted class than idling in a regular class. One student noted that "Being in the gifted program affects my learning attitude a lot. It is exciting and fun. . . . In regular class, it is too slow and too easy." Another student revealed her sense of the different experience, noting that she aspired to go to college and make a decent life for her and her children in the future, something she could not get from her parents. She noted,

> It [participation in the gifted program] expands my college opportunity. I think it can get me into a better college . . . I think we [will] have a better chance to get a good job, it gives you a lot of spaces for what you can do, and you can challenge yourself . . . I want to build a happy family when I am getting older . . . because for me we haven't had a lot of money most of the time while I was growing up . . . I felt like I want something

other people didn't, so I know I can get into college and then get a good job, and I will be able to do those things for my kids when I get older, and provide them what they want . . . they'll have a lot of what they want. For me, all I need is to get it worked out . . .

Program Participation as Confidence Booster

Participation in the program itself had a confidence-boosting effect. The impact appeared to be in both academic and affective areas. In academics, many students were able to maintain a high grade point average (GPA) and were perceived as strong students by their teachers. Low-income gifted students identified by both methods appeared to demonstrate enhanced self-esteem and became proud and more confident about themselves. They became more interested and motivated to learn. One Black boy noted, "The program is a lot of fun. I enjoy the building, the researching, and the computer programs . . . I learned to cooperate and have trust in other people, even to understand myself."

Intellectual Peerage and Social Networks

All students interviewed were asked about their friendship proclivity in both regular and gifted classes. The results seemed to suggest that many of these students adjusted quickly to peer friendships while maintaining old friends in their regular classes; these students apparently enjoyed the intellectual peerage in their gifted classes, citing that "I feels [sic] more connections in the gifted class . . . I feel smarter because we all know what we are talking about." Another student noted her feelings about being placed in the gifted program in the following way:

When they placed me, I thought there would be a good chance to meet people, because you got people from all different classes that will be put in one. Also, [they were] of similar mind when you were talking, the big

words, that the regular kids would not talk to me . . .
nothing [*sic*] that I was smarter, we are all smart in certain things, anybody is smart differently, or learn differently, but we would be talking in words they wouldn't
have known, and we communicate very well.

However, Black students in the sample appeared to present a unique pattern. These students were perceived to desire
continued peer relationships outside of their gifted class, and
were more likely to be perceived as loners by gifted class teachers. They seemed to be facing a pressure from a peer culture
against "acting White," on the one hand, and an increasing
hunger for social life as middle schoolers on the other. Several
Black students interviewed (5 out of 11), however, presented
a high level of maturity in handling peer relationships. One
student demonstrated his sensitivity in dealing with peers and
friendship in and out of his regular classroom and community:
"I don't want to brag about it [being in a gifted class], 'cause
other students might get mad. They are my friends in the regular classroom, and I don't want to break up my friendship."

Discrepancy in Perceptions

In this interview study, we found a somewhat consistent
pattern of differences among students', parents', and teachers'
perceptions about the learning characteristics of these students
in respect to motivation, task-management, and organization
skills. Teachers saw the students more negatively than parents
or students themselves. Understandably, many of these students
were from a disadvantaged family background, complicated by
ethnic membership, single parent families, and socioeconomic
status. A majority of the uneven ability profile and twice-exceptional students were from a middle class background, and their
special learning preference and/or twice-exceptionality often
positioned them in an unfavorable light in a gifted class, where
they often were classified as "hyper" or uninterested by gifted
class teachers.

A contrast thus emerged between students' and parents' more favorable perceptions of the program's impact on learning motivation and teachers' somewhat less favorable perceptions of these special prototype students in their classes. Moreover, a majority of these students articulated strong subject preferences during the interviews, which also might create a tension in teachers' perceptions of their being unmotivated learners or lacking organization skills.

Pros and Cons of the Consequential Validity of Alternative Identification

In any statewide identification system, a mechanism designed to be more inclusive likely will increase the overall percentages of students identified. This situation clearly happened in South Carolina, with the overall percentage of students served inching up to 11% of the population statewide (Feng, VanTassel-Baska, Quek, & Struck, 2003). Moreover, the larger number of students identified created two kinds of problems for districts: (1) the existing gifted service delivery mechanism had to absorb these students, leading to higher pupil-teacher ratios in a pull-out setting and greater diversity in student functional levels and (2) in some locales, the new performance-based protocol neither enhanced ethnic nor SES diversity, thus failing to produce a greater representation of these students in gifted programs at selected local levels (VanTassel-Baska & Feng, 2003). In order to employ equitable identification procedures at the state level, it is apparent that inequalities of the outcome may result at the local level in some districts.

When we examined the implications for individual districts, the results varied, depending on the representation of these underrepresented groups within a given school district. In districts where percentages were small to begin with, little change occurred. In fact, more high-SES White students were identified. In districts where the percentage of low-income and some Black students was greater than 20%, district data reflected higher percentages of change.

Although the academic outcomes on PACT did not show favorable benefits to this alternatively identified gifted student population, the in-depth study on special prototype learners revealed quite a different picture. Program participation brought more opportunities, stimulation, and inspiration into the young lives of many students from disadvantaged families, and hope to their parents as well. The level of appreciation among both students and parents was overwhelming. The elevated self-esteem and motivation to learn among students who would otherwise be bored and daydreaming in a regular class was powerful.

Importantly, the many perspectives shared among teachers, parents, and students themselves suggested the beneficial nature of gifted identification and programming for these students. Many common, yet diverse, characteristics were cited for these students, ranging from being strong learners in several ways to being limited in motivation, organization, and the ability to work with peers. It is fair to conclude, however, after 3–4 years in the gifted program, these students in general had gained important new skills, enhanced their academic performance (i.e., GPA) and felt renewed confidence in their own abilities. The program benefits seemed stronger than what the state standardized test results would suggest.

Cost and Efficiency of Performance-Based Assessment Protocols

The use of performance-based assessment in a state identification protocol raises two issues of interest. One issue relates to the efficiency of the approach. Is it worthwhile to expend the additional funds and resource time of multiple educators to use the approach as opposed to either (1) lowering cutoffs on traditional measures or (2) using an additional nonverbal test? One argument for using performance-based assessment is its authentic nature. Testers are teachers in schools who can see student results and use them to further instruction. Students demonstrated true understanding through these tasks rather than hypothetical understanding through a multiple-choice format. Moreover, the tasks require off-level and higher level thinking and problem solving, specifications not built into traditional measures. Therefore, efficiency in test taking is balanced off against the easy and relevant use of test data to improve instruction directly for specific learners and to model gifted-level task demands. The testing costs for scoring are provided by the state, thus reducing the burden of the cost of testing to individual districts.

The Mismatch Between Area of Identification and Program Intervention

The finding that a large percentage of performance task-identified students are identified in the nonverbal domain (72.5%) raises interesting questions about the nature of program interventions in South Carolina and their flexibility for including students with different profiles and needs. Most programs in the state are pull-out in nature, and many districts require students to be doing well in regular classes as a condition of being in the gifted program. Students with uneven profiles then may suffer doubly for being identified as gifted: (1) they must overcome their deficits sufficiently to function well in the regular classroom and in the pull-out program, and (2) they must try to benefit from a program designed primarily for more evenly functioning gifted students. It seems that merely to find more students from low-income and minority backgrounds is insufficient if programming mechanisms are limited or counterproductive to their success. For students whose major strength lies in the nonverbal domain, crafting program interventions in that domain may be critical to ensuring program success, combined with removing the "sword of Damocles" of contingent high-level performance in the regular classroom in other domains of learning.

The performance of regular gifted students on the statewide PACT test suggests a potential problem or mismatch between gifted programs in the state and the major content areas deemed important on these high-stakes measures. A full 10–20% of these traditionally identified gifted students performed only at the basic level in English or mathematics on the test during

2001–2004. Most educators of the gifted would deplore setting the bar for the gifted on these state tests at an "advanced"
level; however, for high-ability students not to score at least at
the proficient level on these tests suggests a potentially serious
problem in our thinking about what gifted programs might do
to address the standards. For example, 15% of the gifted students were at the basic level on the math portion of the test,
suggesting that gifted interventions for these students may need
to include more archetypal math problems consistent with the
NCTM standards, a basis for both the South Carolina standards
and PACT assessments.

Conclusions and Implications

The studies in South Carolina over a 6-year period suggest
that, in general, performance-based assessment on a statewide
basis has steadily contributed to greater numbers of both low-
income and minority students being identified for gifted programs than would have been found through existing protocols
although the majority of students identified are high-SES and
White. Moreover, the profiles of students identified through
nontraditional means are more heavily weighted toward nonverbal abilities, are slightly more likely to be female, and present
an uneven profile of ability between verbal and nonverbal aptitudes. Performance on high-stakes state testing (PACT) suggests that these gifted students are less proficient and advanced
than their traditionally identified counterparts across 4 years,
although the differences between the two groups were educationally insignificant, compared to the self-reported long-term
positive program impact (VanTassel-Baska et al., 2005).

The follow-up intervention studies of the identification,
performance, and social-emotional profiles of performance
task-identified students have provided an insightful venue to
understand the promise and problems that these gifted students are facing, the challenging tasks that teachers are facing
in accommodating their needs, and strategies we might use to
further develop potential in their strength areas.

At a practical level, these studies continue to demonstrate the importance of using nontraditional assessments in tandem with traditional ones to find and serve underrepresented gifted students. The results also challenge practitioners to match program intervention to ability and aptitude information in order to achieve an optimal match for students in programs.

Finally, it suggests an important subtext for analyzing gifted student performance, especially those students whose level of functioning may be atypical. Adjustment to higher expectations and performance takes time; it is not automatic and may require real effort and struggle for these students to be successful. However, long-term talent development is the goal, not short-term success. Thus, practitioners may need to adjust their own expectations for student success, plan more customized programs, and employ more longitudinal assessments of student progress in order to document growth for these learners from low socioeconomic backgrounds.

References

Campbell, J. R., Hombo, C. M., & Mazzeo, J. (2000). *NAEP 1999 trends in academic progress: Three decades of student performance* (NCES 2000-469). Washington, DC: U.S. Department of Education.

Feuerstein, R. (1986). Learning to learn: Mediated learning experiences and instrumental enrichment. *Special Services in the Schools, 3*, 49–82.

Feng, A. X., VanTassel-Baska, J., Quek, C., & Struck, J. (2003). *A report of Project STAR follow-up study*. Williamsburg, VA: Center for Gifted Education, The College of William and Mary.

Ford, D. Y. (1996). *Reversing underachievement among gifted Black students: Promising programs and practices*. New York: Teachers College Press.

Hyde, J. S., Fennema, E., & Lamon, S. J. (1990). Gender differences in mathematics performance: A meta-analysis. *Psychological Bulletin, 107*(2), 139–155.

Kirschenbaum, R. J. (1998). Dynamic assessment and its use with underserved gifted and talented populations. *Gifted Child Quarterly, 42*, 140–147.

VanTassel-Baska, J., & Feng, A. X. (2003). *Project STAR follow-up study*. Columbia, SC: South Carolina Department of Education.

VanTassel-Baska, J., Feng, A. X., Chandler, K., Quek, C., & Swanson, J. (2005). *Project STAR: A two year research study report*. Williamsburg, VA: Center for Gifted Education, The College of William & Mary.

VanTassel-Baska, J., Feng, A. X., & de Brux, E. (in press). A study of performance task–identified gifted students' identification and achievement profiles over six years. *Roeper Review*.

VanTassel-Baska, J., Johnson, D., & Avery, L. D. (2002). Using performance tasks in the identification of economically disadvantaged and minority gifted learners: Findings from Project STAR. *Gifted Child Quarterly, 46*, 110–123.

VanTassel-Baska, J., Patton, J., & Prillaman, D. (1991). *Gifted youth at risk: A report of a national study*. Reston, VA: Council for Exceptional Children.

Author Note

The author used the terms *performance-based assessment* and *performance tasks* interchangeably in this chapter. Performance tasks is the terminology typically used in the state of South Carolina, where the study was conducted. It is one form of performance-based assessment.

The Rainbow Project: Using a Psychological Theory of Giftedness to Improve the Identification of Gifted Children

Robert J. Sternberg

In the late 19th century, British scientist Sir Francis Galton (1883) proposed a theory of intelligence based upon the notion that more intelligent people have keener sensory capacities. For example, he expected them to have keener eyesight, a firmer grip, greater ability to distinguish between different tones, and so forth. Galton developed a test based on this notion that he gave to people to test their intelligence. A gifted individual, therefore, would be one who has very good eyesight, hearing, tactile skills, and so forth.

French scientists Alfred Binet and Theodore Simon (1916) had different notions about the nature of intelligence and how to measure it. They thought that intelligence was a matter of higher level thinking rather than sensory abilities. They stressed the importance of good judgment. So, they developed tests that they thought would measure judgment, requiring people to interpret proverbs, provide the meanings of words, solve arithmetic problems, among other things. These tests proved to predict school performance better than Galton's test did, so they came to serve as the basis for future tests of intelligence. The test of Binet and Simon thus became the first of what are today known as *IQ tests* (i.e., tests of "intelligence quotient," originally conceived of by Stern [1912] as the ratio of one's mental age divided by one's chronological age multiplied by 100). Thus, giftedness, in their view, is excellent judgment and higher level cognition.

The tests of Binet and Simon were imported to the United States by Lewis Terman at Stanford University (Terman & Merrill, 1937), but in the meantime, testing was taking off in another direction. Binet and Terman had both created other tests designed to be used for measuring the intelligence of individuals. Researchers such as Arthur Otis and Carl Brigham were interested in developing tests that could be used for group testing of individuals. Brigham was the inventor, in the early 20th century, of what is today called the SAT.

The SAT has a long history. Originally, the initials were an acronym for "Scholastic Aptitude Test." This name implied to many people that the test measured innate intellectual qualities, so the name was changed to "Scholastic Assessment Test." It also has been called the "Scholastic Achievement Test," but today, the acronym has largely replaced whatever it once stood for.

Although the SAT is asserted by its owner, the College Board, not to be an ability test, research has suggested that scores on the test are very highly correlated with scores on tests of intelligence (Frey & Detterman, 2004). Indeed, the test is about as related to any one intelligence test as intelligence tests are related to each other. Charles Spearman (1927) argued that all tests of mental abilities are positively related to each other, and the SAT is no exception. The SAT is widely used in the identification of gifted children through the many and diverse projects that now exist for having children enter summer and weekend programs that teach them rigorous academic content (e.g., Brody & Stanley, 2005). This test, like many others, assumes that giftedness is somewhat domain-specific (see VanTassel-Baska, 2005).

The SAT has been a good predictor of college and earlier school performance (Bridgeman, McCamley-Jenkins, & Ervin, 2000; Hezlett et al., 2001), but no test, including this one, provides perfect prediction. Moreover, there is another problem. Tests such as the SAT originally were introduced to counter decisions being made largely on the basis of social class. Before these tests, one's last name, social standing, or private school mattered more to future outcomes than abilities. The idea was to introduce a merit-based rather than class-based system. But, as the diversity of the college applicant pool increased, an unfortunate fact emerged: Test scores are correlated highly with social class standing.

The SAT, ACT, and similar tests are not based on any one particular theory of abilities, and some have hoped that a test based more closely on a psychological theory, especially, a broad theory of abilities, might improve prediction of performance beyond what the SAT currently yields (e.g., Gardner, 1983; Sternberg, 1985). A related hope was that such tests might better recognize the wide diversity of abilities students can bring to college life. One group of researchers set out to devise a test that might turn these hopes into reality.

Devising the Rainbow Assessment

The Underlying Theory

The theory underlying this new "Rainbow Assessment" is the theory of successful intelligence (Sternberg, 1997), which also forms the basis for a theory of giftedness (Sternberg, 2000, 2005). This theory holds that intelligence is one's ability to achieve one's goals in life, within one's sociocultural context by capitalizing on one's strengths and compensating for or correcting one's weaknesses, so as to adapt to, shape, and select environments through a combination of creative, analytical, and practical abilities. One needs creative abilities to generate novel ideas, analytical abilities to evaluate whether the ideas are good ones, and practical abilities to execute one's ideas and to persuade others of their value. People can be gifted, therefore, in multiple ways. They can be analytically (conventionally) gifted, but also creatively and/or practically gifted. Moreover, a person's giftedness will depend on the extent to which he or she succeeds in capitalizing on strengths and compensating or correcting for weaknesses.

According to this theory, conventional tests of intelligence and the SAT, as well, measure primarily analytical abilities, as well as memory. This means that a new test would have the most contribution to make in its assessments of creative and practical abilities, the two kinds of abilities not directly measured by conventional tests.

The Project Team

I describe here the work we did on the Rainbow Project (Sternberg & the Rainbow Project Collaborators, 2006). The team working on the Rainbow assessment was unusual in two ways. First, it had more than a dozen researchers from all around the United States, whose views on intelligence and how to measure it were very different. Most projects have collaborators from a single point of view, or at least, from points of view that differ relatively little. In contrast, the team on this project had views that varied all over the map. Second, the team was highly interdisciplinary, involving cognitive psychologists, measurement psychologists, educational psychologists, developmental psychologists, cultural psychologists, and others from outside psychology altogether. I was the team leader.

The project was funded by the College Board, publishers of the SAT, and some of our collaborators were from the College Board. But, the College Board made no attempt, ever, to influence the results.

The Sample

Students in the Rainbow Project came from diverse schools, ranging from not at all selective in their admissions procedures to highly selective. There were 13 colleges and universities and two high schools that participated.

The Tests

We used a variety of different kinds of tests in order to measure the analytical, creative, and practical skills in which we were interested. Some of the tests were multiple choice and others were based on performance. All of the analytical tests were multiple choice. The performance-based tests were different in kind. They involved students having to solve problems that required more divergent thinking.

There were three creative performance tests. In one, participants had to caption cartoons of the kind found in *The New Yorker* magazine. Cartoons were presented without their captions, and participants had to suggest what they thought a good caption might be. In a second test, participants were given unusual titles for stories, such as *Beyond the Edge* or *The Octopus's Sneakers*, and wrote creative stories. In a third test, participants were shown visual collages, such as of different pictures of musicians, and had to tell a story orally.

There were also three practical tests. One presented participants with situations of the kind they would encounter in college. In one test, they might have to resolve a dispute with a roommate. In a second test, similar scenarios were presented, except these were work-related problems. And, in a third test, scenarios were presented, but this time through movies. For example, in one scenario, a student entered a party, and the expression on his face suggested he did not know anyone else at the party. The participant had to figure out what to do.

The Results

Prediction of Freshman Year Academic Success

So, how did the results come out? Keep in mind that our goal was not, precisely, to achieve excellent prediction of freshman-year performance, but rather, to achieve excellent prediction *above and beyond* what we could get from SATs and high school grade point average (GPA). In other words, the success of our venture would be measured in terms of what it added to already existing predictors, rather than in terms of how well it did when viewed solely on its own. Keep in mind also that our level of prediction would tend to be lower than if only one college were studied, because the dependent (predicted) variable was freshman GPA, and different colleges differ widely in their grading systems. For example, an A in one school counted the same as an A in another, even though they might not mean the same thing.

We did not expect our analytical measures to add much prediction beyond what is obtained from the SAT, because the SAT already is an analytical test. In fact, our analytical measures did not add anything significant: They added only 0.1% prediction over and above the SAT, from 9.8% to 9.9% of the variation in scores explained. (If you imagine a pie, where the whole pie represents perfect prediction and none of the pie represents no prediction, then our analytical measure added only .1% of the pie to our equation.) We hoped, however, that our creative and practical measures would add significant prediction. They did. The creative measures increased prediction from 9.8% to 12.8%, and the practical measures increased prediction from 9.8% to 10.7%. If we allow the measures we used to enter freely into the prediction equation, the combination of all of our new measures increased prediction from 9.8% to 19.9%, roughly doubling our ability to predict freshman success. If we included high school GPA in the equation, prediction increased by roughly 50%.

So, we now knew our measures do seem to make a value-added contribution in predicting freshman academic success in college, at least in our sample. Creative and practical abilities make a difference to academic success in the freshman year of college, beyond the difference made by the analytical abilities measured by the SAT and beyond what high school GPA measures.

Effect on Ethnic-Group Differences

An issue of concern is what would happen to differences among ethnic groups in their potential for admission if new tests were used. Would the new tests increase, decrease, or leave unchanged the level of diversity on college campuses? Most college admissions offices are very concerned with increasing diversity, and hence would view a test that decreased diversity as suspect for practical use.

We found that use of the Rainbow Assessment potentially would increase diversity. We did two different kinds of data analysis in order to assess the impact of our assessment on five ethnic groups: Whites, Hispanics, Blacks, Asian Americans, and Native Americans. Both kinds of data analysis revealed the same results: Ethnic-group differences, overall, *decreased* when assessments of creative and practical abilities were added on to assessments of analytical ones. Why? Because, on average, diverse populations have diverse backgrounds and socializations, and so broader tests are more likely to capture the full range of their abilities than more narrow ones.

Follow-Ups

There have been several follow-ups to the Rainbow Project. These reflect opportunities to turn data into actions.

The Tufts Follow-Up

How can one turn data into action? As Dean of the School of Arts and Sciences at Tufts University, I have been interested in applying the latest findings in psychology to education of students at Tufts. After all, we study psychology, at least in part, so that ultimately we can make a difference to the world with it. Beginning in the Fall of 2006, Tufts has added to its college-specific application an experimental section that encourages students, on an optional basis, to select an activity that gives the students an opportunity to demonstrate their creative, analytical, and practical skills in ways that conventional tests and college applications perhaps have not fully allowed. One item asks applicants what book they would most like on their bookshelf and why (analytical). Another asks applicants to write a story with a title such as "The End of MTV" (creative). A nonverbal item allows students to draw an advertisement for a new product (creative). Another item asks applicants how they would convince other students of an idea to which the other students initially did not respond favorably (practical). The idea is to let students have a fairly free reign so that they can demonstrate the broad kinds of skills needed for college success that college admissions offices want to know about, but often don't.

Putting the items on the college application rather than having them in a separate test (as in the Rainbow Project) has both advantages and disadvantages. An advantage is that students can ponder their responses rather than being forced to produce them rapidly. This is particularly an advantage for creative thinking, which cannot always be produced at the drop of a hat. But, a disadvantage is that parents, counselors, or others may help the students write their answers. There is no way of knowing for sure. In measuring skills, there is no one perfect way to achieve a true reading of what a student can do.

The Aurora Project

The Aurora Project is an attempt to devise an instrument for assessment of gifted children in the 9–12 age range (Chart, Grigorenko, & Sternberg, in press). The test, based on the theory of successful intelligence, has both a general intelligence battery and a successful intelligence battery. To date, we have collected data from several thousand school children, but the analyses of these data are not yet complete.

Conclusion

It is possible to devise assessments that measure a broader range of skills than is traditionally measured by tests such as the SAT and the ACT, as well as conventional tests of IQ. In our case, we measured creative and practical skills. We showed that when these measures were administered to a broad sample of college freshmen, it simultaneously was possible to improve prediction of freshman academic success and to decrease differences in average scores across diverse ethnic groups. The results are currently being used at Tufts University to try out new assessments to broaden the college admissions process, and they are serving as the basis for the Aurora Project to devise an instrument to identify gifted children in the 9–12 age range.

The theory of successful intelligence is certainly not the only theory that could be used to devise new assessments in the gifted world. Theories such as Gardner's (1983), Ceci's (1996), or Carroll's (1993) certainly can provide reasonable bases. But, we believe it is important (a) to go beyond just old wine in new bottles—that is, new ways of packaging measures of general intelligence; (b) to empirically validate tests, rather than just talking about doing so; and (c) to take into account diversity considerations by having theories that recognize that intelligence has broader meanings when interpreted outside the confines of just a single culture (Sternberg, 2004). These new assessments have been built on just such beliefs and values.

References

Binet, A., & Simon, T. (1916). *The development of intelligence in children* (E. S. Kite, Trans.). Baltimore: Williams & Wilkins.

Bridgeman, B., McCamley-Jenkins, L., & Ervin, N. (2000). *Predictions of freshman grade-point average from the revised and recentered SAT I: Reasoning test* (College Board Report No. 2000-1). New York: College Entrance Examination Board.

Brody, L. E., & Stanley, J. C. (2005). Youths who reason exceptionally well mathematically and/or verbally: using the MVT:D^4 model to develop their talents. In R. J. Sternberg & J. E. Davidson (Eds.), *Conceptions of giftedness* (2nd ed., pp. 20–38). New York: Cambridge University Press.

Carroll, J. B. (1993). *Human cognitive abilities: A survey of factor-analytic studies.* New York: Cambridge University Press.

Ceci, S. J. (1996). *On intelligence.* Cambridge, MA: Harvard University Press.

Chart, H., Grigorenko, E. L., & Sternberg, R. J. (in press). The Aurora Battery: Toward better identification of giftedness. In J. Plucker & C. Callahan (Eds.), *Critical issues and practices in gifted education: What the research says.* Waco, TX: Prufrock Press.

Frey, M. C., & Detterman, D. K. (2004). Scholastic assessment or *g*? The relationship between the Scholastic Assessment Test and general cognitive ability. *Psychological Science, 15,* 373–378.

Galton, F. (1883). *Inquiry into human faculty and its development.* London: Macmillan.

Gardner, H. (1983). *Frames of mind: The theory of multiple intelligences.* New York: Basic Books.

Hezlett, S., Kuncel, N., Vey, A., Ones, D., Campbell, J., & Camara, W. J. (2001, April). *The effectiveness of the SAT in predicting success early and late in college: A comprehensive meta-analysis.* Paper presented at the annual meeting of the National Council of Measurement in Education, Seattle, WA.

Spearman, C. (1927). *The abilities of man.* New York: Macmillan.

Stern, W. (1912). *Psychologische methoden der intelligenz-prüfung.* Leipzig, Germany: Barth.

Sternberg, R. J. (1985). *Beyond IQ: A triarchic theory of human abilities.* New York: Cambridge University Press.

Sternberg, R. J. (1997). *Successful intelligence.* New York: Plume.

Sternberg, R. J. (2000). Patterns of giftedness: A triarchic analysis. *Roeper Review, 44,* 231–235.

Sternberg, R. J. (2004). Culture and intelligence. *American Psychologist, 59,* 325–338.

Sternberg, R. J. (2005). The WICS model of giftedness. In R. J. Sternberg & J. E. Davidson (Eds.), *Conceptions of giftedness* (2nd ed., pp. 327–342). New York: Cambridge University Press.

Sternberg, R. J., & The Rainbow Project Collaborators. (2006). The Rainbow Project: Enhancing the SAT through assessments of analytical, practical and creative skills. *Intelligence, 34,* 321–350.

Terman, L. M., & Merrill, M. A. (1937). *Measuring intelligence.* Boston: Houghton Mifflin.

VanTassel-Baska, J. (2005). Domain-specific giftedness: Applications in school and life. In R. J. Sternberg & J. E. Davidson (Eds.), *Conceptions of giftedness* (2nd ed., pp. 358–377). New York: Cambridge University Press.

The Value of Traditional Assessments as Approaches to Identifying Academically Gifted Students

Nancy M. Robinson

Before deciding which assessment approaches are best, we need to make very sure that we know for what—that is, for whom—we are looking, why we are engaging in this enterprise in the first place. I submit that there are two major goals in identifying gifted students—and these are quite different purposes: targeting different students and requiring different approaches.

The first goal is to identify students who are *currently in academic need*—students whose academic advancement is such that they will, from this point forward, be ill-served, undereducated, and miserable, unless their educational trajectory is modified to provide a better fit with the level and pace of their learning.

The second goal is to identify students *of academic promise*, those who are growing up in unsupportive circumstances and who may, if given intensive and probably prolonged intervention, become outstanding students with the same kinds of performance (and needs) as the first group. At this point, we only have sketchy evidence about alternative ways to identify the second group, of which standard psychometric instruments constitute only one, but perhaps not even the most effective approach (although this is yet to be demonstrated).

Even in identifying this second group, traditional aptitude/academic measures have an important role to play. We especially shouldn't overlook those students who, despite signifi-cant barriers to their success, have so far done a pretty good job of learning and show up moderately well on traditional mea-sures. These may well be the students who will respond best to intervention and support (Lohman, 2005a).

But, it is to the first group that this chapter is primar-ily addressed. Academically gifted children are at high risk of suffering discouragement and giving up in the clutches of an ill-fitting, slow-moving educational system. We as a society sentence them there for at least 6 hours a day, 180 days a year, during 13 years that are critical to their development—more than 14,000 precious hours, not including homework. As a society, we are therefore responsible, because we set up the sys-tem, to identify those students whose thinking and skills are too advanced for what is being offered them, the level and pace of their learning being significantly more mature than that of their classmates. Having located these children, we are mor-ally obligated to provide them with a better-fitting educational experience, a rigorous academic program that makes it possible for them to continue to grow and gain satisfaction from their own efforts. We have no better way to identify such students than through traditional psychometric measures, because these measures are targeted specifically at assessing the level of their reasoning abilities and their attained academic skills—precisely those abilities and skills that make them "gifted" and in need of tailored intervention.

Selecting for What?

The programs for which these measures are selection instruments should be created precisely to provide challenges to gifted students in the form of academic depth and advancement (acceleration), rigor, pace, and emphasis on reasoning and inno-vation. The options may consist of differentiation in the regular classroom, promotion to a higher grade or more advanced class, independent study, a summer program, or a specialized pro-gram just for academically advanced students. The options must be tailored to the academic needs of the children they target.

And, just like tailors who measure their customers in order to make alterations in a suit, educators must measure children's readiness, that is, their reasoning abilities and academic skills, to achieve an optimal match (Lohman, 2005a; Robinson & Robinson, 1982).

The programs we should be providing to gifted students who have outgrown the regular programs are, then, very likely to emphasize verbal, quantitative, and scientific reasoning—just as do the regular programs. Appropriate programs demand a high level of traditional skills—reading, calculating, and writing—tools students need to have mastered or for which specific accommodations are effective. The programs certainly go beyond the basics; they encourage visual, as well as verbal strategies, application of conceptual-analytic understanding to real-life situations, creative thinking, leadership, and nontraditional activities, but these accompany and are part of a solid academic core.

To summarize this first section of the paper, the following key points are central in understanding the dynamic role of assessment and programming.

- Traditional measures are the best tools we have to identify and describe these students.
- Appropriate programs for academically gifted students differ from regular programs in precisely those domains in which these gifted students excel.
- Over time, the measures and the programs have prospered in this partnership, meeting identified needs in more and more effective ways, unless they have been distorted by political agendas.

Which Sorts of Measures Work?

Traditional measures of aptitude and achievement are standardized on nationally representative samples of students, with items carefully developed and tested for consistency and efficacy. Items are eliminated that exaggerate differences between ethnic or gender groups. The tests are rewritten and restandardized from time to time so that scores have up-to-date meaning.

Test results are generally reported in terms of standard scores with a mean of 100 and a standard deviation of 15 derived from a normal-curve distribution, and/or by percentiles based on the same distribution. One of the ways we think of gifted children is by the positions on that normal curve that best describe their various aptitudes and skills.

Aptitude tests involve tasks that emphasize reasoning, generally in verbal, mathematical, and/or spatial domains. Most of the tasks presented are of medium novelty—neither so straightforward that the student automatically knows the answer, nor so unusual that the student cannot figure out what is being asked. They are, of course, affected by a student's experience and knowledge, but the emphasis is on problem solving.

Achievement tests focus on proficiency in skills in reading, math, and writing, and often include the use of these tools to reason within their domains. For example, the student may be asked to read paragraphs of increasing complexity and to supply a missing word or answer questions about the passages, or to use knowledge of the number system to reason through word problems.

Obviously, the distinction between these two kinds of measures is inexact and permeable and results are highly correlated. Generally, each is composed of several different kinds of tasks, and sometimes the contrasts in performance are enlightening. For example, some young children arrive at school having "cracked" the symbol codes involved in reading and/or math, but are unable to use these skills to reason at an advanced level. Older children may reason well in the number system but be burdened by counting out basic facts on their fingers every time.

If students are suffering because they are too advanced in reasoning and skills for regular classrooms and ordinary curricular strategies, and if the special programs we provide them are designed to provide a more optimal match along those same dimensions, then measures should be chosen to be as relevant as possible to this academic situation. The closer the tests resemble the kinds of behaviors being promoted in the program, the better they will predict students' success in that class (Lohman,

2005a). These are precisely the "traditional" measures we've been using—the measures of verbal and quantitative reasoning and of academic skills—that are so familiar. As we have said, just as marriage partners and best friends tend to grow more compatible over the years, so too have the members of this partnership (the selection measures and the programs for which they select) grown to be more effective partners.

Of course, these measures aren't perfect, and there may be aspects of students' development besides verbal and quantitative reasoning and academic skills that should be added to the mixture in order to do a better job of describing student need and predicting success. Perhaps we should add standardized measures of practical and creative reasoning to the primarily analytic reasoning measures we are using already (Sternberg, Grigorenko, Ferrari, & Clinkenbeard, 1999). Perhaps we should add measures of organizational skills and self-discipline (Duckworth & Seligman, 2005) that predict success in challenging situations. On the other hand, I would argue that, for students who have been chronically underchallenged, there may have been no opportunity to develop these assets, and that even latent creativity is often squelched in too-conventional families and classrooms. The point remains that, unless we can very carefully specify what students need to have in place to be *ready* for a program, we shouldn't throw in measures that simply will muddy the waters.

Among the traditional measures are the tests of reasoning like the individual intelligence tests (e.g., the Wechslers, the Stanford-Binet, the Differential Aptitude Scales), especially those components of the measures that emphasize verbal and quantitative reasoning. Tests of reasoning that can be administered to groups also fall into this category, tests such as the Cognitive Abilities Test (CogAt), Otis-Lennon School Ability Test (OLSAT), the SAT, the ACT, and others. Individually administered tests of academic skills like the Woodcock-Johnson III, the Wechsler Individual Achievement Test (except for reading comprehension), and the group tests such as the Iowa Tests of Basic Skills, the Stanford Achievement Test, and the Metropolitan Achievement Tests also are useful in identifying gifted students. Unfortunately, because curricula differ so much from state to state and even from district to district, nationally normed achievement tests in the United States cannot assess what children actually *know*. However, tests like the SAT-II, the Advanced Placement tests, and the International Baccalaureate exams can do this. School districts must therefore use course grades and their own curriculum guidelines to plan for students accordingly.

Do These Measures Work?

Generally speaking, educators who conduct programs for gifted students appear reasonably well-satisfied that their students are qualified for them. The precise data we'd like to have do not seem to exist: Is there a high correlation between initial assessments and performance in academically rigorous programs? If we had such predictive validity data, we could adjust selection indices more precisely.

In nearly 30 years of selecting students for the Early Entrance Program at the University of Washington, in which scores on tests like the SAT and the ACT are used for initial screening and then taken into account in conjunction with other information, we have admitted virtually *no* students who were not bright enough to succeed in this highly demanding program that substitutes one year of academic preparation for 4 or 5 years of secondary school. Another program of very early entrance to college did run into problems when it initially ignored psychometric evidence that the students were not ready (Cornell, Callahan, & Loyd, 1991). Test scores generally provide the *only* selection criterion for entry into the summer programs for gifted adolescents that are connected with the regional talent searches and are doing the job quite well (Olszewski-Kubilius, 2004). Tests like the SAT-I and SAT-II demonstrate a substantial correlation, albeit an imperfect one, with subsequent college grades (e.g., Bridgeman, Burton, & Cline, 2001).

Large-scale studies of the relationship of test scores to vocational and economic achievement by adults also confirm the meaningfulness of traditional test scores (Gottfredson, 2004), and even graduate school performance can be predicted effectively by tests like the GRE, LSAT, MCAT, and others used for admission (Kuncel & Hezlett, 2007). Extensive and impressive longitudinal studies of adults who, as young adolescents, scored well on the SAT, demonstrate remarkably high educational attainment and occupational success (e.g., Benbow, 2006; Lubinski & Benbow, 2006; Lubinski, Benbow, Webb, & Bleske-Rechek, 2006; Wai, Lubinski, & Benbow, 2005).

In brief, it appears that the system "ain't broke" from the point of view of selecting candidates who will succeed in rigorous educational programs designed for academically gifted students.

Are We Missing Some Students Who Would Prosper in the Programs?

Do these traditional measures pick up every student who would thrive in an academically rigorous program designed for gifted students, or who could handle a more advanced class? Are students who are ready for the programs being left behind? We should always be on the lookout for three groups of students who might be missed. First, there are those who are fully ready but had a bad day when tested, for any of a number of reasons. These will usually be students whose nonselection comes as a surprise to teachers and parents. They deserve being reassessed immediately. Second are those who are twice-exceptional, whose reasoning is fully advanced but for whom a disability has interfered with test performance. These students need careful reassessment, usually using special accommodations, and thoughtful consideration as to whether they can cope with the more demanding academic option with appropriate instructional accommodations in place. Finally, there are gifted students who still are mastering the English language and are not yet ready to cope with the new option but likely will be within a year, learning the language being enough challenge for the next year but no longer. Indeed, for this last group of students, the speed with which they do master English will be an important tip-off to their exceptional abilities.

Do Other Measures Work Just as Well?

Other measures have been tried and found wanting. In particular, selecting candidates for rigorous educational programs on the basis of high nonverbal, visual-spatial reasoning (in the absence of high verbal and quantitative reasoning) turns out not to be effective. Students so selected tend not to be very successful in the programs (Gohm, Humphreys, & Yao, 1998). Indeed, Lohman (2005b) suggested that spatial strengths may constitute an "*in*aptitude for academic learning," at least in an educational system that emphasizes verbal and linear reasoning, even though they are critical to some occupations (Shea, Lubinski, & Benbow, 2001). Lohman proposed that this, to some extent, negative relationship may occur because of the mismatch of talent and program, or because measures of achievement in such programs do not reflect high spatial ability or a preference for such reasoning modes (see Chapter 3, this volume).

What about adding a nontraditional measure to a traditional battery? VanTassel-Baska and her colleagues (Feng & Chandler, 2006; VanTassel-Baska, Feng, & Evans, 2007) reported data from Project STAR, which admitted students who qualified on two of the three following kinds of instruments: traditional aptitude, traditional achievement, or performance tasks (verbal and nonverbal). Note that here was an instance in which the program was explicitly receptive to students who were so selected. The students who were selected on the basis of performance tests and one of the other measures, rather than a combination of the traditional aptitude and achievement measures, tended to underperform at the advanced level compared with students who qualified on the traditional measures, and showed more uneven profiles that sometimes resulted in learning problems. Teachers tended to identify strengths in spatial reasoning and creativity, but also to identify weaknesses in needed verbal skills, critical thinking, time management, and leadership in those students who qualified in part on the basis of performance measures.

"Bias" in Testing

Up to this point, we have ignored the major reason people have begun looking for nontraditional measures; namely the fact that our usual methods of selection result in ethnic imbalances in programs for gifted students. The assumption is that "fair" tests would identify the same proportions of students from ethnic minorities as are represented in the general local population. Mean group differences are assumed to demonstrate test bias. And yet, this assumption flies in the face of all we know about child development. Socioeconomic differences are more powerful than ethnic differences (Robinson, 2003) and no doubt account for the lion's share of the group differences that turn up over and over, but the point is that group differences do not demonstrate bias *unless* the scores have different implications depending on the group one comes from (Jensen, 1979). There is no evidence that this is the case. It is life, not the tests, that is unfair to children.

Children who grow up in families that are unable to provide positive conditions for child development less often develop along optimal intellectual paths than children who grow up in homes that are less stressed and able to be more supportive. It should be no surprise that these more deprived children are underrepresented among those children who can profit from more advanced school programs (Robinson, 2003). At the same time, children who grow up in marginalized, economically disadvantaged families but whose parents are able to provide more optimal conditions may indeed become children with a special need for advancement (Robinson, Lanzi, Weinberg, Ramey, & Ramey, 2002).

What Else Does a Psychometric Viewpoint Afford Us?

The scientific study of giftedness began with Francis Galton (1869) and was launched in the United States by Lewis Terman (1916, 1921, 1925). Galton had tried to measure aspects of high ability but used mainly physical attributes that had little relationship to intelligence. It was at the beginning of the 20th cen-

tury that Binet and Simon (1905), at the invitation of the board
of education in Paris, created a test to objectively identify children who were intellectually unprepared to profit from standard schooling. They arranged the items of their tests in order
of difficulty and specified age levels, leading to the concept of
mental age. A child's mental age, in terms of test performance, is
defined as mean age of a population of unselected children who
attain the same performance. Once a child's mental age could
be described, it was a short step to derive a simple quotient by
comparing mental age (MA) to calendar age, or chronological
age (CA; Stern, 1914). Using the 1916 version of the Binet-
Simon test he developed, the Stanford-Binet Intelligence Scale,
Terman used a ratio Intelligence Quotient (IQ; $IQ = MA \div CA \times 100$) that expresses a child's *rate* of intellectual development.
One can think of this as the length of time it has taken this child
to achieve this MA—more or less time than it takes the average child. With Terman, the notions of giftedness and cognitive
development began to go hand in hand. Giftedness began to be
defined as *rapid rate of cognitive development*.

Unfortunately, it is incredibly difficult to develop tests primarily according to an age scale, so the concept of mental age
has fallen by the wayside (Robinson, 2005). Today, tests tend
to be divided by types of items rather than by age levels, and to
be manipulated statistically to produce standard scores in the
form of deviation IQs that express children's relative standing in
comparison with others of their own chronological age, rather
than those who are older or younger, as do ratio IQs. Even so,
tests that span several ages still reflect underlying age changes.
Test developers do publish age-equivalents for subtests (only),
and something like a median mental age can be derived, but it is
no longer as easy as it once was to think of test performance in
that way. Yet, the age progression of children's development has
not gone away, nor has the fact that they traverse increasingly
mature developmental tasks at different rates of speed.

Based on this notion of rate of development, IQs can still be
used to derive ball park *estimates* of cognitive maturity. Think of
the IQ as representing rate of development in the form of a percentage. An IQ of 133 would imply that a child's maturity level

is about 133% of CA. A 6-year-old with an IQ of 133 would have a mental age of roughly 8 years; a 6-year-old with an IQ of 150 would have a mental age of roughly 9 years.

Measuring a student's cognitive abilities and academic achievement yields a picture of his or her maturity and readiness in various domains of educational attainment. It affords a sense of what to expect next, for what next steps the student is ready. This is an invaluable concept in creating and selecting educational options. A gifted child's cognitive maturity level, in the context of maturity in other critical aspects of development like social-emotional development, self-regulation, and motor skills, is a critical guide to matching educational experiences with those intended for older students. This is, of course, the conceptual basis for the practice of academic acceleration in all its permutations.

An interesting by-product of considering age progression and maturity is the opportunity to examine ways in which the thought processes of gifted children are simply *quantitatively* ahead on the maturity scale (i.e., like those of older children) and to what extent there may be *qualitative* differences that set them apart not only from age peers but also from older students. Whatever differences there are from the thinking of older children are likely to be subtle. A research design that compares responses of gifted children of a given MA with those of older children of the same MA is critical, but it seldom has been employed. For exceptions, see Kanevsky (1992) and Johnson, Im-Bolter, and Pascual-Leone (2003), who have studied metacognitive strategies and aspects of executive function, respectively, in children at different developmental levels, using the same tasks.

To be sure, the notion of mental age per se, as opposed to readiness and preparation, begins to lose meaning in the early teen years and makes no sense at all for adults.

Tests Do Reflect Real-Life Development

To preserve the value of tests and to avoid redeveloping them every time they are administered, there must be secrecy about the specific items on standardized tests. The tasks rely on an element of novelty to elicit children's ability to reason, strategize, and problem solve. They may, therefore, seem isolated from "real life." We have evidence from several longitudinal studies of young children that this is not the case, however. In each study, we asked parents to nominate children who showed precocity in general cognitive development or a specific domain (Robinson & Robinson, 1992), precocity in language (Robinson, Dale, & Landesman, 1990), or precocity in mathematical thinking (Robinson, Abbott, Berninger, & Busse, 1996). Parents were quite accurate in nominating children who fit the description. For example, the first study enrolled 550 children ages 2–5 years; more than half of the children attained IQs of 132 or higher on a brief form of the then-new 1972 Stanford-Binet and others showed precocity in specific domains. In the study of language-precocious toddlers, nominated by age 18 months, mother's initial reports of their children's language at home correlated 0.63 with verbal items of the Bayley Mental Scale and 0.37 with a sample of 50 utterances during play with toys, despite an attenuated range of scores. Finally, in the study of math-precocious children nominated at the end of preschool or kindergarten, parental descriptions of the kindergarten children's advanced math abilities related 0.48 and 0.41 with two brief screening measures (Pletan, Robinson, Berninger, & Abbott, 1995).

These findings confirm the accuracy of parental descriptions of their children's behavior. They tell us to trust parents who think that their children's behavior is advanced—whether or not we have seen that behavior in school. But, the studies also do something else. They confirm that the results of standardized tests *are strongly correlated with the children's actual behavior at home.* Furthermore, each of the above studies had a 2- to 5-year longitudinal aspect, and in each case, the scores initially attained by the children were predictive over time for the group as a whole.

Criticisms of a Psychometric Approach

Of course, tests are not perfect, and we can't rely on them altogether in high-stakes situations such as a child's admission to a special class or a decision about grade-skipping (Dale, Crain-Thoreson, & Robinson, 1995; Robinson, Abbott, Berninger, Busse, & Mukhopadhyay, 1997, Robinson & Robinson, 1992). Here are some reasons:

- Too much weight can be placed on single-episode testing. This is a misuse of the approach. Test results always should be taken in the context of a child's school performance and any other evidence such as portfolios, grades, or previous tests that could reveal talent. On the other hand, students we had ignored occasionally surprised us with their high performance and their hidden abilities.

- Students seldom make scores that are significantly "too high," with the result that they are rarely admitted to situations they are unable to handle, but they certainly can make scores that are inaccurately low. Some sources of error lie in children's failure to take the situation seriously, their inexperience in taking tests (e.g., spending too much time with single items or moving along too quickly and failing to check answers), test anxiety or feeling threatened in the situation, errors such as missing whole pages, becoming disoriented on separate answer sheets, not feeling well, or even needing to use the bathroom.

- More systematic errors may occur if children who are still mastering English are asked to take verbal tests, or if children with disabilities are not given accommodations during testing.

- Users of tests are at the mercy of test developers. For example, publishers may be more interested in identifying children at risk for poor achievement than those who are advanced, so that test ceilings may be too low and high levels of abstract reasoning may be underrepresented. Test developers also may include measures of other functions, such as memory and processing speed that detract from the power of the summary scores to reflect maturity of reasoning. This has occurred on the popular Wechsler Intelligence Scale for Children, Fourth Edition, for example, so an alternative summary, the General Ability Index, is recommended for selection purposes by the test publisher.

- Tests may miss talents important for children with advanced development but not children in general. For example, the Wechsler Preschool and Primary Scale of Intelligence, Third Edition (WPPSI-III) includes no measure of arithmetic reasoning because most young children are not yet interested in numbers.
- The ceilings of tests may be too low to permit students to show their "true colors." This is less a problem in selecting students for programs, where the cutoff is usually pegged to "moderate" rather than "exceptional" degrees of giftedness, than in gaining an accurate picture of the advancement of truly exceptional students. Differences among students who are at the far upper tail of the distribution will be masked by ceilings that are too low, yet there are so few such individuals that no test standardized on their age-mates will ever be able to describe them accurately. We therefore cannot know from the standard measures how accurately the theoretical parameters of the normal curve describe the frequency of occurrence of truly exceptionally gifted individuals.
- Finally, the tests will not by themselves be able to pick out *children of promise*, whose modest test scores actually represent unusual growth, given their limited experience and support. To find children who might profit from intensive intervention will require getting to know individual children and their families. Yet, even these traditional measures have their place in identifying promising youngsters. Children who are reading at an average to above-average level for their age but whose homes have no books and whose parents are alienated from the educational system might well be better bets than children from similar backgrounds who are reading below grade level.

Conclusion

Identification of gifted students has two purposes: First, means are needed to identify students who, by reason of their developmental maturity, are ready for much greater challenges than they are likely to receive unless educational changes are made. Second, means are needed to identify students who may, with intensive and prolonged intervention, grow to resemble the first group. This chapter addressed the first purpose.

Not all students selected for gifted programs will proceed to become gifted adults or world-class performers, to be sure. It would be wrong to criticize selection measures because they do not, by themselves, locate as children those adults who will change the world. For such success, a number of personality factors, high-quality instruction, deep and protracted commitment to one's talent development through both good times and bad, opportunities for advancement, and an appropriate configuration of genes all are required (Gagné, 2007; Simonton, 2005; Subotnik & Jarvin, 2005). The instructional opportunities we provide to students are but one component of such careers, but they are a critical step along the way.

Provision of curriculum modifications and programs for gifted students is a response to real need, both for their benefit and for ours. If these students are to grow in a healthy way, to learn to weather and overcome challenges, to gain the inner strength that comes with such experience, and to figure out that the world was not necessarily designed so that they always know the answers before anyone else, we need to identify them and provide alternatives matched to the level and pace of their learning. Conventional ability and achievement tests can be critical to the process. Other alternatives simply don't do the job as well.

References

Benbow, C. P. (2006, May). *Studying the development of math/science talent for 35 years through SMPY: Implications for the flat world.* Julian C. Stanley Keynote Address, Eighth Biennial Wallace International Research Symposium.

Binet, A., & Simon, T. (1905). Méthodes nouvelles pour le diagnostic du niveau intellectuel des anormaux. *Année Psychologique, 11,* 191–244.

Bridgeman, B., Burton, N., & Cline, F. (2001). *Substituting SAT-II: Subjects tests for SAT-I: Reasoning Tests: Impact on admitted class composi-*

tion and quality (College Board Report 2001–2003, ETS RR-01-07). Princeton, NJ: College Entrance Examination Board.

Cornell, D. G., Callahan, C. M., & Loyd, B. H. (1991). Socioemotional adjustment of adolescent girls enrolled in a residential acceleration program. *Gifted Child Quarterly, 35,* 58–66.

Dale, P. S., Crain-Thoreson, C., & Robinson, N. M. (1995). Linguistic precocity and the development of reading: The role of extra-linguistic factors. *Applied Psycholinguistics, 16,* 173–187.

Duckworth, A. L., & Seligman, M. E. P. (2005). Self-discipline outdoes IQ in predicting academic performance of adolescents. *Psychological Science, 16,* 939–944.

Feng, A. X., & Chandler, K. (2006, May). *A longitudinal study of performance task-identified gifted learners.* Paper presented at the Eighth Biennial Wallace International Research Symposium.

Gagné, F. (2007). Ten commandments for academic talent development. *Gifted Child Quarterly, 51,* 93–118.

Galton, F. (1869). *Hereditary genius: An inquiry into its causes and consequences.* New York: Macmillan.

Gohm, C. L., Humphreys, L. G., & Yao, G. (1998). Underachievement among spatially gifted students. *American Educational Research Journal, 35,* 515–531.

Gottfredson, L. S. (2004). Realities in desegregating gifted education. In D. Boothe & J. C. Stanley (Eds.), *In the eyes of the beholder: Critical issues for diversity in gifted education* (pp. 139–155). Waco, TX: Prufrock Press.

Jensen, A. R. (1979). *Bias in mental testing.* New York: Free Press.

Johnson, J., Im-Bolter, N., & Pascual-Leone, J. (2003). Development of mental attention in gifted and mainstream children: The role of mental capacity, inhibition, and speed of processing. *Child Development, 74,* 1594–1614.

Kanevsky, L. (1992). The learning game. In P. S. Klein & A. J. Tannenbaum (Eds.), *To be young and gifted* (pp. 204–241). Norwood, NJ: Ablex.

Kuncel, N. R., & Hezlett, S. A. (2007). Standardized tests predict graduate students' success. *Science, 315,* 1080–1081.

Lohman, D. F. (2005a). An aptitude perspective on talent: Implications for identification of academically gifted minority students. *Journal for the Education of the Gifted, 28,* 333–360.

Lohman, D. F. (2005b). The role of nonverbal ability tests in identifying students for participation in programs for the academically gifted. *Gifted Child Quarterly, 49,* 111–138.

Lubinski, D., & Benbow, C. P. (2006). Study of mathematically precocious youth after 35 years. *Perspectives in Psychological Science, 1*,
316–345.

Lubinski, D., Benbow, C. P., Webb, R. M., & Bleske-Rechek, A.
(2006). Tracking exceptional human capital over two decades.
Psychological Science, 17, 194–199.

Olszewski-Kubilius, P. (2004). Talent search: Purposes, rationale, and
role in gifted education. In D. Boothe & J. C. Stanley (Eds.), *In
the eyes of the beholder: Critical issues for diversity in gifted education* (pp.
251–262). Waco, TX: Prufrock Press.

Pletan, M. D., Robinson, N. M., Berninger, V. W., & Abbott, R. D.
(1995). Parents' observations of kindergartners who are advanced
in mathematical reasoning. *Journal for the Education of the Gifted,
19*, 30–34.

Robinson, N. M. (2003). Two wrongs do not make a right: Sacrificing
the needs of academically talented students does not solve society's unsolved problems. *Journal for the Education of the Gifted, 26*,
321–328.

Robinson, N. M. (2005). In defense of a psychometric approach to the
definition of academic giftedness: A conservative view from a die-
hard liberal. In R. J. Sternberg & J. E. Davidson (Eds.), *Conceptions of
giftedness* (2nd ed, pp. 280–294). New York: Cambridge University
Press.

Robinson, N. M., Abbott, R. D., Berninger, V. W., & Busse, J. (1996).
The structure of abilities in young, math-precocious children:
Gender similarities and differences. *Journal of Educational Psychology,
88*, 341–352.

Robinson, N. M., Abbott, R. D., Berninger, V. W., Busse, J., &
Mukhopadhyay, S. (1997). Developmental changes in mathemat-
ically precocious young children: Matthew and gender effects.
Gifted Child Quarterly, 41, 145–159.

Robinson, N. M., Dale, P. S., & Landesman, S. J. (1990). Validity
of Stanford-Binet IV with young children exhibiting precocious
language. *Intelligence, 14*, 173–186.

Robinson, N. M., Lanzi, R. G., Weinberg, R. A., Ramey, S. L., &
Ramey, C. T. (2002). Factors associated with high academic com-
petence in former Head Start children at third grade. *Gifted Child
Quarterly, 46*, 281–294.

Robinson, N. M., & Robinson, H. B. (1982). The optimal match:
Devising the best compromise for the highly gifted student. In D.
Feldman (Ed.), *Developmental approaches to giftedness and creativity* (pp.
79–94). San Francisco: Jossey-Bass.

Robinson, N. M., & Robinson, H. B. (1992). The use of standard-ized tests with young gifted children. In P. S. Klein & A. J. Tannenbaum (Eds.), *To be young and gifted* (pp. 141–170). Norwood, NJ: Ablex.

Shea, D. L., Lubinski, D., & Benbow, C. P. (2001). Importance of assessing spatial ability in intellectually talented young adolescents: A 20-year longitudinal study. *Journal of Educational Psychology, 93,* 604–614.

Simonton, D. K. (2005). Genetics of giftedness: The implications of an emergenic-epigenetic model. In R. J. Sternberg & J. E. Davidson (Eds.), *Conceptions of giftedness* (2nd ed., pp. 312–326). New York: Cambridge University Press.

Stern, W. (1914). *The psychological methods of testing intelligence* (G. M. Whipple, Trans.). Baltimore: Warwick & York.

Sternberg, R. J., Grigorenko, E. L., Ferrari, M., & Clinkenbeard, P. (1999). A triarchic analysis of an aptitude-treatment interaction. *European Journal of Psychological Assessment, 15,* 1–11.

Subotnik, R. F., & Jarvin, L. (2005). Beyond expertise: Conceptions of giftedness as great performance. In R. J. Sternberg & J. E. Davidson (Eds.), *Conceptions of giftedness* (2nd ed., pp. 343–357). New York: Cambridge University Press.

Terman, L. M. (1916). *The measurement of intelligence: An explanation of and a complete guide for the use of the Stanford revision and extension of the Binet-Simon intelligence scale.* Boston: Houghton Mifflin.

Terman, L. M. (1921). Intelligence and its measurement: A symposium. *Journal of Educational Psychology, 12,* 127–133.

Terman, L. M. (1925). *Genetic studies of genius: Vol. I. Mental and physical traits of a thousand gifted children.* Stanford, CA: Stanford University Press.

VanTassel-Baska, J., Feng, A., & Evans, B. (2007). Patterns of identifi-cation and performance among gifted students identified through performance tasks: A three-year analysis. *Gifted Child Quarterly, 51,* 218–231.

Wai, J., Lubinski, D., & Benbow, C. P. (2005). Creativity and occupa-tional accomplishments among intellectually precocious youths: An age 13 to age 33 longitudinal study. *Journal of Educational Psychology, 97,* 484–492.

Nontraditional Applications
of Traditional Testing

Sylvia Rimm, Barbara Gilman, & Linda Silverman

In Chapter 9, Nancy Robinson substantiated the value of traditional IQ and achievement tests for the goal of identification of gifted children who are in academic need. She stated a second goal as one of identifying academic promise among children who are growing up in unsupportive circumstances. In this chapter, the authors will expand on how traditional individual IQ tests can be administered and interpreted in nontraditional ways to improve the identification of gifted children who are in academic need. It also will recommend ways to identify those with academic promise. A third goal also can be achieved by the nontraditional application of individual IQ testing results—improved, appropriate educational and psychological support programs can be organized for those children based on the knowledge gained in such testing and may, in fact, provide the most important value of traditional testing for gifted children.

The Gold Standard

Individual IQ tests have seen their most extensive use in education as part of comprehensive evaluations for special education services. Programming for special needs children with deficits has been planned only after comprehensive testing, with individual IQ tests providing the gold standard for assessment of cognitive strengths and weaknesses. Standardized individual ability tests tap a balance of verbal, visual-spatial, and mathematical reasoning, as well as working memory and processing skills, and are administered one-on-one by highly qualified examiners who can observe the way the child approaches each task and generates answers. Such tests are based on extensive research and utilize normative samples comprising thousands of children from diverse racial, ethnic, and socioeconomic groups. Group-administered IQ tests for the entire school may be used for more general screening but are not sufficient for such high-stakes testing as the identification of giftedness and provide inadequate information for the development of educational programs to support strengths and accommodate weaknesses.

Gifted children are viewed as *special needs* students in many states because regular curriculum and instructional approaches typically do not meet their needs. Individual IQ tests are an essential part of the comprehensive battery used to identify and serve such students. They are especially useful when some of the new administration and scoring options are utilized. However, because many school districts lack the financial resources for comprehensive testing of the gifted, they resort to ability screening tools that can be administered more easily by teachers to groups of children. The largely multiple-choice screening tests locate some gifted children, but offer little information about specific strengths and weaknesses that can help shape a child's individual learning plan. Screening tests generate many false negatives; for example, when the test emphasizes one type of ability and the child's strengths lie in another domain or if the child has processing speed problems and cannot complete the test within the time limit. Twice-exceptional children, who are both gifted and learning disabled, are frequently missed because their disabilities depress their IQ scores below the threshold for admission to programs. Individual IQ scales are used in special education evaluations because they are more reliable and valid than group tests. Their conspicuous absence in the identification of the gifted is purely economic.

Testing Gifted Children Using Individual IQ Tests

When using traditional individual IQ tests with the gifted, certain approaches yield better results. For example, if subtest and scoring choices exist, decisions should be made with gifted needs in mind. The gifted show advanced development in verbal, visual-spatial, and mathematical reasoning; however, their processing skills (short-term memory, processing speed on paper-and-pencil tests) are not necessarily as strong. Testers need to utilize the most effective reasoning tests to cull out those children who will be at risk when exposed to a typical curriculum inadequate in terms of advancement and pace. Processing skill deficits may need accommodation, but accommodations should be added to gifted programming, rather than prevent identification for that programming. Following such guidelines can improve assessment by clarifying strengths and weaknesses and offer information beyond labeling to plan programs.

Newly revised and renormed versions of major IQ tests require that the tester stay abreast of best practices in testing the gifted. Testing considerations for the two major individual IQ tests on the market follow.

Stanford-Binet, Fifth Edition (SB5)

The SB5, released in 2003, is a completely redesigned test. It is based upon the popular Cattell-Horn-Carroll theory of intelligence and employs sophisticated Item Response Theory as pioneered by Rasch (Roid, 2003b). SB5 test items are designed to assess five areas of ability: Fluid Reasoning, Knowledge, Quantitative Reasoning, Visual-Spatial Processing, and Working Memory. Each type of ability is assessed both verbally and visually, resulting in 10 subtests. Although it appears that half of the subtests measure verbal abilities, there is insufficient emphasis on classic verbal reasoning and language items. Verbal subtests include Verbal Quantitative Reasoning (math questions presented verbally) and Verbal Visual-Spatial Reasoning.

For the gifted, the SB5 has challenging mathematical and spatial reasoning items, which can document unusual abilities.

Like the Stanford-Binet Intelligence Scale Form L-M (SBL-M), the SB5 is virtually untimed—a plus for gifted children, who may be reflective thinkers. The major processing skill assessed is visual/auditory memory.

The main drawback of the SB5 is that when the Full Scale IQ (FSIQ) scores are used for admission to gifted programs, many gifted children will be missed. Lovecky, Kearney, Falk, and Gilman (2005) found that the SB5 FSIQ would *not* have identified 17 out of the 47 children in a gifted program where the cutoff for identification was 130. Instead of an FSIQ of 130, the authors recommended an FSIQ, Verbal IQ, or Nonverbal IQ score of 120. There also are other scoring modifications for the gifted, such as the Rasch Ratio IQ score (see Carson & Roid, 2004; Roid & Barram, 2004; Roid & Carson, 2004; Ruf, 2003).

The Wechsler Intelligence Scale for Children, Fourth Edition (WISC-IV)

The Wechsler IQ scales are the most popular individual IQ tests for identification of giftedness. The Wechsler Intelligence Scale for Children, Fourth Edition (WISC-IV; Wechsler, 2003), the latest revision of this test, has changes that have a great impact on the selection of gifted students. Substantially different from its predecessor, this version has eliminated the Verbal and Performance IQ scores. The WISC-IV provides a Full Scale IQ score and four index scores: Verbal Comprehension, Perceptual Reasoning, Working Memory, and Processing Speed. The Verbal Comprehension Index is an excellent indicator of verbal abstract reasoning ability, conceptual thinking, and language. Children who score in the gifted range on this portion (including the core subtests of Similarities, Vocabulary, and Comprehension) are well-prepared for gifted programs that emphasize advanced concepts, discussion, debate, and in-depth writing. The Perceptual Reasoning portion (Block Design, Picture Concepts, and Matrix Reasoning), which measures nonverbal reasoning, visual abstract reasoning, spatial reasoning, and pattern recognition, can locate children with strong visual-spatial abilities—long overlooked in gifted programs (Dixon,

1983; Lubinski, 2003). As such, the Perceptual Reasoning Index better identifies giftedness than the WISC-III's Performance IQ, which emphasized visual perception more than visual reasoning and was heavily timed.

Both the Verbal Comprehension and Perceptual Reasoning portions are excellent indicators of intelligence, with only one timed subtest among the six core subtests in these two areas. Reduced emphasis on timing helps gifted children with more reflective response styles.

Fewer core subtests now comprise the Verbal Comprehension and Perceptual Reasoning Composite areas because additional core subtests have been added to the Working Memory and Processing Speed Indices. Because the WISC-IV features a number of subtest additions and deletions, the Indices now assess somewhat different abilities. They also are assigned a different weight in the calculation of the FSIQ score. This situation also proves to be significant for the gifted. The weighting of processing skills (working memory and processing speed) has doubled from 20% to 40%. These may be weak areas for some gifted children and are not as related to general intelligence (g) as Verbal Comprehension and Perceptual Reasoning. Gifted children are not necessarily fast processors (Reams, Chamrad, & Robinson, 1990). The impact of this new weighting is that many children who were identified by the WISC-III as gifted no longer meet the IQ criteria for gifted programs in their schools. This could prevent schools from serving thousands of gifted children who legitimately need services.

The gifted group in the WISC-IV normative sample earned discrepant composite/index scores when compared with the control group (Wechsler, 2003). Although scores of the control group varied by less than 4 points across the indices, scores for the gifted group varied by more than 14 points. Table 10.1 shows these scores.

Similar scoring patterns with even greater disparities were found in a study of 103 children at the Gifted Development Center (GDC) in Denver (Gilman & Kearney, 2004; Silverman, Gilman, & Falk, 2004) and in a sample of 42 children from the

Table 10.1
Subscores From the WISC-IV Normative Sample

WISC-IV Normative Sample, Gifted Group ($n = 63$)		
	Gifted Group	Control Group
Verbal Comprehension	124.7	106.6
Perceptual Reasoning	120.4	105.6
Working Memory	112.5	103.0
Processing Speed	110.6	102.8
Full Scale IQ	123.5	106.7

Family Achievement Clinic (FAC; Rimm, 2006). Index scores from these psychological clinics are shown in Table 10.2.

The variance of index scores exceeded 27 points at the GDC and 19 points at the FAC. Flanagan and Kaufman (2004) advise against the use of the FSIQ as a global estimate of ability when the disparity between index scores is equal to or greater than 1.5 standard deviations (23 points). In such cases, they argue that the FSIQ is not a unitary construct and is, therefore, not interpretable.

How frequently does this happen? In 79% of GDC and 74% of FAC cases, the Full Scale IQ score was not interpretable due to extreme discrepancies (> 23 points) between index scores. Flanagan and Kaufman (2004) state that in those cases the General Ability Index (GAI) provides a better overall indicator of the child's reasoning abilities. The GAI combines the scores of the Verbal Comprehension and Perceptual Reasoning indices (which should vary by less than 23 points), eliminating Working Memory and Processing Speed (Raiford, Weiss, Rolfhus, & Coalson, 2005).

Use of the GAI increased the identification of children for gifted programs (with scores ≥ 130), but more particularly for highly gifted programs (with scores ≥ 145). GDC identified 44 children with FSIQ scores of 130, whereas when using the

Table 10.2
Comparative WISC-IV Index Scores

	Gifted Development Center (*n* = 103)	Family Achievement Clinic (*n* = 42)
Verbal Comprehension	131.7	130.0
Perceptual Reasoning	126.4	126.7
Working Memory	117.7	119.9
Processing Speed	104.3	111.9

GAI, 61 children were identified with scores of 130 or higher, and the percentage increased from 43% to 59%. The differential was not as great for FAC's smaller sample, with 19 identified by FSIQ and 22 by GAI, and the percentage increasing from 45% to 52%. Greater differences were found for highly gifted students. The GDC identified only 8 students with FSIQs of 145 or higher, compared to 21 children with GAIs of 145 or higher (from 8% to 20%). At FAC, only 2 had been found with FSIQs above 145, while 10 children were identified as highly gifted using GAIs (from 5% to 24%).

Significant disparities among the four indices of the WISC-IV exist for a large percentage of gifted children. Thus, the Full Scale IQ score does *not* yield a valid global estimate of ability and should not be required for admission to gifted programs.

The definition of standardization of scores by test makers implies that there always will be an upper 1% or 3%; so, theoretically, if intelligence fits a normal curve, the use of the Full Scale IQ should continue to identify many gifted children. However, by reducing the emphasis on reasoning and doubling the weight of Working Memory and Processing Speed, the wrong children may be identified as gifted. The GDC study found only 4 of 103 children scored 130 or above on the visual-motor tasks that measure Processing Speed (Gilman & Falk, 2005; Silverman

Good Measures of g

Vocabulary	(.82)
(Information)	(.79)
Similarities	(.79)
(Arithmetic)	(.74)
(Word Reasoning)	(.70)
Comprehension	(.70)

Fair Measures of g

Matrix Reasoning	(.68)
Block Design	(.67)
(Picture Completion)	(.63)
Letter-Number Sequencing	(.60)
Symbol Search	(.58)
Picture Concepts	(.57)
Digit Span	(.51)

Poor Measures of g

Coding	(.48)
(Cancellation)	(.25)

Figure 10.1. Relationships of WISC-IV subtests to general intelligence (g).

Note. Adapted from Flanagan & Kaufman, 2004, p. 309. Subtests in parentheses are not *core* subtests (used to compute composite or Full Scale IQ scores), but are diagnostic or substitute subtests only.

et al., 2004). The emphasis on physical development seems a throwback to the earliest IQ measurement attempts put forth by Francis Galton (1883).

The relationship between tasks on an individual IQ test and general intelligence (g) can be experimentally determined. Strong measures of g, or general intelligence, predict school and life success, and most effectively locate gifted children seriously in need of accommodations. Figure 10.1 shows all of the WISC-IV subtests as they relate to g.

Although administration of Working Memory and Processing Speed subtests (which have lower g-loadings) provide helpful diagnostic information (e.g., a child may need to type his or her compositions), subtests with the highest g-loadings (primarily Verbal Comprehension and Perceptual Reasoning subtests) best identify the gifted. As two subtest substitutions are allowed in different indices, substituting Arithmetic for Letter-Word Identification or Digit Span is preferable for gifted children who are not mathphobic (Gilman & Falk, 2005). Arithmetic has the fourth highest g-loading of all subtests, is a meaningful memory test, suggests mathematical talent, and was the second highest-scoring subtest for the gifted group in the normative study.

Recommendations for Use of the WISC-IV
in Identification for Gifted Programs

Either the General Ability Index (GAI), which emphasizes reasoning ability, *or* the Full Scale IQ Score (FSIQ) should be acceptable for selection to gifted programs. The GAI should be derived using the table provided on the Harcourt Assessments Web site (Technical Report 4; http://harcourtassessment.com/ hai/Images/pdf/wisciv/WISCIVTechReport4.pdf). The Verbal Comprehension Index (VCI) and the Perceptual Reasoning Index (PRI) also are independently appropriate for selection to programs for the gifted, especially for culturally diverse, bilingual, twice-exceptional students, or visual-spatial learners. It is important that a good match be made between the strengths of the child and the attributes of the program. Students who have special learning needs should be admitted to gifted programs, provided that there are other indications of giftedness and instructional modifications are made to fit the needs of the students.

Finding the Unmeasured Gifted

In 1922, Columbia University's Leta Hollingworth studied and taught, with assistance, 50 students divided into two classes. The average IQ score of one class was 145 and the other 165 (Gray & Hollingworth, 1931). Further, she observed that children with 140 IQs typically wasted about half their time in regular schools and those with IQs in the 170s wasted practically all of their time (Hollingworth, 1939). If the Binet tests of the 1920s could separate gifted students into two such extremely different categories, one wonders why our present standardized

IQ tests can't discern such differences. The original ratio formula (Stern, 1911) yielded scores for some gifted children as high as or higher than 200. The Binet tests included increasingly difficult items that were assigned age values. Months were added to a child's mental age, representing the number of items completed. Julian Stanley (1990), founder of the nationwide talent searches, referred to the Binet-type scale as "the original examination suitable for extensive out-of-level testing" (p. 167). Approximations of ratio IQs of brilliant persons have been estimated by Cox (1926a). Figure 10.2 includes IQ scores of such leaders.

Present-day tests yield standard IQ scores (deviation IQs) only as high as 155 or 160, depending on the edition of the tests. Most IQ tests have a mean of 100 and a standard deviation of 15. Two standard deviations above the mean, or 130, typically represents the cutoff point for the very superior or gifted range of intelligence. Three standard deviations above the mean, or 145, is regarded as highly gifted. There is little concern within the fields of assessment or education about identifying children with higher abilities than current tests can measure. Only the occasional child earns an IQ score of 145, 149, or rarer still, 152—skirting the ceiling of one of today's tests. Do children with even higher abilities exist, and does it matter? At that level, would a higher score have any meaning?

Surprising to many is the fact that exceptionally gifted children are our highest risk gifted population—not our most successful. So different from their age peers that it is truly difficult to connect with classmates socially, they seek support groups or much older friends for the rare opportunity to meet a "like-minded peer" with similar interests. As typical curricula cannot begin to meet their educational needs, they are desperate for options in school. They may awe their teachers, intimidate them, or disappoint them when they fail to meet the teacher's expectations for a top student. Their intensity, sensitivity and a host of other characteristics of extreme giftedness, enhanced at their IQ level, can appear pathological to teachers. There is a pressing need to identify and support these students.

Name	Nationality	Activity	Ratio IQ
Johann Wolfgang von Goethe	Germany	Poet/Writer	210
John Stuart Mill	England	Philosopher/ Economist/ Political Theorist	200
Blaise Pascal	France	Mathematician/Physicist/ Religious Thinker	195
Bobby Fischer	U.S.	Chess player	187
Galileo Galilei	Italy	Physicist/Astronomer/ Philosopher	185
René Descartes	France	Philosopher/ Mathematician	180
Madame de Stael	France	Woman of Letters/Novelist/ Political Philosopher	180
Immanuel Kant	Germany	Philosopher	175
Linus Carl Pauling	U.S.	Chemist (Double Nobel Prize Winner)	170
Sofia Kovalevskaya	Russia/ Sweden	Mathematician/Writer	170
Charles Darwin	England	Naturalist	165
Wolfgang Amadeus Mozart	Austria	Composer	165
George Eliot (Mary Ann Evans)	England	Writer	160
Nicolaus Copernicus	Poland	Cleric/Astronomer	160
Albert Einstein	U.S.	Physicist	160
Rembrandt van Rijn	Holland	Painter/Etcher	155
Anna Lindh	Sweden	Foreign Minister	152
George Sand (Aurore Dupin)	France	Writer	150

Figure 10.2. Estimated ratio IQ scores of famous persons.

Note. From *Estimated IQs of Some of the Greatest Geniuses*, by C. M. Cox (1926b). Table created by Ulf Norlinger, retrieved December 18, 2006, from http://hem.bredband.net/b153434/Index.htm. Reprinted with permission.

The Stanford-Binet L-M

A longstanding method, still supported by Riverside Publishing (Carson & Roid, 2004), is to administer its older Stanford–Binet Intelligence Scale Form L-M (SBL–M; Terman & Merrill, 1973) as a retest after a child scores at or near the ceiling of a current test. Because the SBL–M has a higher ceiling and a ratio-based metric, it can further differentiate children whose scores cluster around the 140s—near the ceilings of current tests or slightly higher—but have widely varying levels of ability. When retested, some will score about the same, others a bit higher, some much higher. The test is an excellent measure of abstract reasoning (especially verbal) and language, with minimal processing skills emphasis—an excellent vehicle for gifted assessment.

Although these authors strongly recommend the use of the SBL–M for children already identified as gifted, it also is appropriate to mention some concerns regarding its use. First, a few items may be missed because they are dated and seem a little strange to children today. Second, psychologists often assert that its scores are inflated compared to present day norms due to the Flynn effect (1984, 1987). The Flynn effect found that IQ scores of children in the world increased approximately three points a decade. Explanations for the increase include better education, smaller families, improved nutrition, and greater environmental complexity (Minigroni, 2004). Thus, for a test like the SBL–M, normed in 1972, it might be prudent to subtract six to nine points when comparing results to today's IQ scores, although a like number of points is usually lost due to dated items that are missed. In his recent review of the Flynn effect, Wasserman (2007) writes, "there is no substantive evidence for [the Flynn effect's] validity with high ability individuals (particularly those who are intellectually gifted)" (p. 1). And, the fact that Rasch-Ratio scores on the SB5 yield somewhat higher scores than the SBL–M (Lovecky et al., 2005) further suggests that the SBL–M may underestimate rather than overestimate scores. Teasdale and Owen (2005) and others propose that the Flynn effect may have ended beginning in the 1990s (see Wasserman, 2007).

Ratio-Based Metrics

Ratio-based metrics, such as the SBL-M utilizes, offer the best hope of differentiating higher levels of giftedness than current tests measure. Based on the original concept of an Intelligence Quotient (IQ), comparing mental age and chronological age, they reflect what a child actually can do, compared with developmental expectations for a child of that age. This approach has been helpful in locating exceptionally and profoundly gifted children, not found by tests with normative scaling.

Talent searches, which discriminate among students scoring $\geq$ 97th percentile, demonstrate that differentiation of scores at the high end predicts specific needs of children. Children with IQ scores in the 150s usually require acceleration—probably at least one grade skip and multiple opportunities for subject-area acceleration. Honors classes and some individualization in the classroom are inadequate at this level. As IQ scores rise to 160 and 175, the need for acceleration increases (Gross, 2004). For the rare child with an IQ above 200, traditional schooling may not be suitable at all—at least partial homeschooling is often the best option to address such a child's needs and interests. Just as the talent search out-of-level testing finds middle schoolers functioning at the level of entering college students, ratio-based scores on individual IQ tests offer a way to find young children functioning at the level of much older children. The approach breaks down once children can answer the most difficult items on the test, so care must be taken to limit its use to optimal age ranges, which differ with the test. Used appropriately, ratio-based metrics can identify our most highly gifted students and provide some hope of meeting their unique educational needs.

Ratio-Based Scores for SB5

Ratio-based and criterion-referenced scoring options have been included in the SB5 to address children at both extremes of the ability spectrum. Gale Roid (2003a), author of the Stanford Binet 5, offers alternative scoring methods for the SB5 that utilize Change Sensitive Scores (CSS).

In addition to norm-referencing, where the child is compared to peers of the same age, the CSS scale allows for criterion-referencing to task complexity and age-related milestones such as the achievement of reading fluency or the various stages in mathematical competence (p. 21).

Roid further notes that, "Unfortunately, conventional normative scoring systems (such as the normalized standard scores for subtests and composites) do not provide fine distinctions among the exceptionally high scoring or extremely low scoring individuals" (p. 22). When the raw scores of these individuals are examined, considerable variability is still present. This approach utilizes raw scores, taking into account all points earned beyond the minimum needed to yield the highest scaled score.

Roid cautions that ratio scores must be interpreted carefully by psychologists. Comparing normative and ratio-based scores would be similar to comparing Fahrenheit to Centigrade scales that have different intervals, although they both measure temperature.

Ratio-Based Scores for the WISC-IV

Scores comparing a child's performance or mental age (designated as Test-Age Equivalent) and chronological age can be quite effectively utilized with the WISC-IV. The WISC-IV provides age-equivalent scores (see Table A-9; Wechsler, 2003, p. 253), which take into account all items answered correctly for each subtest. It is possible to convert age-equivalent scores to months, average them to derive a mental age, and, using the ratio formula (mental age divided by chronological age multiplied by 100), calculate a Rimm Ratio score. This could further differentiate highly gifted children who appear to have abilities beyond the limits of the test, potentially making them eligible for services for the exceptionally and profoundly gifted. Thus, a quotient, rather than a normative standard score, can again function to identify highly gifted children.

Figure 10.3 is an example of a student's testing where the ceiling effect of scores prevents differentiation of his extreme

Name: FAC DH Male
Date of Birth:
Age at Testing: 8:2
Grade at Testing:
Date Tested:

Wechsler Intelligence Scale for Children (4th ed., WISC-IV)

Verbal Comprehension:	152	>99.9 percentile	Profoundly Gifted
Perceptual Reasoning:	147	99.9 percentile	Profoundly Gifted
Working Memory:	116	86 percentile	High Average
Processing Speed:	112	79 percentile	High Average
Full Scale IQ:	144	99.8 percentile	Very Superior

Verbal Comprehension		Perceptual Reasoning:	
Similarities:	19 (+8) VS	Block Design:	15 S
Vocabulary:	19 (+13) VS	Picture Concepts:	19 (+2) VS
Comprehension:	18 VS	Matrix Reasoning:	19 (+0) VS

Working Memory		Processing Speed	
Digit Span:	11 A	Coding:	10 A
Arithmetic:	15 S	Symbol Search:	14 S

Scale Score
16 and up: Very Superior
14–15: Superior
12–13: Above Average
9–11: Average
8 and below: Below Average

Figure 10.3. Summary of assessment, FAC DH Male.

giftedness: It is clear from this figure that a scaled score of 19 (the highest possible) is not always the same. Although all four tests are counted equally in computing this child's IQ score, he actually has scored 8 extra raw score points above the ceiling (beyond what is required to yield the highest scaled score) for Similarities, 13 extra points for Vocabulary, no extra points for Picture Concepts, and 2 extra points for Matrix Reasoning. This is an excellent example of a child whose FSIQ score, 144, is a gross underrepresentation of his ability both because his

---

Name: FAC RB Female
Date of Birth:
Age at Testing: 7:6
Grade at Testing:
Date Tested:

Wechsler Intelligence Scale for Children (4th ed., WISC-IV)

Verbal Comprehension:	142+	Very Superior
Perceptual Reasoning:	147+	Profoundly Gifted
Working Memory:	123	Superior
Processing Speed:	126	Superior
Full Scale IQ:	146+	Profoundly Gifted

Verbal Comprehension		Perceptual Reasoning:	
Similarities:	19+ VS	Block Design:	16 S
Vocabulary:	15 S	Matrix Reasoning:	19+ VS
Comprehension:	17 VS	Picture Concepts:	18 VS

Working Memory		Processing Speed	
Digit Span:	13 AA	Coding:	15 S
Letter–Number Seq.:	15 S	Symbol Search:	14 S

Scale Score
16 and up: Very Superior
14–15: Superior
12–13: Above Average
9–11: Average
8 and below: Below Average

Figure 10.4. Summary of assessment, FAC RB Female.

Verbal Comprehension scores were not credited sufficiently and because his Working Memory and Processing Speed Index scores were so heavily weighted. When age equivalent scores are applied to this child's scores, a truer representation of his abilities emerges.

Figures 10.4 and 10.5 compare the Standard IQ scores of a highly gifted child to her scores when calculated using the age-equivalent scores provided by Harcourt. RB achieved the ceiling score of 19 on two subtests and very superior range scores in

Name: FAC RB Female
Date of Birth:
Age at Testing: 7:6
Grade at Testing:
Date Tested:

Wechsler Intelligence Scale for Children (4th ed., WISC-IV)

Results:	MA	IQ Score
Verbal Comprehension:	13:0	171, Extraordinarily Gifted
Perceptual Reasoning:	16:3	214, Extraordinarily Gifted
Working Memory:	12:0	158, Profoundly Gifted
Processing Speed:	14:8	195, Extraordinarily Gifted
Full Scale IQ:	14:1	186, Extraordinarily Gifted

Verbal Comprehension		Perceptual Reasoning:	
Similarities:	15:10	Block Design:	13:2
Vocabulary:	10:6	Matrix Reasoning:	18:10
Comprehension:	12:6	Picture Concepts:	16:10

Working Memory		Processing Speed	
Digit Span:	10:10	Coding:	13:6
Letter-Number Seq.:	13:2	Symbol Search:	15:10

Figure 10.5. Summary of assessment by age equivalent IQ scores.

Note. Derived from formula of mental age divided by chronological age times 100.

two other subtests. Her FSIQ, 146, communicates lesser ability than her ratio-calculated IQ score of 186. Thus, parents and educators can plan very differently for educational challenge based on these finer-grained results.

Rimm Ratio scores were calculated on a sample of 42 students who represented three different schools and Family Achievement Clinic clients who were brought in for assessment of giftedness (Rimm, 2006). Figure 10.6 demonstrates how gifted programming would be affected in schools where there are programs for highly gifted children. Using the standard score metric, 45% would have been qualified for gifted programs compared to 79% that would be qualified using the ratio-based metric. Nine times the number of students would

Changes in Admission to Gifted Programs $n = 42$					
Regular Gifted Programs 130+		**Highly Gifted Programs 145+**		**Total Qualified Gifted**	
FSIQ	RRFS	SFSIQ	RRFS	SFSIQ	RRFS
17 (40%)	15 (36%)	2 (5%)	18 (43%)	19 (45%)	33 (79%)

Figure 10.6. Changes in admission to gifted programs when Rimm Ratio Full Scale IQ (RRFS) scores are substituted for standard Full Scale IQ (FSIQ).

be qualified for the program for highly gifted students. Because this study was an exploratory one and these students' placements were never actually changed, it is not possible to determine if their needs would be better met if their ratio IQ scores were used for placement.

Risks Related to Ratio IQ Scores

Robinson (2005) points out that it is difficult to develop tests specifically for an age scale as was done for the Stanford-Binet L-M (Terman & Merrill, 1973). According to Larry Weiss, "father of the WISC-IV," most test companies interpolate age-equivalent tables, rather than basing them on actual medians or means for grade level performance (personal communication, November 28, 1996). Thus, the concept of age-equivalent scores admittedly is shaky and probably was in the early days of IQ test construction, as well. However, using a standardized norm, which assumes that there are no major differences among the top one percent of gifted children, also is questionable.

There is some risk that too many children would be identified as highly gifted and too much could be expected of them using age-equivalent scores. However, with experience in using these ratio IQs, new cutoffs could easily be established for programs for highly gifted children, much as they were in Leta Hollingworth's day (Gray & Hollingworth, 1931). Because children in the highly gifted IQ range often require an individ-ualized educational plan, that risk is not so great as it may first appear. Weiss did not rule out reconsideration of age-equivalent scores; he also indicated that the psychometricians at Harcourt would explore the development of a new metric to differentiate further among highly gifted students using a higher score range (personal communication, November 28, 2006). It appears that the major test publishers, Harcourt and Riverside, are inter-ested in assisting gifted educators in improving identification. When scoring becomes more adequate for the identification of highly gifted children, more of these children will be discovered and hopefully educated appropriately.

Finding and Serving Twice-Exceptional Students

Both traditional and nontraditional assessments may miss twice-exceptional children who only may be located by uncon-ventional analysis of IQ tests. It is estimated that 10% to 15% of the school-age population suffers from learning disabilities (Springer & Deutsch, 1998) and a similar percentage has been found among the gifted (Rogers & Silverman, 1997). It is essen-tial that gifted programs be "handicapped accessible."

Selection to gifted programs often requires that students achieve a specific cutoff score on a standardized group or indi-vidual IQ test, as well as demonstrating high performance on major sections of an achievement test. These criteria discrimi-nate against twice-exceptional children. Group IQ tests should never be used with students who are dyslexic, have processing speed deficits, are distracted in group settings, or have other issues that may depress their IQ scores. Students who show extraordinary ability in some areas and weaknesses in others need to be referred for comprehensive assessment, including standardized individual IQ tests. But, even when these students are administered individual measures, they can be missed due to the misinterpretation of their scores (Silverman, 1989).

There are federal laws to protect disabled students; however, many school districts deny accommodations, as well as access to gifted programs, to students who are performing at the level of average students. This is a catch-22 for twice-exceptional children. Their disabilities depress their IQ scores below the cutoff for gifted programs, yet their high intelligence enables them to compensate so that they can attain average grades. Too often, these students are seen as average, "lazy," and unmotivated, when, in fact, they are working twice as hard as their classmates to keep up.

Several radical departures from accepted practice are needed to find twice-exceptional children. First, it is necessary to look at strengths separately from weaknesses, rather than averaging highly discrepant scores. If the student's highest scores are in the superior range on subtests richly loaded on general intelligence (g), and the discrepancies between the student's strengths and weaknesses are greater than three standard deviations, the student is likely to be both gifted and learning disabled. Yet, traditional interpretation of intelligence scales would deny him or her both types of services. The following example illustrates the problem. An average child with learning disabilities might attain a high subtest score of 13 on a WISC-IV and a low score of 4, clearly in the disabled range. This nine-point discrepancy—three standard deviations—is taken seriously. However, a gifted child might attain a high subtest score of 17, and a low subtest score of 8, also a discrepancy of three standard deviations, but because the lowest subtest score is within the average range, the child does not qualify for accommodations. And, the high and low scores cancel each other out, so the child does not qualify for gifted services either (Silverman, 1989, 2002).

Second, a different diagnostic question needs to be asked. All diagnosticians, including school psychologists, are trained to ask, "How does this child's scores compare to the scores of average children?" Twice-exceptional children also are missed using this criterion. Instead, the question needs to be raised, "To what extent does the discrepancy between the child's strengths and weaknesses cause *frustration* and interfere with the full development of the child's abilities?" (Silverman, 1998). This is an *intrapersonal* interpretation of test scores, rather than a *normative* perspective.

Third, the role of compensation needs to be taken into account in test interpretation. The greater an individual's intelligence, the more abstract reasoning is available to enable the person to cover up real weaknesses by finding other ways to solve problems (Silverman, 2000). For example, children with visual weaknesses talk their way through items they ought to be able to solve visually (Silverman, 2001). Children with auditory weaknesses may become excellent at lip reading. And, some children have developed such strong intuition as a compensation mechanism that they can guess correctly, preventing diagnosis of even severe disabilities. Some clever psychologists test a child for giftedness in the morning when she is fresh and better able to compensate for weaknesses; they test for disabilities in the late afternoon, when the child is tired and less capable of compensating.

Perhaps the most radical departure from accepted practice comes from the understanding that scores for twice-exceptional children are inconsistent over time and can be dramatically affected by many factors: tests that are heavily timed, tests that emphasize their weaknesses, cumulative lack of confidence, rapport with the examiner, inadequate rest, fluctuating attention, fear of failure, and so on. Some twice-exceptional individuals earn progressively higher IQ scores as they get older, others have lower scores with each succeeding test, and still others have great variation in IQ scores depending on the test. Therefore, the highest score attained *at any time* by a gifted child with learning disabilities is the best estimate of the child's abilities, rather than the most recent score (Silverman, 2003).

Gifted children with learning disabilities may need gifted programs even more than gifted children without disabilities. There are many cases of children who flounder in the regular classroom and shine in the gifted program. When they are properly challenged, they are able to concentrate more effectively. When their strengths are appreciated, these students are likely to be more successful than when the focus of instruction is on remedying their weaknesses. Accommodations, such as use of a keyboard, extended time for tests, reduced assignments, and graphic organizers, can enable twice-exceptional children to be highly successful in gifted programs, and this opportunity can change their lives.

Use of Traditional Testing to Identify and Serve Gifted Children With Other Problems

A great advantage of individual testing, compared to group testing, is the opportunity to observe the child who is being tested. Although the assumption that the test environment is a sample of classroom behavior is not always true, an experienced psychometrist or psychologist recognizes that the final scores, whether standardized or age equivalent, are only as important as the tester's observations of the child in the test environment. Uncovering some typical issues can be useful in understanding how to guide these children.

Perfectionism

Perfectionistic children often fear giving responses unless they are very certain they are correct. They are hesitant about guessing and worry that a mistaken guess may show them to be unintelligent. They may manage to cover problem areas or even areas of disability when their work is unchallenging, but may suddenly stop achieving and even become rebellious and angry when they can no longer compensate for their weakness with reasonably hard work. The combination of observation during testing and large differentials in index scores uncovers this problem (see the case example found below).

Mr. and Mrs. Brown came to Family Achievement Clinic with serious concerns about their only child, Yolanda, age 12. Since her recent entrance to middle school, the parents had observed dramatic behavioral changes. In elementary school, Yolanda had been a happy child and an all-A student, although she was perfectionistic and had difficulty accepting criticism. Her first quarter progress reports this year showed missing assignments and grades that were C's, D's and F's. Her dress style had changed to all black gothic. She had new friends, and was angry and oppositional at home and particularly defiant toward her mother. She also was depressed at times. The parents intercepted Yolanda's writing on the computer and discovered letters that suggested serious depression and even thoughts of potential suicide.

The results of Yolanda's WISC-IV and WIAT-R indicated that Yolanda is a gifted child whose abilities were uneven. While scoring in the 99.8 percentile for the Verbal Comprehension Index (144), her Perceptual Reasoning Index scores were only in the average range (104). A similar disparity showed itself in her achievement test scores with verbal skills being at the 98th percentiles and math skills at the 42nd percentile. This was a surprising finding to her parents. Although the math curriculum was not complex in elementary grades, Yolanda's motivation was sufficient to overcome the difficulties, and she earned excellent grades. With the higher level of complexity expected at middle school, Yolanda struggled, gave up on all efforts, and distracted herself with a less positive peer group and a peer culture of depression, loneliness, and rebellion.

Anxiety and Pressure

Children who continually ask if their answer is correct are experiencing feelings of pressure. Some children actually try to peek at the tester's manual in hopes of finding the correct answer. Gifted children who feel pressure may change the subject when they don't know answers. Instead, they deliver an oration on a different topic, sometimes totally unconnected to the question. It's as if they are trying to proclaim to the tester that they are, indeed, gifted children and that a gap in their knowledge should be discounted because they know so much about another topic.

Culturally Diverse Children

Children brought up in homes where English is not their first language are at a distinct disadvantage in verbal testing. Their Verbal Comprehension Index scores should be assumed to be an underestimate of their true verbal ability, particularly during their young years. They may also have problems understanding instructions for nonverbal tests. Caution should be used in interpreting such test scores. In some cases, a parent may need to attend the testing to translate for the child. Although final test scores will not be entirely valid, they are nevertheless useful for planning.

For children brought up in culturally diverse homes, dynamic assessment (Kirschenbaum, 1998) has been found to be effective in improving identification for gifted programs. Traditional tests can be followed by an intervention on test-taking skills, and that can be followed by a retest. Thus, traditional tests can continue to be useful for both identification and planning despite cultural differences.

Conclusion

Individual IQ tests are the gold standard for assessment of cognitive strengths and weaknesses of all learners. When individual IQ tests are used with the gifted, certain approaches in testing yield better results. The gifted show advanced development in verbal, visual-spatial, and mathematical reasoning; however, their processing skills are not necessarily as strong. Allowable choices of subtests and scoring can maximize our ability to find the truly gifted. Processing skill deficits may need accommodation, but accommodations should be added to gifted programming, rather than preventing the identification of students for that programming.

A discussion of the two major individual IQ tests noted strengths and weaknesses, as well as specific recommendations for use of the newest editions of the Stanford-Binet Fifth Edition (SB5) and the Wechsler Intelligence Scale for Children-Fourth Edition (WISC-IV). A strength of the SB5 is advanced spatial and mathematical reasoning items. Drawbacks include limited verbal abstract reasoning and a tendency for children who scored above 130 on other tests to score lower on the SB5. FSIQ scores of 120 best identify children for gifted programs.

The WISC-IV has doubled the weighting of processing skills from 20% to 40%. These often yield only average/high average scores for gifted children and are not as related to general intelligence (g) as verbal comprehension and perceptual reasoning.

In 79% of GDC and 74% of FAC cases, the Full Scale IQ score was not interpretable due to extreme discrepancies between index scores. Flanagan and Kaufman (2004) stated that when index scores vary by 23 points or more, the General Ability Index (GAI) provides a better overall indicator of the child's reasoning abilities. The GAI combines the scores of Verbal Comprehension and Perceptual Reasoning Indices, but does not include Working Memory and Processing Speed. Use of the GAI increases identification of children for gifted programs, but, more particularly, for highly gifted programs.

As the Full Scale IQ (FSIQ) score on the WISC-IV often does not present a unitary construct, requiring gifted-level FSIQs for admission to gifted programs is inappropriate. It is the recommendation of these authors that when using the WISC-IV, the GAI, the FSIQ, the Verbal Comprehension Index, or the Perceptual Reasoning Index should be acceptable for selection to gifted programs.

Twice-exceptional children also can only be located by unconventional analysis of individual IQ tests. A process for assessing gifted learners who exceed current normative tables on individual intelligence tests was discussed and procedures for processing such scores was outlined.

This chapter has shown that the individual IQ test offers far more than a single IQ score. The gold standard for assessing the strengths and weaknesses of gifted children, it is most effective in the hands of an experienced tester, who has tested many gifted children. As choices on modern individual IQ tests increase, testers must make every effort to stay abreast of test options and learn how to use multifaceted individual IQ tests optimally for the gifted child.

References

Carson, D., & Roid, G. H. (2004). *Acceptable use of the Stanford-Binet Form L–M: Guidelines for the professional use of the Stanford-Binet Intelligence Scale, Third Edition (Form L-M)*. Itasca, IL: Riverside

Cox, C. M. (1926a). *Genetic studies of genius: Vol. 2. The early mental traits of three hundred geniuses*. Stanford, CA: Stanford University Press.

Cox, C. M. (1926b). *Estimated IQs of some of the greatest geniuses.* Retrieved December 18, 2006, from http://hem.bredband.net/b153434/Index.htm

Dixon, J. (1983). *The spatial child.* Springfield, IL: Charles Thomas.

Flanagan, D. P., & Kaufman, A. S. (2004). *Essentials of WISC-IV assessment.* Hoboken, NJ: John Wiley & Sons.

Flynn, J. R. (1984). The mean IQ of Americans: Massive gains 1932 to 1978. *Psychological Bulletin, 95,* 29–51.

Flynn, J. R. (1987). Massive IQ gains in 14 nations: What IQ tests really measure. *Psychological Bulletin, 101,* 171–191.

Galton, F. (1883). *Inquiries into human faculty and its development.* London: J. M. Dent & Sons.

Gilman, B., & Kearney, K. (2004, November). *From conceptual to practical: Making gifted testing relevant.* Paper presented at the 51st annual convention of the National Association for Gifted Children, Salt Lake City, UT.

Gilman, B., & Falk, R. F. (2005, August). *Research-based guidelines for use of the WISC-IV in gifted assessment.* Paper presented at the 16th Biennial Conference of the World Council for Gifted and Talented Children, New Orleans, LA.

Gray, H. A., & Hollingworth, L. S. (1931). The achievement of gifted students enrolled and not enrolled in special opportunity classes. *Journal of Educational Research, 24,* 255–261.

Gross, M. U. M. (2004). *Exceptionally gifted children* (2nd ed.). London: Routledge Falmer.

Hollingworth, L. S. (1939). What we know about the early selection and training of leaders. *Teachers College Record, 40,* 575–592.

Kirschenbaum, R. J. (1998). Dynamic assessment and its use with underserved gifted and talented populations. *Gifted Child Quarterly, 42,* 140–147.

Lovecky, D. V., Kearney, K., Falk, R. F., & Gilman, B. J. (2005, August). *A comparison of the Stanford-Binet 5 and the Stanford-Binet Form LM in the assessment of gifted children.* Paper presented at the 16th Biennial Conference of the World Council for Gifted and Talented Children, New Orleans, LA.

Lubinski, D. (2003). Exceptional spatial abilities. In N. Colangelo & G. A. Davis (Eds.), *Handbook of gifted education* (3rd ed., pp. 521–532). Boston: Allyn & Bacon.

Minigroni, M. A. (2004). The secular rise in IQ: Giving heterosis a closer look. *Intelligence, 32,* 65–83.

Raiford, S. E., Weiss, L. G., Rolfhus, E., & Coalson, D. (2005). *Wechsler Intelligence Scale for Children–Fourth edition: General Ability*

Index (Technical Report No. 4). Retrieved December 15, 2006, from https://harcourtassessment.com/hai/Images/pdf/wisciv/WISCIVTechReport4.pdf

Reams, R., Chamrad, D., & Robinson, N. M. (1990). The race is not necessarily to the swift: The validity of WISC-R bonus points for speed. *Gifted Child Quarterly, 34*, 108–110.

Rimm, S. (2006, November). *Breaking the ceiling scores for profoundly gifted children using the WISC-IV*. Paper presented at the 53rd Annual Convention of the National Association of Gifted Children, Charlotte, NC.

Robinson, N. M. (2005). In defense of a psychometric approach to the definition of academic giftedness: A conservative view from a die-hard liberal. In R. J. Sternberg & J. D. Davidson (Eds.), *Conceptions of giftedness* (2nd ed., pp. 280–294). New York: Cambridge University Press.

Rogers, K. B., & Silverman, L. K. (1997, November). *Personal, medical, social and psychological factors in 160+ IQ children*. Paper presented at the 44th annual convention of the National Association for Gifted Children, Little Rock, AR.

Roid, G. H. (2003a). *Stanford-Binet Intelligence Scales interpretive manual: Expanded guide to the interpretation of SB5 test results*. Itasca, IL: Riverside.

Roid, G. H. (2003b). *Stanford-Binet Intelligence Scales, Fifth Edition, Technical manual*. Itasca, IL: Riverside.

Roid, G. H., & Barram, R. A. (2004). *Essentials of Stanford-Binet (SB5) assessment*. New York: Wiley.

Roid, G. H., & Carson, A. (2004). *Special composites scores for the SB5* (Assessment Service Bulletin No. 4). Itasca, IL: Riverside.

Ruf, D. L. (2003). *Use of the SB5 in the assessment of high abilities* (Assessment Service Bulletin No. 3). Itasca, IL: Riverside.

Silverman, L. K. (1989). Invisible gifts, invisible handicaps. *Roeper Review, 12*, 27–42.

Silverman, L. K. (1998). Through the lens of giftedness. *Roeper Review, 20*, 204–210.

Silverman, L. K. (2000). The two-edged sword of compensation: How the gifted cope with learning disabilities. In K. Kay (Ed.), *Uniquely gifted: Identifying and meeting the needs of the twice exceptional student* (pp. 153–165). Gilsum, NH: Avocus.

Silverman, L. K. (2001). Diagnosing and treating visual perceptual issues in gifted children. *Journal of Optometric Vision Development, 32*, 153–176.

Silverman, L. K. (2002). *Upside-down brilliance: The visual-spatial learner.* Denver, CO: DeLeon.

Silverman, L. K. (2003). Gifted children with learning disabilities. In N. Colangelo & G. Davis (Eds.), *Handbook of gifted education* (3rd ed., pp. 553–543). Boston: Allyn & Bacon.

Silverman, L. K., Gilman, B. J., & Falk, R. F. (2004, November). *Who are the gifted using the new WISC-IV?* Paper presented at the 51st Annual Convention of the National Association for Gifted Children, Salt Lake City, UT.

Springer, S. P., & Deutsch, G. (1998). *Left brain/right brain: Perspectives from cognitive neuroscience* (5th ed.). New York: W. H. Freeman.

Stanley, J. (1990). Leta Hollingworth's contributions to above-level testing of the gifted. *Roeper Review, 12,* 166–171.

Stern, W. (1911). The supernormal child. *Journal of Educational Psychology, 2,* 143–148, 181–190.

Teasdale, T. W., & Owen, D. R. (2005). A long-term rise and recent decline in intelligence test performance: The Flynn Effect in reverse. *Personality and Individual Differences, 39,* 837–843.

Terman, L. M., & Merrill, M. A. (1973). *Stanford-Binet Intelligence Scale: Manual for the third revision form L–M.* Boston, MA: Houghton Mifflin.

Wasserman, J. D. (2007). *The Flynn effect in gifted samples: Status as of 2007.* Unpublished manuscript available online at http://www.gifteddevelopment.com/Whats_New/flynn.htm

Wechsler, D. (2003). *The WISC-IV technical and interpretive manual.* San Antonio, TX: The Psychological Corporation.

The Role of Creativity Tools and Measures in Assessing Potential and Growth

Bonnie Cramond & Kyung Hee Kim

"Imagination is more important than knowledge. For knowledge is limited to all we now know and understand, while imagination embraces the entire world, and all there ever will be to know and understand." Albert Einstein

"How do you catch a cloud and pin it down?" This line from the lyrics of Rodgers and Hammerstein's song "Maria," from the musical *The Sound of Music*, expresses the way many people feel about the measurement of creativity. How is it possible to measure something as ineffable as creativity? It is perplexing that the same people who express shock, disbelief, and sometimes indignation at the idea of measuring creativity have no trouble trusting in the measurement of intelligence, personality, or any of a number of equally elusive psychological constructs.

Assessing Creative Potential

Of course, we cannot assess creativity—no more than we can assess intelligence—but with both constructs we can measure some thinking skills that are used, or some personal traits that correlate with the construct, or the products of that kind of thinking.

Just as there are many very bright people, as measured on IQ tests, without the motivation, perseverance, energy, or opportunity to bring their intellectual potential to fruition, so too, are there people who will not develop their creative potential.

Yet, intelligence and creativity measures are used because they are good predictors of certain behaviors. Intelligence measures tend to be good predictors of school success (Jensen, 1998; Sternberg, Grigorenko, & Bundy, 2001), which makes sense when you consider that the Binet tests, the mother of intelligence tests upon which many others are based and validated (Binet, Simon, & Kite, 1916), were themselves based upon school activities. They were designed to predict school performance.

Different kinds of creativity measures, such as divergent thinking tests and creativity inventories, generally are predictive of creative activities, interests, and accomplishments later in life (Cline, Richards, & Needham, 1963; Kogan & Pankove, 1974; Rimm & Davis, 1976; Russ, Robins, & Christiano, 1999; Torrance, 2002). As indicated by the 40-year longitudinal study, the Torrance Tests of Creative Thinking (TTCT), based upon behaviors that individuals use in the creative process, are good predictors of adult creative performance (Cramond, Matthews-Morgan, Bandalos, & Zuo, 2005; Torrance, 2002).

According to Kim's meta-analysis (in press), creativity test scores predicted creative achievement ($r = .22$) better than IQ did ($r = .17$). Further, 51.8% of the 274 correlation coefficients incorporated in the study used the TTCT, and the TTCT predicted creative achievement ($r = .33$, $p < .0001$) better than other measures of creative potential (e.g., Wallach and Kogan's Divergent Thinking Tasks, Guilford's Divergent Thinking Tasks, sounds and images, word association tests). In this meta-analysis, art, music, writing, science (including mathematics, medicine, and engineering), leadership, and social skills were used to measure creative achievement. Among these different types of creative achievement, musical achievement was predicted better by IQ than by measures of creative potential, whereas art, science, writing, and social skills were predicted by measures of creative potential better than by IQ. This finding suggests that creativity test scores account for more variance in creative achievement than IQ, and therefore may predict overall creative achievement better.

Still, both measures, IQ and creativity, are not as good with certain populations. Much has been written about the various performances of different ethnic or SES groups on intelligence tests (Rushton & Jensen, 2006; Turkheimer, Haley, Waldron, D'Onofrio, & Gottesman, 2003). The longitudinal studies on the Torrance Tests of Creative Thinking, however, have shown that the children from a housing project in Minneapolis scored comparably to other students on the tests, but they did not have the adult success that their scores should predict. Torrance concluded that they just didn't have the same opportunities (Millar, 2002). This also was true for the girls in this cohort, who grew up in the late 1950s and early 1960s (Cramond, 1993).

Of course, it should always be clear that any test is just a snapshot—taken at one point in time under very unusual circumstances for most children. No single score on any test should be taken as a complete measure of any individual's ability. Therefore, another similarity between creativity and intelligence measures is that there are false negatives, but not false positives. In other words, there are intelligent and creative individuals who do not score high on intelligence and creativity measures for many reasons related to the person, the test, and the conditions of testing. However, given valid, reliable measures, it is not likely that a student will get a high score on an intelligence test and not be intelligent, or a high score on a creativity test without having a high capacity for creative thinking.

Torrance (1960, 1962) observed that if we use intelligence and achievement tests alone to look for talent, we miss 70% of the top 20% of creative students. A recent study with Korean students had similar findings, but indicated that the proportion of top creative students missed may be as high as 80% of the top 20% (Kim & Cramond, 2007). That is a tremendous loss of potential!

Guilford (1950, 1962, 1966, 1968) argued that traditional intelligence tests do not measure creative abilities, and he hypothesized that creative individuals possess divergent thinking abilities including idea production, fluency, flexibility, and originality. Guilford's theories spawned an array of divergent thinking (DT) tests such as the Torrance Tests of Creative Thinking (TTCT), Wallach and Kogan Divergent Thinking Tasks, and the Guilford Divergent Thinking Tasks. They also spawned research that correlates scores on these DT tests with creative potential.

Many studies have been conducted that illustrate that creative potential is independent of IQ (Getzels & Jackson, 1958; Gough, 1976; Helson, 1971; Rossman & Horn, 1972; Rotter, Langland, & Berger, 1971; Torrance, 1977a). However, many researchers agree with the threshold theory, which assumes that above a critical IQ level, which is usually thought to be about 120, there is no correlation between measured creativity and intelligence (Barron, 1961; Getzels & Jackson, 1962; Guilford, 1967; Guilford & Christensen, 1973; Hall, 1972; MacKinnon, 1961, 1962, 1967; Simonton, 1994; Walberg, 1988; Walberg & Herbig, 1991; Yamamoto, 1964). The threshold theory is based upon the thought that creativity and intelligence are separate constructs (e.g., more intelligence does not necessarily mean greater creativity beyond a minimum level). Kim's (2005) meta-analysis indicated that the relationship between creativity test scores and IQ ($r = .17$) is negligible, which undermines the threshold theory, but supports the underlying belief that creativity and intelligence are separate constructs.

A Rationale for Finding Creative Potential

In all fields of endeavor, outstanding success requires the demonstration of creativity (Torrance, 1962). Creativity is important in scientific discovery, invention, and the arts. Striking advances in human affairs such as in the creative arts, political and military leadership, and in scientific discovery and invention are mainly due to a few exceptionally creative gifted individuals (Simonton, 1994). Achievement is dependent on multiple factors, including the interaction between environmental conditions and the particular manifestation of specific creative characteristics (Amabile, 1983; Csikszentmihalyi, 1988; Mellou, 1996; Torff, 1999). Creativity is important to gifted students' development because it has the power to transform giftedness to eminence (Khatena, 1983).

Yet, if we were only looking for the eminent, the effort hardly would be worthwhile because so few people reach that level. There are many reasons that we should be assessing and developing the creativity of all of our students. As Sawyer (2006) and others have pointed out, in the last several decades the most developed countries are moving away from an industrial economy and toward a knowledge economy (p. 1). A major keystone of this knowledge economy is innovation, or in psychological and educational terms, creativity. As pointed out in the recent report from the National Center on Education and the Economy (NCEE; 2006), we must change our curriculum if we hope to compete in the global economy. While our corporations are outsourcing low-skill jobs to third world countries, we continue to emphasize such basic skills rather than the critical and creative thinking that will allow our children to find employment in the future.

Other countries, most notably the United Kingdom (National Advisory Committee on Creative and Cultural Education, 1999; Robinson, 2001), as well as the Scandinavian countries (Florida, 2002) and the countries of East Asia (Friedman, 2005; Korean Educational Development Institute, 2003), have recognized this shift in the economy and the resulting need for a shift in education. If we hope to continue to be economically competitive, we, too, must try to recognize and cultivate our most creative citizens (Florida, 2002). In fact, we must try to keep them here to prevent a reverse brain drain from the U.S. to other countries who are more conducive to creative productivity (Florida, 2005).

As important as economic competition is, though, it is not the only nor, necessarily, the most important reason for identifying creative talent. Our schools, which were built on the factory model, are filled with faculty who operate on the medical model—using the diagnostic and prescriptive rule. If someone is different, he or she must have a problem, or in the words of the Japanese adage, "The nail that sticks up will be hammered down." This can be seen in the fact that teachers are well-versed in the behaviors associated with various diagnostic categories of the fourth edition of the Diagnostic and Statistical Manual of Mental Disorders (DSM-IV; American Psychiatric Association [APA], 1994), and much less aware of characteristics of highly creative students. Because of this, teachers may misidentify highly creative students as having some behavior or mental disorder. For example, creative students who may be alternately energetic and dreamy, as well as unconventional loners, often are seen as having Attention Deficit/Hyperactivity Disorder because of their activity level, inattention, and impulsivity (Cramond, 1994).

Many traits of creative individuals do not fit well into the classroom. Teachers are apt to prefer students who are achievers and teacher pleasers rather than disruptive or unconventional creative students (Davis & Rimm, 1994; Oliphant, 1986; Rimm & Davis, 1976; Ritchie, 1980; Robinson, 1980; Rudowicz, 2003; Rudowicz & Yue, 2000; Scott, 1999; Westby & Dawson, 1995). Teachers see creative children as a source of interference and disruption (Scott, 1999). Westby and Dawson (1995) found that teachers' judgment of their favorite students was negatively correlated with scores on creativity tests. Teachers prefer students who exhibit traits such as unquestioning acceptance of authority, conformity, logical thinking, and responsibility that make students easy to manage in the classroom. Several studies have shown that most teachers' images of the ideal student have emphasized traits that are conformist and socially acceptable (Bachtold, 1974; Kaltsounis, 1977; Kaltsounis & Higdon, 1977; Torrance, 1963).

In older classic studies on creativity, Anderson (1961) found that the teachers in his study preferred students with a high IQ rather than students who were both highly creative and highly intelligent. Similarly, Torrance (1962) found that teachers rated children with high IQs as more desirable, better known, or understood, and more studious than children with high creativity. In a paper in which she categorized gifted students into certain types based upon their characteristics, Drews (1961) noted that the studious achievers attained the highest teacher grades while the creative intellectuals attained the lowest among three types of gifted high school students: social leaders, studious achievers, and creative intellectuals.

Just a few years before Drews and Anderson wrote about negative teacher attitudes toward the creative, Getzels and Jackson (1958) had found that highly creative adolescents were estranged not only from their teachers, but also from their peers. This feeling of being different and isolated can cause intense loneliness and pain, especially among highly creative students who are frequently described as being very emotionally sensitive (Feist, 1999; Piechowski, 2006). It may be assumed that such feelings led a very creative Edgar Allen Poe (1875) to reflect upon his own childhood and write:

"Alone"

From childhood's hour I have never been
As others were—I have not seen
As others saw—I cannot bring
My passions from a common spring.
From the same source I have not taken
My sorrow—I could not awaken
My heart to joy at the same tone
And all I lov'd—I lov'd alone

Creative children may be more vulnerable to such negative reactions to their ideas than adults are. Children have not completed their identity development, and they usually have not reached a point of creative productivity where their odd behaviors can be viewed as eccentricities rather than as problems. Also, as previously discussed, school children are more likely to have their behaviors viewed as pathological. Some examples may help illustrate this point.

Robert Frost's daydreaming was not seen as creative; instead he was put out of school. Frank Lloyd Wright was said to go into such trancelike daydreams that he had to be shouted at or slapped to bring him out of them. Their inattention caused them problems in school but may have enabled their imaginations. Samuel Taylor Coleridge and Virginia Woolf were both known to be constant talkers—a trait that is often a problem in school—yet, this verbal ability was clearly an asset to their writing. The energy of Thomas Edison and Nikola Tesla got them into trouble in childhood but undoubtedly aided them in working the long hours that they did, reportedly around the clock for days at a time while aides collapsed in exhaustion (Cheney, 1981). All of these highly creative individuals evidenced behaviors that resulted in school problems (Cramond, 1995).

Observations of contemporary creative children included a 2-year-old who conducted lively conversations with herself in different voices while in her car seat. She also went through a period when she took on the persona of a character, either one she created or one from literature, movies, or television, and would stay in character all day, failing to respond to her real name, responding only to the name of the character. Her preschool teachers worried and disallowed this; her psychotherapist aunt suggested she may be the earliest recorded case of a multiple personality. She grew up to be an actor, writer, and musician—all part of the same single personality.

Another child loved to play with sticks. That may not seem unusual, but it is the imaginative way that he played with sticks, weaving stories, walking and talking with the stick while alone in the yard for an hour or two at a time, that was unusual. A teacher suggested that the behavior may be on the autism spectrum, but anyone who recognizes creativity can see that his imaginative storytelling is no different from the creative writing of another child, but his product has taken a different form because of his current expressive outlets—psychomotor and oral.

If children like these are assessed and seen as creative, it is easier for them to retain their creativity into adulthood and develop it into other products, as the first girl did. These children were lucky; their families recognized their creativity and encouraged it. Others are less fortunate. One little girl was always getting into trouble in her elementary school. Two particular instances of her behavior lost her unsupervised restroom privileges. On the first occasion, she was found hitting the pipes in the restroom and making a racket. The other time, she had jammed the toilet with paper and objects so that it wouldn't flush. She was punished. When asked curiously by an observer in the school why she had done those things, the girl explained that the first time she was trying to see if the sound would carry in the pipes all the way down to her classroom. The second time, she was trying various types of paper and objects to see which would float. This child was demonstrating curiosity, experimentation, and a rudimentary use of the scientific method. She chose to experiment in the lavatory because it was the only place where she had the time, access to materials, and freedom to explore in the whole school day. She lost that privilege. Whether she loses her creativity, only time will tell.

If creative children are more likely to be seen in a negative light by teachers, and if their behaviors often are seen as symptomatic of problems, then it seems reasonable to predict that creative children from minority populations are at even greater risk for being unidentified as gifted and misunderstood. The evidence from one state supports the effectiveness of adding creativity and other measures for identifying gifted students, especially those from underserved populations.

In the early 1990s, a group of Georgia educators led by the research of Dr. Mary Frasier of the University of Georgia piloted a multiple criteria rule for identifying gifted students. Although a cadre of educators in Georgia had long recognized that the identification of gifted students by IQ and achievement tests alone was missing many gifted students, the state was not compelled to work toward changing the rule until the Office of Civil Rights in Georgia threatened action because of the gross ethnicity inequities in the state's gifted program (Williams, 2000). The resulting multiple criteria rule prescribes four areas through which a student may show giftedness, and to qualify for the program, a student must reach the criteria in three of the four areas (Georgia State Board of Education, 1996). The areas are mental ability, achievement, creativity, and motivation. Therefore, the new rule added two areas, creativity and motivation, to areas assessed for the gifted program. In addition, the new rule allows students to show giftedness through performances and products, as well as by tests. However, at least one standardized test must be part of the identification protocol (Georgia Department of Education,

2005). Because IQ and achievement tests are the only standard-ized tests besides creativity tests that are allowed, students from underserved populations who do not traditionally score high on IQ and achievement tests can qualify with a creativity test in addi-tion to products and performances in at least two other areas.

As indicated in the following statistics, the use of the mul-tiple criteria rule has had a profound impact on the gifted pro-gram in Georgia. Although the resulting change in numbers of students participating in the gifted program must be viewed in light of shifting demographics, there still has been a remark-able increase in the numbers of African American and Hispanic students who are being served in the gifted program. Also, it appears that the addition of a creativity test as an option to meet the standards for identification has been very helpful in identi-fying students from underserved populations.

> As a result of that multiple-criteria eligibility rule, from January 1997 to October 2005, the number of African-Americans participating in Georgia's programs for gifted students has increased by over 200%; the number of Hispanic gifted students has increased by 570%. The impact of more inclusive identification and program-ming practices and a statewide focus on more demand-ing coursework for all students is now being felt at the high school level, with many more students from under-represented groups reaching the highest level of rigorous coursework: From 2002–2006 alone, there was a 71% increase in the number of African-Americans students enrolled in Advanced Placement (AP) courses. Hispanic participation in AP courses increased 180% in the same time period. ("The Georgia Story," n.d., last 10 lines)

Using Creativity Measures to Assess Growth

The Theoretical Basis

Whether one believes that creativity can grow depends upon one's belief in the nature of creativity. Researchers disagree as to whether creativity is fixed or developmental, general or domain-specific, within the reach of everyone or a characteristic of genius. These are the same arguments that plague research in intelligence. Currently, most researchers see creativity as dynamic, and Runco (2004) has described it as a syndrome or complex to emphasize its intricate and changeable nature. Runco also stressed the importance of originality for innovation and of flexibility for adapting to all of the innovations in the changing world. Thus, he stressed the importance of creativity for all humans' physical and psychological health and optimal human functioning (Runco, 2004, p. 3). So, here creativity will refer to both the creativity of the eminent (Simonton, 1984, 1994) and to everyday creativity that allows us to solve problems, adapt to our world, and express ourselves (Runco, 2004).

The systems approaches such as those of Sternberg (Sternberg & Lubart, 1999) and Gardner (1988) also inform the theoretical framework for this discussion because such views recognize the multifaceted nature of creativity. These approaches allow for the most inclusive view of creativity and represent the latest thinking about it.

The theoretical basis of universal, dynamic, general creativity allows for the most inclusive productive approach for education because it allows us to address the need for creative thinking by all students, as well as those most able in this area. Additionally, it recognizes the necessity of nurturing creative thinking in all areas of our lives. As Maslow (1998) explained, a good soup can be more creative than a poem.

Learning Outcomes From Creativity Programs

Torrance (1988) indicated that he learned about the nature of creativity through testing and teaching creative behavior. Assessment of creativity was not one of Torrance's goals—instead his main focus was in understanding and nurturing qualities that help people express their creativity. As such, Torrance's tests were not designed to simply measure creativity, but instead to serve as tools for the enhancement of creativity (Hébert, Cramond, Speirs Neumeister, Millar, & Silvian, 2002). Regardless of whether it is the TTCT or other measures, measures of creative potential can be used to measure creative growth.

It often has been shown that creative thinking also can be taught (Guilford, 1950; Torrance & Torrance, 1973). However, important questions about what is being taught by creativity training and how best to enhance creativity by training remain. Some research indicates that a part of creativity, innate creative abilities, cannot be taught, while another part of creativity, creative skills, can be taught (Huang, 2005; Rose & Lin, 1984). Other research indicates that creativity training enhances creativity in general (Scott, Leritz, & Mumford, 2004). Most likely there are components of creativity that cannot be significantly affected by training and can be thought of as innate abilities. However, there are other aspects of creativity—skills and dispositions—that can be enhanced by training.

Several reviews of research have incorporated measures of creative potential and showed that creativity can be enhanced by creativity training programs. Torrance (1972) analyzed 142 studies to review the effectiveness of the creativity training programs studied. Of these studies, 72.5% used the TTCT scores to measure such effectiveness. He assessed the training effectiveness, based on a judgment of whether the study attained its initial objectives. Rose and Lin (1984) incorporated 46 studies that used the TTCT scores in their meta-analysis. Scope (1999) incorporated 30 studies in his meta-analysis. All of the studies that Torrance (1972), Rose and Lin (1984), and Scope (1999) analyzed used students as participants, whereas Scott et al. (2004) and Huang (2005) did meta-analyses of studies that used both students and nonstudents.

Scott et al. (2004) incorporated 70 studies in their meta-analysis to investigate the effectiveness of creativity training programs. They concluded that creativity training is effective in enhancing creativity overall and enhancing each of the individual criteria that make up creativity in general: divergent thinking, problem solving, performance, and attitude/behavior. One limitation of this study was that it did not investigate the differences in the creativity measures used in the underlying studies, whereas both Huang (2005) and Rose and Lin (1984) found significant differences in how creativity training affects the scores on the TTCT-Verbal and Figural.

Scott et al. (2004) found that creativity training has a particularly strong influence on problem solving and divergent thinking, especially originality; however, the effect of training on fluency, flexibility, and elaboration also was sizeable. Rose and Lin (1984) also found that creativity training has the greatest impact on originality scores. Scott et al. (2004) found that creativity training equally was effective in both the short term and long term (6–12 months) for enhancing creativity. They also found that creativity training benefited everyone in academic and occupational settings, across all ages, and at all different intellectual levels. With regard to intellectual levels, the results were most striking for the nongifted and low achievers who benefited from creativity training by strongly enhancing both divergent thinking and problem solving. Gifted and high-achieving students showed enhancement in divergent thinking but not problem-solving skills. Cognitive training that was based upon a single model or theory of creativity (rather than an ad-hoc approach) and that stressed specific analytic techniques (rather than exploratory techniques) produced the greatest overall enhancement of creativity. Whole-group approaches to learning such as lectures, and even video- or audiotapes, were positively related to the success of creativity training, especially divergent thinking, whereas problem solving was more strongly enhanced with practice and individualized coaching.

Finally, Huang's (2005) meta-analysis incorporated 51 studies that investigated the effectiveness of creativity training programs. Huang looked at the effectiveness of different kinds of programs, on different groups of participants, and as measured by different types of assessments.

Huang found mean effect sizes that ranged from a low of .61 for School Programs and .67 for Other Creative Training Programs, to a high of 1.13 for the Creative Problem Solving program. Thus, he concluded that various types of creativity training programs can effectively improve participants' scores on measures of creative thinking. Among the creativity training programs analyzed, the Creative Problem Solving program had the biggest increase on creativity scores. Torrance (1972) also found that creativity training programs that used the Creative Problem Solving program were the most frequently used and had the highest percentage of success in children's creativity. Rose and Lin (1984) also found that the Creative Problem Solving program increased scores on measures of creative potential in general more than any other creativity training program, whereas the Purdue Creative Thinking Program effected the biggest increase in the Figural score.

In order to investigate the differential effects of creative thinking programs on different groups, Huang (2005) looked at studies that included gifted students, regular students, students with disabilities, and nonstudents. Therefore, the meta-analysis included 8.1% of 51 studies with gifted students (ES: 0.50), 66.1% of 51 studies with regular students (ES: 0.77), 16.1% of 51 studies with nonstudents (e.g., workers, teachers, nurses, scientists: ES: 0.91), and 9.7% of 51 studies with special groups of students (e.g., with a learning disability, mental handicap, or hearing impairment: ES: 0.73). As the mean effect sizes indicate, the effectiveness of creativity training programs is robust across various kinds of participants.

In addition, Huang (2005) looked at studies that included various types of creativity measures. The studies analyzed included those using the TTCT-Verbal (12.9% of 51 studies, ES: 1.22); the TTCT-Figural (24.2% of 51 studies, ES: 0.69; the TTCT-Verbal and Figural (25.8% of 51 studies, ES: 0.53); Other Scales (22.6% of 51 studies, ES: 0.75); Judges' Rating (6.5% of 51 studies, ES: 0.68); and Measuring Attitudes (8.1% of 51 studies, ES: 1.07) as measures of creativity. Among the measures of creative potential analyzed, the TTCT-Verbal had the biggest increase after the creativity training programs. This agrees with Rose and Lin's (1984) finding that the scores on the TTCT-Verbal (ES: 0.60) were increased more than those on the Figural (ES: 0.37).

This might be explained by the fact that the TTCT Verbal and Figural tests measure different creative abilities in addition to assessing the construct of two different modalities (Cramond, 1999). In fact, performance on the TTCT-Verbal and Figural show very little correlation (Cramond, 1993; $r = .06$), which suggests that the TTCT-Figural is not simply a nonverbal measure of the same creative potential as measured on the TTCT-Verbal. It also may be explained by the fact that most of the creativity training techniques emphasize verbal creativity. Given the differences in what various creativity measures assess, it would be wise for investigators to heed the advice of Hunsaker and Callahan (1995) to carefully consider the content of the training program in choosing an appropriate measure of growth, and to use several measures of creativity, if possible, in order to assess as much of the creativity syndrome as possible.

Huang (2005), like Scope (1999) and Scott et al. (2004), did not find a significant positive relationship between the length of training and learning impact. However, Huang (2005) found that the Creative Problem Solving program spent the least amount of time on training and had the highest effect. All of the cited meta-analytic studies concluded that creativity training programs have a strong positive effect on measures of creative potential in general. Torrance (1972) concluded that about 72% of the studies that he reviewed showed creativity training was effective. In addition, he concluded that successful creativity training included cognitive and emotional functioning and provided motivation and opportunities to be involved. Motivating and facilitating conditions made a difference in creativity, but differences were greatest and most predictable when deliberate teaching was involved (Huang, 2005; Rose & Lin, 1984; Scope, 1999; Scott et al., 2004). In addition, researchers concluded that creativity training programs can have a strong positive effect on measures of creative potential at all ages (children to adults), in all situations (academic or occupational), and across all intelligence levels (low achievers to the gifted).

Five large meta-analytic studies, which investigated the effects of creativity programs on the enhancement of creativity, have indicated that scores on creativity measures generally are enhanced regardless of program, participants, or measures used to assess growth. Whether these skills will be retained and generalized to other situations is not clear. However, research on the transfer of thinking skills indicates that frequent and extended practice in a variety of domains with specific transfer strategies infused will best enable students to retain and apply the learned thinking skills (Cramond, Martin, & Shaw, 1990).

Conclusion

Top economists are warning that we must change our educational system to maintain our competitive position in the new global economy. The knowledge explosion and the easy availability of information on the Web have made it impossible and irrelevant to teach in our old fact-based, content-divided way. We know that we are dependent upon creative responses to find solutions to the problems our world faces and to adapt to the changes such problems and solutions bring. We know that we miss many of our most creative students when we test them in only traditional ways, and by missing them, we may be failing to nurture our most valuable resources. Creativity assessment allows individuals to respond from their own knowledge base rather than from some predetermined knowledge base, and therefore is fairer to individuals from diverse cultures, especially when the assessment minimizes verbal components (Jellen & Urban, 1989; Torrance, 1977b; Voss, 1998). In addition, there is the personal loss that highly creative individuals may face due to the pain of being different, alienated, and alone. Recognizing their creativity and encouraging them to express it in positive ways can help alleviate this pain and result in positive methods of dealing with stress. All of our students should be learning to solve problems and express themselves creatively for their own mental and physical health and well being.

We can assess creative abilities, we can nurture them, and we can measure their growth. We must do so. Although we can't know what the future will bring, we can open our students' minds toward it.

References

Amabile, T. M. (1983). *The social psychology of creativity.* New York: Springer-Verlag.

American Psychiatric Association. (1994). *Diagnostic and statistical manual of mental disorders* (4th ed). New York: Author.

Anderson, K. E. (1961). *Research on the academically talented student.* Washington, DC: National Education Association Project on the Academically Talented Student.

Bachtold, L. M. (1974). The creative personality and the ideal pupil revisited. *Journal of Creative Behavior, 8,* 47–54.

Barron, F. (1961). Creative vision and expression in writing and painting. In D. W. MacKinnon (Ed.), *The creative person* (pp. 237–251). Berkeley, CA: Institute of Personality Assessment Research, University of California.

Binet, A., Simon, T., & Kite, E. S. (1916). *The development of intelligence in children* (The Binet-Simon Scale). Baltimore: Williams & Silkins.

Cheney, M. (1981). *Tesla: Man out of time.* New York: Prentice Hall.

Cline, V. B., Richards, J. M., Jr., & Needham, W. E. (1963). Creativity tests and achievement in high school science. *Journal of Applied Psychology, 47,* 184–189.

Cramond, B. (1993). The Torrance Tests of Creative Thinking: From design through establishment of predictive validity. In R. F. Subotnik & K. D. Arnold (Eds.), *Beyond Terman: Contemporary longitudinal studies of giftedness and talent* (pp. 229–254). Norwood, NJ: Ablex.

Cramond, B. (1994). Attention-Deficit Hyperactivity Disorder and creativity—What is the connection? *Journal of Creative Behavior, 28,* 193–210.

Cramond, B. (1995). *The coincidence of Attention Deficit Hyperactivity Disorder and creativity* (RBDM 9508). Storrs, CT: National Research Center on the Gifted and Talented, University of Connecticut.

Cramond, B. (1999). The Torrance Tests of Creative Thinking: Going beyond the scores. In A. S. Fishkin, B. Cramond, & P. Olszewski-Kubilius (Eds.), *Investigating creativity in youth.* (pp. 307–327). Cresskill, NJ: Hampton Press.

Cramond, B., Matthews-Morgan, J., Bandalos, D., & Zuo, L. (2005). The Torrance Tests of Creative Thinking: Alive and well in the new millennium. *Gifted Child Quarterly, 49,* 283–291.

Cramond, B., Martin, C. E., & Shaw, E. (1990). Generalizability of the Creative Problem Solving process to real-life problems. *Journal for the Education of the Gifted, 13*, 86–98.

Csikszentmihalyi, M. (1988). Society, culture, and person: A systems view of creativity. In R. J. Sternberg (Ed.), *The nature of creativity: Contemporary psychological perspectives* (pp. 325–339). New York: Cambridge University Press.

Davis, G. A., & Rimm, S. B. (1994). *Education of the gifted and talented* (3rd ed.). Needham Heights, MA: Allyn & Bacon.

Drews, E. M. (1961). *Creative intellectual style in gifted adolescents.* East Lansing, MI: Michigan State University.

Feist, G. J. (1999). The influence of personality on artistic and scientific creativity. In R. J. Sternberg (Ed.), *Handbook of creativity* (pp. 273–296). New York: Cambridge University Press.

Florida, R. (2002). *The rise of the creative class: And how it's transforming work, leisure, community and everyday life.* New York: Basic Books.

Florida, R. (2005). *The flight of the creative class: The new global competition for talent.* New York: HarperCollins.

Friedman, T. (2005). *The world is flat.* New York: Farrar, Straus, & Giroux.

Gardner, H. (1988). Creativity lives, creative works: A synthetic scientific approach. In R. J. Sternberg (Ed.), *The nature of creativity* (pp. 298–325). Cambridge, England: Cambridge University Press.

The Georgia story: One state's approach to the underrepresentation issue. (n.d.). Retrieved April 1, 2007, from http://www.gifted.uconn.edu/sem/The_Georgia_Story.html

Georgia State Board of Education. (1996). *Education program for gifted students.* Retrieved April 17, 2007, from http://www.doe.k12.ga.us/DMGetDocument.aspx/160-4-2-.38.pdf?p=4BE1EECF99CD364EA5554055463F1FBB77B0B70FECF5942E12E123FE4810FFF53501CAAE8CB828385D2BCE08D0A1A4EA&Type=D

Georgia Department of Education. (2005). *Education program for gifted students.* Retrieved January 23, 2005, from http://www.doe.k12.ga.us/_documents/doe/legalservices/160-4-2-.38.pdf

Getzels, J. W., & Jackson, P. W. (1958). The meaning of 'giftedness': An examination of an expanding concept. *Phi Delta Kappan, 40*, 75–77.

Getzels, J. W., & Jackson, P. W. (1962). *Creativity and intelligence.* New York: John Wiley & Sons.

Gough, H. G. (1976). Studying creativity by means of word association tests. *Journal of Applied Psychology, 61*, 348–353.

Guilford, J. P. (1950). Creativity. *American Psychologist, 5*, 444–454.

Guilford, J. P. (1962). Factors that aid and hinder creativity. *Teachers College Record, 63*, 380–392.

Guilford, J. P. (1966). Intelligence: 1965 model. *American Psychologist, 21*, 20–26.

Guilford, J. P. (1967). *The nature of human intelligence.* New York: McGraw-Hill.

Guilford, J. P. (1968). *Intelligence, creativity, and their educational implications.* San Diego, CA: Robert R. Knapp.

Guilford, J. P., & Christensen, P. R. (1973). The one-way relation between creative potential and IQ. *Journal of Creative Behavior, 7,* 247–252.

Hall, W. B. (1972). A technique for assessing aesthetic predispositions: Mosaic Construction Test. *Journal of Creative Behavior, 6,* 225–235.

Hébert, T. P., Cramond, B., Speirs Neumeister, K. L., Millar, G., & Silvian, A. F. (2002). *E. Paul Torrance: His life, accomplishments, and legacy.* Storrs: National Research Center on the Gifted and Talented, University of Connecticut.

Helson, R. (1971). Women mathematicians and the creative personality. *Journal of Consulting and Clinical Psychology, 36*, 210–220.

Hunsaker, S. L., & Callahan, C. M. (1995). Creativity and giftedness: Published instrument uses and abuses. *Gifted Child Quarterly, 39,* 110–114.

Huang, T.-Y. (2005) Fostering creativity: A meta-analytic inquiry into the variability of effects. *Dissertation Abstracts International,* 66 (04A), 2348A.

Jellen, H., & Urban, K. (1989). Assessing creative potential worldwide: The first cross-cultural application of the Test for Creative Thinking-Drawing Production (TCT-DP). *Gifted Education International, 6*(2), 78–86

Jensen, A. R. (1998). *The g factor: The science of mental ability.* Westport, CT: Praeger.

Kaltsounis, B. (1977). Middle Tennessee teachers' perceptions of ideal pupils. *Perceptual and Motor Skills, 44*, 803–806.

Kaltsounis, B., & Higdon, G. (1977). Student teachers' perceptions of ideal pupils. *Perceptual and Motor Skills, 44*, 160.

Khatena, J. (1983). What schooling for the gifted. *Gifted Child Quarterly, 27*, 51–56.

Kim, K. H. (2005). Can only intelligent people be creative? A meta-analysis. *Journal of Secondary Gifted Education, 16*, 57–66.

Kim, K. H. (in press). Meta-analyses of the relationship of creative achievement to both IQ and divergent thinking test scores. *Journal of Creative Behavior.*

Kim, K. H., & Cramond, B. (2007, April). *The relationship between creativity and behavior problems among Korean elementary and high school underachievers.* Paper presented at the Annual Meeting of the American Educational Research Association, Chicago.

Kogan, N., & Pankove, E. (1974). Long-term predictive validity of divergent-thinking tests: Some negative evidence. *Journal of Educational Psychology, 66,* 802–810.

Korean Educational Development Institute. (2003). *Current status of teaching and learning at educational institutions for the gifted.* Seoul, South Korea: Korean Educational Development Institute.

MacKinnon, D. W. (1961). Creativity in architects. In D. W. MacKinnon (Ed.), *The creative person* (pp. 291–320). Berkeley, CA: Institute of Personality Assessment Research, University of California.

MacKinnon, D. W. (1962). The nature and nurture of creative talent. *American Psychologist, 17,* 484–495.

MacKinnon, D. W. (1967). Educating for creativity: A modern myth? In P. Heist (Ed.), *Education for creativity* (pp. 1–20). Berkeley, CA: Center for Research and Development in Higher Education.

Maslow, A. H. (1998). *Toward a psychology of being.* New York: Wiley.

Mellou, E. (1996). Can creativity be nurtured in young children? *Early Child Development and Care, 11,* 119–130.

Millar, G. W. (2002). *The Torrance kids at mid-life: Selected case studies of creative behavior.* Westport, CT: Ablex.

National Advisory Committee on Creative and Cultural Education. (1999). *All our futures: Creativity, culture, and education.* London: Department of Education and Employment.

National Center on Education and the Economy. (2006). *Tough choices or tough times: The report of the new commission on the skills of American workforce.* Washington, DC: Jossey-Bass.

Oliphant, C. C. (1986). A descriptive study of factors associated with teacher identification of gifted students (Doctoral dissertation, Temple University, 1986). *Dissertation Abstracts International, 47,* 1691.

Piechowski, M. M. (2006). *"Mellow out they say." If I only could: Intensities and sensitivities of the young and bright.* Madison, WI: Yunasa.

Poe, E. A. (1875, September). Alone. *Scribner's Monthly Magazine, 10,* 691.

Rimm, S., & Davis, G. A. (1976). GIFT: An instrument for the identification of creativity. *Journal of Creative Behavior, 10,* 178–182.

Ritchie, S. P. (1980). Creativity and risk-taking in young children (Doctoral dissertation, University of North Carolina at Greensboro, 1980). *Dissertation Abstracts International, 42,* 539.

Robinson, A. W. (1980). A study of the effectiveness of a special class for academically gifted elementary students on the enhancement of the characteristics of giftedness (Doctoral dissertation, State University of New York at Buffalo, 1980). *Dissertation Abstracts International, 41,* 1380.

Robinson, K. (2001). Mind the gap: The creative conundrum. *Critical Quarterly, 43*(1), 41–45.

Rose, L. H., & Lin, H. T. (1984). A meta-analysis of long-term creativity training programs. *Journal of Creative Behavior, 18,* 11–22.

Rossman, B. B., & Horn, J. L. (1972). Cognitive, motivational and temperamental indicants of creativity and intelligence. *Journal of Educational Measurement, 9,* 265–286.

Rotter, D. M., Langland, L., & Berger, D. (1971). The validity of tests of creative thinking in seven-year-old children. *Gifted Child Quarterly, 15,* 273–278.

Rudowicz, E. (2003). Creativity and culture: A two way interaction. *Scandinavian Journal of Educational Research, 47,* 273–290.

Rudowicz, E., & Yue, X.-d. (2000). Compatibility of Chinese and creative personalities. *Creativity Research Journal, 14,* 387–394.

Runco, M. A. (2004). Creativity. *Annual Review of Psychology, 55,* 657–687.

Rushton, J. P., & Jensen, A. R. (2006). The totality of available evidence shows the race IQ gap still remains. *Psychological Science, 17,* 921–922.

Russ, S. W., Robins, A. L., & Christiano, B. A. (1999). Pretend play: Longitudinal prediction of creativity and affect in fantasy in children. *Creativity Research Journal, 12,* 129–139.

Sawyer, R. K. (2006). Educating for innovation. *Thinking Skills and Creativity, 1,* 41–48.

Scope, E. E. (1999). A meta-analysis of research on creativity: The effects of instructional variables. *Dissertation Abstracts International, 59*(7), 2348A.

Scott, C. L. (1999). Teachers' biases toward creative children. *Creativity Research Journal, 12,* 321–328.

Scott, G., Leritz, L., & Mumford, M. (2004). The effectiveness of creativity training: A quantitative review. *Creativity Research Journal, 16,* 361–388.

Simonton, D. K. (1984). *Genius, creativity, and leadership: Historiometric inquiries.* Boston: Harvard University Press.

Simonton, D. K. (1994). *Greatness: Who makes history and why*. New York: Guilford Press.

Sternberg, R. J., Grigorenko, E. L., & Bundy, D. A. (2001). The predictive value of IQ. *Merrill-Palmer Quarterly, 47*(1), 1–41.

Sternberg, R. J. & Lubart, T. (1999). The concept of creativity: Prospects and paradigms (pp. 3–15). In R. J. Sternberg (Ed.), *Handbook of creativity*. Cambridge, England: Cambridge University Press.

Torff, B. (1999). Encouraging the creative voice of the child. *The NAMTA Journal, 25*, 194–214.

Torrance, E. P. (1960). *Eight partial replications of the Getzels-Jackson study* (Research Memo BER-60-18). Minneapolis, MN: Bureau of Educational Research, University of Minnesota.

Torrance, E. P. (1962). *Guiding creative talent*. Englewood Cliffs, NJ: Prentice-Hall.

Torrance, E. P. (1963). The creative personality and the ideal pupil. *Teachers College Record, 65*, 220–226.

Torrance, E. P. (1972). Can we teach children to think creatively? *Journal of Creative Behavior, 6*, 114–143.

Torrance, E. P. (1977a). *Creativity in the classroom*. Washington, DC: National Education Association.

Torrance, E. P. (1977b). *Discovery and nurturance of giftedness in the culturally different*. Reston, VA: Council for Exceptional Children.

Torrance, E. P. (1988). The nature of creativity as manifest in its testing. In R. J. Sternberg (Ed.), *The nature of creativity* (pp. 43–73). New York: Cambridge University Press.

Torrance, E. P. (2002). *The manifesto: A guide to developing a creative career*. Westport, CT: Ablex.

Torrance, E. P., & Torrance, J. P. (1973). *Is creativity teachable?* Bloomington, IN: Phi Delta Kappa Educational Foundation.

Turkheimer, E., Haley, A., Waldron, M., D'Onofrio, B., & Gottesman, I. I. (2003). Socioeconomic status modifies heritability of IQ in young children. *Psychological Science, 14*, 623–628.

Voss, D. H. (1998). *Determining test fairness and differential validity of scores for the Torrance Tests of Creative Thinking for kindergarten students* (Doctoral dissertation, Texas Tech University, 1997). *Dissertation Abstracts International,* DAI-A 58/10, 3828.

Walberg, H. A. (1988). Creativity and talent as learning. In R. J. Sternberg (Ed.), *The nature of creativity* (pp. 340–361). New York: Cambridge University Press.

Walberg, H. A., & Herbig, M. P. (1991). Developing talent, creativity, and eminence. In N. Colangelo & G. A. Davis (Eds.), *Handbook of gifted education* (pp. 245–255). Needham Heights, MA: Allyn & Bacon.

Westby, E., & Dawson, V. L. (1995). Creativity: Asset or burden in the classroom? *Creativity Research Journal, 8,* 1–10.

Williams, E. (2000). *The history of the evolution of gifted identification procedures in Georgia* (Doctoral dissertation, University of Georgia, 2000). *Dissertation Abstracts International, 160,* 153.

Yamamoto, K. (1964). Threshold of intelligence in academic achievement of highly creative students. *Journal of Exceptional Education, 32,* 401–405.

Portfolio Assessment of Gifted Students

Susan K. Johnsen

Assessment is defined as the process of gathering and organizing information about student work from a variety of sources for the purpose of making sound educational decisions. According to the National Academies, assessment rests on three connected and interrelated pillars: cognition, observation, and interpretation (Pellegrino, Chudowsky, & Glaser, 2001). The first pillar, *cognition*, focuses on the knowledge and competence that a student has in a particular domain. The domain is defined by standards-based curriculum that is implemented across contexts. What does the student know and how is that knowledge represented? The second pillar involves the teacher's ability to create tasks and situations that provide *observation* opportunities in the classroom and in other settings for the students to exhibit their knowledge and competence. In what ways and in what contexts do the students demonstrate their understanding? Third, the teacher and/or the students make *interpretations* based upon observations of the performance evidence and review of the products. What is the quality of the work and to what degree have the students met the standards? Moreover, the Academies emphasize the importance of involving the student in the assessment process: "Students learn more if instruction and assessment are integrally related. In the classroom, providing students with information about particular qualities of their work and about what they can do to improve is crucial for maximizing learning" (Pellegrino et al., 2001, p. 8).

In the assessment process, teachers therefore must use a variety of tasks and methods that focus on the domain(s) of interest, involve repeated observations across multiple contexts, and engage students, professionals, and other stakeholders in conversations and interpretations of the evidence. Researchers suggest that the compilation of these tasks, observations, interactions, and interpretations that emerge from this type of assessment can be organized into a portfolio that provides a developmental record that is more authentic, naturalistic, and educationally useful than other forms of traditional assessments such as paper-and-pencil tests (Shaklee, Barbour, Ambrose, & Hansford, 1997; Valencia, 1992). Moreover, Borland and Wright (1994) emphasize the significant role that portfolio assessment is able to play in gifted education because it provides opportunities for assessing growth in areas such as creativity and critical thinking with implications for curriculum development, program evaluation, and identification. This chapter will examine the characteristics and purposes of portfolio assessment, the process of portfolio assessment, theoretical underpinnings, uses in identification and instruction, benefits, and challenges.

Characteristics and Purposes of Portfolio Assessment

A portfolio is a purposeful and systematic collection of student work that samples a student's abilities, progress, and accomplishments in a given area or areas (Arter, 1990; Black, 1993; Meyer & Schuman, 1990; Valencia, 1992). Portfolios have been used for a long time by writers, artists, architects, photographers, models, and other professionals to showcase achievements and skills (Belanoff & Dickson, 1991; Gilbert, 1993).

To differentiate the portfolio from files of students' tests and work such as cumulative folders, researchers have identified critical characteristics of portfolio assessments (Arter & McTighe, 2001; Borland & Wright, 1994; Duffy, Jones, & Thomas, 1999; Farr, 1992; Hadaway & Marek-Schroer, 1992;

Hanson & Gilkerson, 1999; Meyer & Schuman, 1990; Paulson, Paulson, & Meyer, 1991; Valencia, 1992; Valencia & Place, 1994; Wiggins, 1989, 1993; Wiig, 2000). The portfolio assessment:

- has a specific purpose;
- aligns with standards, curriculum, instruction, and overall assessments;
- shows growth in a variety of ways over time;
- uses multiple sources and multiple contexts;
- represents student's performance in the field in one or more domains;
- actively engages the students in their own learning, evaluations, and reflections; and
- actually guides teaching and learning.

In summary, portfolio assessment is multidimensional, capitalizes on the actual work of students over an extended time period, enhances student involvement, and is useful in making decisions about the individual student's educational program.

The Portfolio Assessment Process

In developing and implementing a portfolio assessment system, professionals will want to consider the guidelines that follow (Damiani, 2004; Fogarty, 1996; Hanson & Gilkerson, 1999; Jardine, 1996; Moersch & Fisher, 1995; Paulson et al., 1991; Shaklee et al., 1997; Stuhlmann, Daniel, Dellinger, Denny, & Powers, 1999; Wiggins, 1993; Wiig, 2000).

Decide on a Purpose and Type of Portfolio

Portfolios may be used for identification, curriculum and instruction, and program evaluation. For any of these uses, it is important to decide specifically what will be assessed. For example, when identifying gifted students, what type of characteristics will be identified? For curriculum and instruction, what types of knowledge or competencies do the students need to demonstrate? For program evaluation, how will students

show that they have met the program's goals? The answers to
these questions may be identified frequently from the school's
gifted education program plans and curricula.

Consider the Contents

In contrast to traditional tests that may have a ceiling, cover
a limited sampling of the content area, and not represent what
gifted students actually have learned, portfolios sample a wide
range of student work within a given domain, allow for student
differences, and focus on growth over time. The teacher will
need to decide what types of work will be selected and how it
relates to the purpose. Although certainly not exhaustive, the
following items have been suggested as possibilities for inclusion in portfolios (Hadaway & Marek-Schroer, 1992; Hanson &
Gilkerson, 1999; Shaklee et al., 1997):

- baseline sample or pre-instruction inventory;
- anecdotal records;
- journals or logs that focus on a variety of topics that interest
  the student or reactions to books, projects, field trips, and
  class and home activities;
- observations (interests, use of free time, social interactions,
  learning strategies);
- projects (photos and recordings of student projects);
- artwork (publishing projects, graphic representations, self-
  portraits, collages);
- writing (spontaneous or assigned under timed and untimed
  conditions; narrative and expository, book reports, papers,
  personal letters and correspondence, successive drafts);
- samples from home (hobbies, collections, artwork, interactions with family);
- audiotapes, videotapes, or CDs (class discussion, performances, presentations, interactions, interviews, conferences, peer interchanges, cooperative learning activities);
- photos (creative work, displays, art exhibits, engagement in
  activities);
- concept webs of student's knowledge;

- peer and other professional reviews (audience responses, mentor observations); and
- student reflections (written narrative, oral presentation).

Certain items within a portfolio also may enhance the assessment of gifted minority students (Hadaway & Marek-Schroer, 1992). For example, gifted students from different cultural backgrounds may communicate their ideas through their creative projects, share culturally specific information about their families and lifestyle at home using logs, and show their progress toward learning a new language through their written and oral work.

In all cases, the teacher will need to design a learning environment that allows the students to demonstrate their knowledge and competence. A classroom that primarily uses lecture and note taking will not provide the opportunities for students to show creative projects or responses to ill-defined problems.

Determine the Selection of the Samples or Artifacts

Decisions also need to be made about the selection of the samples or artifacts that will be collected in the portfolio. Who will select the items? Will the teacher require certain items? Will the items be completed products or in various stages of completion? Will they show the students' "best" works or a series of works to show their improvement? How will the samples be used—formatively, summatively, or for identification for gifted programs? Will there be criteria for evaluating the overall portfolio or for specific samples? Will all of the samples be evaluated? Will the criteria relate to district, state, and/or national standards, to identification characteristics, to program goals? In what ways will the students reflect about their work?

Because the selection of artifacts is driven by different purposes, Duffy et al. (1999) have described four different types of portfolios with varying degrees of student and teacher involvement in the selection process. The *Everything* or *Developmental Portfolio's* purpose is to evaluate a student's progress throughout an entire semester or year and may contain examples of a student's work in all of the various stages of completion. Students and teachers may select a variety of pieces of evidence that are representative of the student's work. It is typically used during conferences in a formative and summative fashion. The *Product Portfolio's* purpose is to evaluate a set of skills using specific criteria that are aligned with standards. The teacher provides a student with a table of contents that identifies the required products and the student submits work samples that match each of the standards. The teacher and the student then conference regarding how the products match the standards and select the student's best pieces. The purpose of the *Showcase* or *Exemplary Portfolio* is for the students to identify examples of their best work that meet the requirements. The teacher may provide the students with a table of contents with required topics, but the student primarily selects the products and provides a rationale for the selection. When the teacher and student conference, they enhance the student's reflection by discussing not only the items in the portfolio but also the student's rationale for their inclusion. The *Objective* or *Goal-Based Portfolio* (Swicegood, 1994) focuses on the student's selection of items that match a specific objective such as writing a persuasive essay or making oral presentations. Again, the student selects work that best represents the objective and the identified standards for performance. Similar to the Showcase Portfolio, the teacher and student conference about the items and the student reflects on his or her reasons for selecting the piece. If the pieces do not meet the objective, then the teacher provides individual qualitative feedback so that the student gains a better understanding of the objective.

In reviewing these types of portfolios, it is clear that variations might exist for other purposes such as identification and program evaluation. For example, an Exemplary Portfolio also might be used in identifying students for a gifted program with a professional committee making decisions regarding the quality of the items and their relationship to the characteristics needed for entrance into a specific program. Similarly, a program evaluation committee might use the Everything Portfolio to assess the value of a program's curriculum in developing a student's talent.

Decide What Aspects of the Samples or Artifacts Will Be Assessed

Assessing the content, process, and/or product may require different procedures (Damiani, 2004). For example, if only final products or performances will be evaluated, then assessments will be designed that focus on examining tangible evidence. How did the product show innovation? How relevant or significant is the product to the student's domain of study? How professional is the product? How did the performance communicate an understanding of the important ideas? On the other hand, if process is to be considered, then samples other than final products or performances will need to be included in the portfolio. How did the student develop the product? What type of method did he or she use? In what ways did he or she collaborate with other students? Samples such as videos of students' interactions, scientific logs, written steps in solving problems, reflections, and so on may provide a window into the student's ways of learning. Assessment of the process also will require accurate documentation and a separate scoring system. Content assessments may be embedded within the product or process assessment rubrics or may even be assessed using more traditional tests. Assessments need to be aligned with the aspects of the samples being evaluated.

Develop a Scoring System

Portfolios may be scored holistically with the entire set of samples being given a single score or they may be scored in a more focused manner to provide more detailed information to the teacher and the student (Wiig, 2000). Because focused approaches tend to provide better information regarding the gifted student's growth, they are used more frequently in portfolio assessment. Focused scoring systems generally use checklists, rating scales, and rubrics to assess portfolio samples (Arter & McTighe, 2001). Checklists describe simple criteria that identify whether or not the characteristic is present or absent, but do not have any judgments regarding the qualities of the characteristics. An example criterion might be, "Did the gifted student include multiple perspectives regarding the topic?" Rating scales use characteristic checklists but add a rating. For example, a rating of 1 (*infrequently*) to 5 (*frequently*) might be added to the gifted student's incorporation of multiple perspectives in the product or performance. Rubrics include not only criteria and a measurement scale but also describe the characteristics of each point on the scale. The highest quality work generally receives more point values. For example, in the Gifted Students' Performance Standards Project, a student might receive 5 points for "multiple perspective" that (a) separates personal opinions from those of others, (b) represents an understanding of a situation from another's perspective, (c) demonstrates empathy for others, (d) synthesizes multiple points of view, and (e) suggests solutions for conflicts and disparities (Texas Education Agency, 2001). In each case, the scores provide information about the essentials of the product/performance, process, and/or content that guides teaching and learning (Wiggins, 1989).

On the other hand, Royer, Cisero, and Carlo (1993) suggest that portfolios be examined using a more hermeneutic approach where a committee that shares a common, well-trained perspective assesses students' assembled collections of work that they think best documents their progress over time. In this case, each committee member examines the full set of samples independently and then makes an integrative judgment about the candidate. Royer et al. cite Glaser's (1984) dimensions of cognitive assessment as a possible framework for this more holistic approach: knowledge organization and structure, depth of problem representation (e.g., principles that underlie a problem rather than surface structure), quality of mental models (e.g., complex vs. simple models that guide performance), efficiency of procedures (e.g., problem solving that eliminates unnecessary steps), automaticity of performance (e.g., conscious vs. unconscious reasoning); and metacognitive skills (e.g., learners' abilities to plan, monitor, reflect on, and control their performance in a useful and efficient manner). In deciding whether to use a more holistic or focused-holistic approach, the teacher and the students will want to engage in a discussion of the descriptors. If the descriptors are clear and carefully explained to the students, they can act as guideposts for their growth, the selection of items to place in their portfolios, and the presentations of their work that shows what they understand and can do.

Engage the Learner Throughout the Process

One of the critical characteristics of portfolio assessment is to engage the student throughout the entire process. In this way, students understand the goals for learning, the particular characteristics needed for high-quality work, the types of samples that will best showcase these characteristics and their progress, how to reflect on their best work and themselves as learners, and how to communicate their progress to others. As opposed to high-stakes assessments where students have limited control, Hill (2004) has reported that students actually "look forward" to portfolio assessments that provide an "opportunity to show what they know and could do" (p. 1116). Moreover, because students are involved in their assessment, they assume more responsibility for their learning. Duffy et al. (1999) reported that the level of personal reflection required in portfolio evaluation increases the students' understanding of the processes and products of learning. They become more aware at a metacognitive level of the audience and context for constructing a portfolio, personal learning strategies, the development of skills necessary to complete a task, transfer across contexts, how to communicate knowledge within a particular domain, and understanding the conditions for success.

Self-assessments can be elicited during teacher-student conferences, interviews, structured question-answer interactions or checklists, categorically focused performance reflections, anecdotal accounts, or written summaries. For example, during conferences, gifted students might assume a leadership role, using portfolios to tell about their progress toward particular goals, how they made decisions about the selected samples, or how they view themselves as learners. The teacher might create conference questions for note taking or ask the gifted students to compare their observations with the teacher's judgments. The teacher might ask, "How would you describe your knowledge? Your skills?

Your teamwork? What problems are you having in achieving your desired goals? What would you select as an example of your best work?" These notes could summarize progress and future directions and be kept in the portfolio. Throughout the process, the teacher would focus on the student's accomplishments and potential growth, not problems or failures.

The students also might share their portfolios with their parents and/or professionals in their field. For these activities, the students would need to learn how to organize and present their work samples to show their knowledge, competence, and progress toward their goals. Opportunities should be provided for parents or professionals to share their reflections regarding the students' portfolios. What do they see as the special strengths of the students' works? What items tell the most about the students' achievements? What could be improved? What suggestions might they offer?

Student-led portfolio assessments help students think about themselves as learners, assess their own accomplishments, and establish future directions for their work.

Identify a Method for Managing the Portfolio

Researchers have provided practical suggestions for managing portfolios (Belanoff & Dickson, 1991; Fogarty, Burke, & Belgrad, 1996; Hadaway & Marek-Schroer, 1992; Moersch & Fisher, 1995; Paulson et al., 1991; Shaklee et al., 1997). Some decisions the teacher may need to make are how to store portfolios, the type of container that will be used, the labeling technique for each item, the order of items in the portfolio, and the overall look (Fogarty et al., 1996). Will the teacher use a notebook, box, cubby, sack, envelope, file folder, or photo album? Will the samples be stored electronically? Will there be a table of contents, tabs, registry, or labels attached to each item? Will the items be arranged in a sequential, thematic, prioritized, or random order? Will all of the portfolios be similar in appearance, or will they reflect the personality of the student?

With technological advances, more and more portfolios are becoming electronic (Moersch & Fisher, 1995). Multimedia tools such as scanners, digital cameras, personal digital assistants, and bar code readers afford students with opportunities to import and export large quantities of data and attach a variety of work samples. Electronic portfolios can be stored on the Web and/or on recordable CDs for sharing with peers, parents, professionals, and even future employers.

Every item should be dated and described so that those who review the portfolio will understand its inclusion. The description may include directions given, choice of tools, the student's verbal or nonverbal response, and details on the importance of the sample and its relationship to the purpose of the portfolio. No matter how the portfolios are stored, they need to be managed regularly to avoid large piles of items or improve the alignment of selections to specific goals or objectives.

Theoretical Foundations

Portfolio assessment is well-grounded in theory and operational models of education. Its focus on students as active agents who build personal understandings through their experiences places it within the constructivist theory of Vygotsky (1934/1962, 1978) and the individual conceptual change model of Posner and his colleagues (Posner, Strike, Hewson, & Gertzog, 1982; Strike & Posner, 1985, 1992). In these theories and models, learning occurs through interactions between the students and their environments. Individual learning in classroom environments is not isolated but greatly influenced by peer and teacher interactions (Pintrich, Marx, & Boyle, 1993). In the case of Vygotsky's theory, the students discover their zones of proximal development, the distance between the student's actual developmental level and the higher level of potential development, through interacting with more capable peers or adults (Vygotsky, 1978). Within the conceptual change model, cognitive factors such as knowledge in a specific domain, learning or problem-solving strategies, and metacognitive and self-regulation strategies result in deeper cognitive processing in academic tasks.

Pintrich and colleagues (1993) pose this problem: How might schools and classrooms be restructured to foster the development of a community of intentional, motivated, and thoughtful learners (p. 193)? They suggest creating a mastery goal orientation (Dweck & Elliot, 1983) where (a) tasks are authentic, (b) students have choice or control over their activities, (c) evaluation procedures foster a conceptual understanding of the content, (d) classroom activities are more open-ended, (e) students learn about their own learning and thinking strategies, and (f) ultimately students gain confidence in their abilities. The portfolio meets many of these researchers' recommendations for a more student-directed, reflective model of assessment that encourages deeper cognitive processing about academic tasks rather than focusing on external performance goals such as grades, which appear to result in more surface processing. Students are involved in selecting samples that relate to academic goals, interacting with adults and professionals in the field to review their accomplishments, and reflecting on their growth. In addition, developmental portfolios allow gifted students to examine their growth of expertise within a specific domain (Sternberg & Grigorenko, 2002). Because gifted students are constantly in the process of developing expertise when they work in a given domain, the portfolio provides an avenue for evaluating their work over time.

Using the Portfolio With Gifted Students

The use of portfolios for identification of and programming for gifted students has been reported in several studies in the literature (Coleman, 1994; Duncan & Dougherty, 1991; Johnsen & Ryser, 1997; Shaklee, 1993; Shaklee & Viechnicki, 1995; Wright & Borland, 1993). In all of these cases, the portfolios were used primarily to identify younger students and those from economically disadvantaged backgrounds.

In Project Synergy (Wright & Borland, 1993), standard samples—common activities that all students responded to; teacher-selected samples—items that were exemplary of the student's ability, potential, or growth in developmental domains; and child-selected samples—items that were "special" to them—were placed in the portfolio of kindergarten children throughout the year (p. 207). The children completed a sentence that was dictated to the teacher for each of the items they chose: "I chose this for my portfolio because . . . ; I like this because . . . ; My plan for this was . . . ; When I made this, I felt . . ." In addition to these samples, Notable Moment Cards that allowed teachers to record "illuminating, adventitious occurrences" (p. 207) and Let-Me-Tell-You-About-My Child Cards that allowed parents to describe their child's interests, activities, and notable behaviors also were included. At the end of the academic year, the teacher completed a Portfolio Profile that summarized the student's development in various domains. This profile assisted not only with the identification of potentially gifted students but also in developing individualized curriculum and programming. Professional development and conferences between the teacher and the child, between the teacher and parents, and between children were an integral part of the process that allowed all participants to view the growth of the child. Borland and Wright (1994) reported that the portfolios also showed predictive validity for future academic giftedness in a school for gifted students.

In the Early Assessment for Exceptional Potential project (EAEP), Shaklee and Viechnicki (1995) used 18 primary identifiers of exceptional potential, which included a definition and examples of behaviors, to inform the teachers' collection of six types of evidence from four audiences (child, peers, parents/community members, teachers) over a 6-week time frame. Evidence included

> (a) teacher-recorded anecdotal records recorded a minimum of one child per week; (b) systematic teacher observations of class members during six demonstration lessons; (c) peer/self nomination questionnaire; (d) a parent/guardian home-community survey; (e) samples of products produced by the child which could be selected by the child, teacher(s) and/or parent; and (f) additional information provided by resource specialists, teachers or parents. (p. 164)

Products included illustrations, essays, pictures, self-evaluations, worksheets, and books (Coleman, 1994).

Once all of the information was collected, the teachers developed individual and group profiles that consisted of children who needed support in the classroom, options to provide, resources needed, and an action plan that connected the students' characteristics with classroom activities. Again, professional development was extensive with 45 hours of in-service sessions that focused on the primary identifiers and elements of observational assessment, peer teaching, and biweekly visits by project staff (Shaklee & Viechnicki, 1995).

A "Me at My Best" portfolio identification system and curriculum was used to identify students at the kindergarten level (Duncan & Dougherty, 1991). During each fall, the gifted teacher presented three unit lessons from the portfolio curriculum that were used with all of the kindergarten students, which were supplemented with classroom and home extension activities. The first lesson focused on how classmates' similarities and differences produce individual talents with students identifying their own talents, another child's talents, and their families' talents. The second lesson focused on each child's personal talent and a method for collecting examples of these talents—a portfolio. The teacher, the student, and the parents then contributed items for the portfolio for 3 months. A label was attached to each portfolio item that stated, "I chose my (product) for my portfolio because it shows I (skill/talent)." The third lesson focused on original products that all of the students created in responding to two stories about "Sad Sack" and "The Original Toy." These products were included in the portfolio, along with the other items that had been selected by the teacher, student, and parents. Trained classroom teachers rated the portfolio samples on eight different characteristics: high-quality work, advanced vocabulary, leadership skills, in-depth understanding, advanced work, detailed presentation, creative responses, and keen sense of humor. The teacher's ratings and the student portfolios were reviewed at program placement meetings attended by the teacher, counselor, gifted program coordinator or resource teacher, and the principal. The committee then rated each port-

Table 12.1
Portfolio Contents for Identifying a Special Needs Student

1. Writing sample with teacher's anecdotal remarks about interactions with the student during the writing process.
2. Tests with records of responses and descriptions of the student's reactions to challenge.
3. A functional behavior analysis (i.e., observation) describing the context and the student's interactions with other students and tasks.
4. Oral language sample—a taped interview describing relationships with peers and adults.
5. Math problems worksheets that compare growth over time with student reflection.
6. Social studies exam with student's strategies described.
7. Photo of a student's arts and crafts project with a description of methods used.
8. Response to intervention anecdotal teacher journal.

Note. From Swicegood (1994). The portfolio describes the student's adaptations in a variety of subject areas and focuses on the student's relationships with others, which includes the teacher, adults, and other students. Each item is dated with a description of the context in which it was collected.

folio using a checklist on a scale from 1–8, with 8 points being the maximum score a student might receive. Similar to Borland and Wright (1994), this portfolio approach positively related to future achievement 4 years later (Johnsen & Ryser, 1997).

Not much empirical research has been reported in the gifted literature since these promising beginnings. However, researchers have described the use of portfolios at a variety of levels and for a variety of purposes:

1. *Identifying special needs.* Portfolios were adapted and used with sixth-grade students who had learning disabilities (Boerum, 2000). Students collected drafts, final copies, reflections, assessment checklists and rubrics, and videotaped presentations and were able to clarify their strengths and weaknesses as learners. Portfolios also were used with students who have behavioral disorders to assess adaptive functioning, academic growth, strategic learning and self-regulation, language, and cultural aspects (Swicegood, 1994; see Table 12.1).

2. *Formative self-assessment of progress.* In one district, students have used portfolios as a self-assessment of their learning in a variety of ways. Students led portfolio conferences and shared their progress with the teacher, their peers, parents, other professionals in the school, and district administration (Paulson & Paulson, 1996; see example rubric for student-led conference in Table 12.2). Students also used portfolios to document progress in a physical education program at the elementary level (Melograno, 1994). Students in grades 2 and 3 collected writing in portfolios, regularly assessing their work, and developed self-regulated learning (SRL) in high-SRL classrooms (Perry, 1998). Teachers also have used portfolios for formative assessments. Arts Propel, a 5-year, collaborative effort involving Harvard Project Zero, the Educational Testing Service (ETS), and the teachers and administrators of the Pittsburgh Public Schools, focused on using portfolios to track student progress in music, the visual arts, and imaginative writing. The project now disseminates model curricular units and assessment guidelines (Gardner, Wolf, & Gitomer, 2006). Early childhood teachers used a Progress Profile to document children's growth in literacy and numeracy from kindergarten through the fourth grade and collected samples of artifacts such as reading journals from home, exploratory reading projects, and drafts, using a portfolio system (Hill, 2000).

3. *Evaluating overall student performance.* Portfolios also serve as a useful tool for summative self-evaluation of student growth. Students assessed their own writing and their progress as the basis for the final exam in a high school English classroom (Ballard, 1992) and collected a set of writing samples that identified their passions and reflected and evaluated the cumulative whole (Fueyo, 1994). Students also prepared for graduation by developing a portfolio of their work in 14 curricular areas to present to a graduation committee, comprised of teachers from different subjects and grade levels, an outside examiner, and a student peer (Darling-Hammond, 1993).

4. *Program accountability.* Program accountability is another purpose for using portfolios. A state department of education, for example, designed a statewide system of portfolio assess-

Table 12.2
Rubric for a Student-Led Portfolio Conference

Characteristics	Developing	Competent	Proficient
Preparation	Student does not send invitation to parent or guardian.	Student sends invitation to parent or guardian that describes location of the conference, but does not communicate goals of conference.	Student sends invitation to parent or guardian that communicates goals and location for the conference.
Organization of the Portfolio	Artifacts do not show clearly the progress of student in different subject areas. Descriptions of artifacts' inclusion are vague or are not included.	Artifacts show progress of student in most of the subject areas that are representative of the work. Descriptions of artifacts' inclusion are somewhat clear.	Artifacts show progress of student in each subject area and are representative of the work. Student has attached a description to each of the artifacts that explains why it was included.
Communication	Student does not accurately self-assess strengths and weaknesses.	Student accurately self-assesses strengths and weaknesses, but does not focus on the knowledge or skill or how it was learned.	Student accurately self-assesses strengths and weaknesses, focusing on what and how the knowledge or skill was learned.
Reflection	Student does not accept responsibility for work. Goals vaguely relate to student's progress.	Student accepts responsibility for work, describes progress, but is unable to identify goals that link to strengths and weaknesses.	Student accepts responsibility for work, describes progress, and is able to identify future goals that link to strengths and weaknesses.

ment as one way of evaluating a new writing program and math progress (Black, 1993). Along with staff and teachers, school districts set assessment goals, described performance tasks in specific curriculum areas, and established rubrics. The stakeholders, including the students, judged the students' portfolios (Paulson & Paulson, 1996). Students, with limitations in cognitive functioning and who were receiving special education services in Kentucky, were assessed through participation in an alternate portfolio system (Denham & Lahm, 2001). The alternate portfolio was scored at the regional level by a trained team of scorers using a double blind method.

5. *School reform.* In collaboration with the Massachusetts Department of Education, Project Zero at Harvard University helped individual elementary and middle schools adopt portfolio assessment as part of a statewide school reform effort, which examined the fit between curriculum, pedagogy, and assessment practices (Seidel, 2006). The materials were shared with the New Standards Project (2006), which disseminates a system of performance standards and assessments for students at the elementary, middle, and high school levels. The performance standards are internationally benchmarked and indicate the level of performance that students should demonstrate in English and language arts, mathematics, science, and applied learning. Project APPLE (Assessing Projects and Portfolios for Learning) examined ways of fair assessment of student performance and ways that portfolio assessment might be implemented in schools. The New England Regional Assessment Network was formed to disseminate findings (Walters, Gardner, & Seidel, 2006).

More recently, portfolios are being used in teacher preparation programs in gifted education (Johnsen, VanTassel-Baska, & Robinson, 2007). Spurred by new student/candidate-driven assessment requirements from the National Council for Accreditation of Teacher Education (NCATE), universities are developing electronic portfolio systems to show candidate growth on benchmarks that are based on national standards (CEC-TAG, 2006). Teachers or preservice candidates who are seeking an initial certificate in gifted education gather evidence from the classroom and from courses to show their level of proficiency on specific knowledge and skills. Depending upon the standard, evidence may include lesson plans, differentiated units, observations, case studies, student progress data from the classroom, reflections, parent–teacher conferences, workshop presentations, and so on. The candidate, mentor teachers, university faculty, and/or other members of the professional team review the evidence to determine the candidate's progress and assess their strengths and weaknesses (see Table 12.3 for a rubric used in assessing preservice teacher portfolio artifacts).

Benefits

A number of benefits have been identified in the literature that distinguish portfolios from more traditional forms of assessment. First, the use of portfolios contextualizes assessment so that the teacher can readily identify the environmental conditions under which a gifted student's optimal learning occurs and recognize cultural and other factors that might influence performance and/or products (Hadaway & Marek-Schroer, 1992; Melograno, 1994; Sternberg & Grigorenko, 2002; Wiggins, 1989). Second, a wide range of samples can be gathered from multiple sources across a variety of contexts over time (Arter, 1990; Shaklee et al., 1997). This cumulative body of work assists the teacher in observing how the gifted student is developing expertise within a particular domain of talent or interest (Sternberg & Grigorenko, 2002). Third, the use of portfolios integrates assessment with instruction. Through conferences and examination of items within the portfolio, the teacher not only is able to assess content knowledge but also procedural or process knowledge. How does the gifted student organize knowledge within the domain? What problem-solving strategies does the gifted student use? How does the gifted student transfer learning across different content domains and contexts? Through careful observations and interactions with the gifted student, the teacher is able to adapt instructional strategies to promote greater growth. Fourth, portfolio assessment encourages a deeper understanding of knowledge

Table 12.3

Rubric for Assessing Preservice Teacher Portfolio Artifacts

Benchmark 8: Assessment method matches knowledge (curriculum) and student characteristics.

Characteristic	Developing	Competent	Proficient	Not Applicable
Candidate selects curriculum-based, alternative, criterion- and/or norm-referenced methods to assess student(s) that matches the knowledge and student characteristics.	Selection does not match knowledge or the student characteristics.	Selection does match knowledge and characteristics of some of the students.	Selection does match knowledge and characteristics of all of the students.	
Candidate designs/organizes curriculum-based, alternative, and/or criterion-referenced methods to assess student(s) that matches the knowledge and student characteristics.	Design does not match knowledge or the student characteristics.	Design does match knowledge and characteristics of some of the students.	Design does match knowledge and characteristics of all of the students.	
Type and form of assessment varies based on student(s) characteristics.	Assessment is not related to student(s).	Assessment varies for some of the students.	Assessment varies for all of the students.	

Benchmark 9: Formative assessment provides information regarding student(s)' achievement level.				
Characteristic	Developing	Competent	Proficient	Not Applicable
Candidate uses multiple assessment methods that provide formative information about the student(s).	Methods do not discriminate with any students.	Methods discriminate with the majority of the students.	Methods discriminate with all of the students.	
Candidate involves student in self-assessment.	Student is not involved in any self-assessment.	Student is involved in self-assessment during pre– and posttests only.	Student is involved in self-assessment continuously.	
Assessment information is used in the referral process for special programs.	Assessment is not used.	Assessment provides some information about students' strengths and weaknesses that is used in the referral process.	Assessment provides specific information about students' strengths and weaknesses that is used in the referral process.	
Assessment is continuous throughout the instructional process.	No assessment is used for planning instruction.	Occurs at the beginning and/or end of instruction only.	Is continuous.	

Table 12.3 Continued

Benchmark 10: Assessment information is communicated to students, parents, and other professionals.

Characteristic	Developing	Competent	Proficient	Not Applicable
Candidate communicates information in professional contexts (e.g., ARD, team meetings, disciplinary purposes).	No communication with professional.	Communicates general information about student's strengths and weaknesses.	Communicates specific information about student's strengths and weaknesses.	
Candidate communicates progress to student.	No communication with student.	Communicates information about student's strengths and weaknesses at the beginning and end of the semester.	Communicates specific information about student's strengths and weaknesses throughout the semester.	
Candidate communicates progress to parents.	No communication with parent.	Communicates information about student's strengths and weaknesses at the beginning and end of the semester.	Communicates specific information about student's strengths and weaknesses throughout the semester.	

Note: This rubric is for the assessment strand. Three other strands are evaluated—Creating a Positive Learning Environment, Curriculum Planning and Instruction, Professional Development and Communication. From *School of Education Benchmarks*, Baylor University, School of Education (2007). Reprinted with permission.

(Damiani, 2004). Products and performances that do not focus on a single right answer and have longer periods of time for completion tend to facilitate more cognitive activity and conceptual change (Pintrich et al., 1993). Fifth, portfolios actively engage the gifted student in the assessment process. Students are more likely to understand and share expectations and goals for learning. They are more likely to focus on the essentials of the performance or product, which fosters attention to strengths, independence, and self-evaluation (Ballard, 1992; Duffy et al., 1999; Perry, 1998). Moreover, when they share their progress with others, they learn how to communicate and defend their knowledge within a particular domain. Sixth, portfolio assessment provides for individual differences and offers an alternative to students with special needs (Boerum, 2000; Damiani, 2004; Hadaway & Marek-Schroer, 1992; Wiig, 2000; Wright & Borland, 1993). With no ceiling that inhibits their performance, gifted students not only have an opportunity to share their progress in a specific interest or talent area but also in a variety of ways. This variation supports gifted students who may be twice-exceptional by providing time and optional response modes that are not present in norm-referenced assessments. Finally, portfolio assessment is a teaching tool (Black, 1993). By becoming aware of the effectiveness of his or her instructional practices, the teacher is involved in ongoing professional development, action research, and data-based adaptations in instruction.

Challenges

Although it has many benefits, portfolio assessment also presents challenges. These challenges may be categorized into three major areas: time, technical adequacy, and competition with high-stakes assessment.

Time

Implementing portfolios does take time—"time to learn, time to practice, and time to implement" (Shaklee et al., 1997, p.

143). Because teachers often need to shift to different assessment paradigms, create new classroom environments, and adopt new teacher roles, professional development can be extensive with initial weeklong workshops followed by peer teaching and ongoing assistance (Shaklee & Viechnicki, 1995). On top of learning new assessment techniques and instructional practices, Kampfer, Horvath, Kleinert, and Kearns (2001) identified the following areas as most time consuming for the teacher in implementing portfolio assessment: the portfolio entry, facilitating social relationships, documenting progress, developing supports, and accessing multiple settings. They noted that teachers often spent time outside of the school setting assessing portfolios.

However, other researchers suggest that when portfolio assessment is embedded within instruction and students assume more responsibility for evaluation, portfolios do not take any more time than scoring papers after school (Paulson & Paulson, 1996; Shaklee et al., 1997). Unfortunately, the majority of teachers still use portfolios only in a summative fashion (McNair, Bhargava, Adams, Edgerton, & Kypros, 2003).

Technical Adequacy

Assessment specialists also find it difficult to apply rigorous psychometric standards of reliability and validity to portfolio assessment (Paulson & Paulson, 1996). Because reliability requires consistency, the variation in items selected and in sources selecting items creates considerable challenges to those seeking an internal consistency statistic. Are the samples consistent across contexts? Are they consistent across portfolios? Do the samples consistently assess the area of talent or set of standards? Do different examiners score the products the same or observe the same behavior? Stuhlmann et al. (1999) have reported improvements in raters' abilities to reliably interpret scoring items (.60–.87), using a specific rubric of children's writing where the teachers were trained. Rater agreement on a single sample does appear to produce acceptable levels when rater agreement is calculated, and raters are acceptably trained. However, rater agreement across tasks is much more difficult to estimate. It's not clear if an "all-purpose" rubric could be used to assess a wide spectrum of skills and concepts consistently.

In terms of validity, does the sample adequately represent the area of talent? Does it address the standards effectively? Does the sample generalize to other areas that would be expected? Does it relate to other norm-referenced assessments? Does the sample predict future performance? Some researchers have reported that holistically scored portfolios that are used for identification do predict future performance in gifted programs (Borland & Wright, 1994; Johnsen & Ryser, 1997). Other researchers suggest that more qualitative approaches be used in determining portfolios' technical adequacy (Royer et al., 1993). However, if major decisions are going to be made using portfolios, then the technical adequacy issue must be addressed.

Competition With High-Stakes Assessments

Although authentic types of assessment have gained popularity because of the dissatisfaction and frustration with more standardized assessments, ironically, these more traditional assessments may be the greatest challenge to advocates of portfolios. For example, teachers are less likely to use more authentic forms of assessment such as portfolios when faced with high-stakes state assessments (Hill, 2004). They are more likely to use professionally prepared coaching materials that not only are aligned with the state assessments but also have a similar format than to allow students to lead discussions about their progress as evidenced in their portfolios. Teachers are more interested in covering the material that will be on the test rather than assessing the student's depth of understanding. Damiani (2004) points out,

> a written test can include questions from an entire unit with a sample of items from all areas taught. Because of the time it takes to produce products, it is not possible to have a portfolio that represents every aspect of a unit (p. 3).

With pressures on teachers and students alike to perform well on these assessments, portfolios are less likely to be used because of these challenges.

Conclusions

Portfolio assessment provides useful information that is helpful to teachers, families, and other professionals who are identifying and planning programs for gifted students. It is grounded in the theoretical foundations of Vygotsky and in cognitive models such as those of Posner and his colleagues. It incorporates the National Academies' three pillars of assessment—cognition, observation, and interpretation, by using a variety of tasks and methods that focus on knowledge domains, repeated observations over time across multiple contexts, and teachers', students', and other professionals' judgments regarding the qualities of the work samples. It is particularly useful for the assessment of gifted students because it provides a way of observing higher level cognitive strategies and does not suffer from ceiling effect, a test condition that can limit the gifted students' opportunities to show what they actually know and can do.

The portfolio process is complicated and takes time, training, and effort on the part of the participants. Faculty must be committed to ensure implementation that will realize the benefits that often are cited by researchers: contextualized assessment, a wide range of assessment samples, integration of assessment with instruction, deeper understandings of knowledge, engagement of the student in the assessment process, provisions for individual differences, and ongoing professional development.

Although portfolios appear to be a viable option for assessing gifted students, empirical research showing effectiveness is quite limited. Explanations for this gap in the literature may rest with the formidable challenges that accompany the portfolio assessment's implementation: time, technical adequacy, and high-stakes assessments. If the assessment is not embedded within the instructional process, teachers may find more and more time spent after school hours organizing and rating portfolio items, ultimately viewing workload requirements as more important than any benefits accrued from the alternative assessment process. Moreover, researchers who use quantitative approaches are less likely to use portfolio assessments in their studies because they are neither standardized nor meet limited technical requirements. Finally, along with other authentic approaches, portfolio assessments may be viewed as superfluous to the more important evaluations for schools—those that determine state rankings and funding. This latter challenge appears critical because portfolio assessment has seen resurgence in teacher preparation programs at the university level where NCATE requirements for system assessments need to show candidate growth over time.

If professionals are able to address these challenges, portfolios can make important contributions to engaging gifted students in the assessment process, in communicating their progress with others, furthering their opportunities for developing their talents to help them achieve their personal best, and demonstrating authentic learning at key stages of the process.

References

Arter, J. (1990). *Using portfolios in instruction and assessment: State of the art summary*. Portland, OR: Northwest Educational Research Laboratory.

Arter, J., & McTighe, J. (2001). *Scoring rubrics in the classroom: Using performance criteria for assessing and improving student performance*. Thousand Oaks, CA: Corwin Press.

Ballard, L. (1992). Portfolios and self-assessment. *English Journal, 81*(2), 46–48.

Belanoff, P., & Dickson, M. (Eds.). (1991). *Portfolios: Process and product*. Portsmouth, NH: Boynton/Cook.

Black, S. (1993). Portfolio assessment. *The Executive Educator, 15*(1), 28–31.

Boerum, L. J. (2000). Developing portfolios with learning disabled students. *Reading and Writing Quarterly, 16*, 211–238.

Borland, J. H., & Wright, L. (1994). Identifying young, potentially gifted, economically disadvantaged students. *Gifted Child Quarterly, 38*, 164–171.

CEC-TAG. (2006). *Council for Exceptional Children, The Association for the Gifted final version of the initial knowledge and skills standards for gifted and talented education.* Retrieved December 15, 2006, from http://www.cectag.org

Coleman, L. J. (1994). Portfolio assessment: A key to identifying hidden talents and empowering teachers of young children. *Gifted Child Quarterly, 38,* 65–70.

Damiani, V. B. (2004). *Portfolio assessment in the classroom.* Bethesda, MD: National Association of School Psychologists.

Darling-Hammond, L. (1993). Setting standards for students: The case for authentic assessment. *National Association of Secondary School Principals Bulletin, 77*(556), 18–26.

Denham, A., & Lahm, E. A. (2001). Using technology to construct alternate portfolios of students with moderate and severe disabilities. *Teaching Exceptional Children, 33*(5), 10–17.

Duncan, J., & Dougherty, E. (1991). Using product portfolios for student assessment for gifted programs. In *Update on Gifted Education* (pp. 12–16). Austin: Texas Education Agency, Division of Gifted/Talented Education.

Duffy, M. L., Jones, J., & Thomas, S. W. (1999). Using portfolios to foster independent thinking. *Intervention in School and Clinic, 35*(1), 34–38.

Dweck, C. S., & Elliott, E. S. (1983). Achievement motivation. In E. M. Hetherington (Ed.), *Handbook of child psychology: Vol. 4. Socialization, personality, and social development* (pp. 643–691). New York: Wiley.

Farr, R. (1992). Portfolios: Assessment in language arts. *Texas Reading Report, 14,* 10–12.

Fogarty, R. (1996). *Student portfolios: A collection of articles.* Palatine, IL: IRI/Skylight Training and Publishing.

Fogarty, R., Burke, K., & Belgrad, S. (1996). The portfolio connection: Real-world examples. In R. Fogarty (Ed.), *Student portfolios: A collection of articles* (pp. 89–100). Palatine, IL: IRI/Skylight Training and Publishing.

Fueyo, J. (1994). "What do you really care about here?": Portfolios as rites of passage. *Language Arts, 71,* 404–410.

Gardner, H., Wolf, D. P., & Gitomer, D. (2006). *Arts PROPEL.* Retrieved December 13, 2006, from http://www.pz.harvard.edu/Research/PROPEL.htm

Gilbert, J. C. (1993). *Portfolio resource guide: Creating and using portfolios in the classroom.* Ottawa, KS: The Writing Conference.

Glaser, R. (1984). Education and thinking: The role of knowledge. *American Psychologist, 39*, 93–104.

Hadaway, N., & Marek-Schroer, M. F. (1992). Multidimensional assessment of the gifted minority student. *Roeper Review, 15*, 73–78.

Hanson, M. F., & Gilkerson, D. (1999). Portfolio assessment: More than ABCs and 123s. *Early Childhood Education Journal, 27*, 81–86.

Hill, C. (2000). The progress profile: Constructivist assessment in early childhood education. In A. L. Costa (Ed.), *Teaching for intelligence II* (pp. 211–230). Chicago: Skylight Publishing.

Hill, C. (2004). Failing to meet the standards: The English Language Arts Test for fourth graders in New York state. *Teachers College Record, 106*, 1086–1123.

Jardine, A. S. (1996). Key points of the authentic assessment portfolio. *Intervention in School and Clinic, 31*, 252–253.

Johnsen, S. K., & Ryser, G. R. (1997). The validity of portfolios in predicting performance in a gifted program. *Journal for Education of the Gifted, 20*, 253–267.

Johnsen, S. K., VanTassel-Baska, J., & Robinson, A. (2007). *Guidebook for CEC-NAGC standards for gifted education in teacher preparation programs. Volume 1: University programs.* Washington DC: National Association for Gifted Children.

Kampfer, S. H., Horvath, L. S., Kleinert, H. L., & Kearns, J. F. (2001). Teachers' perceptions of one state's alternate assessment: Implications for practice and preparation. *Exceptional Children, 67*, 361–374.

McNair, S., Bhargava, A., Adams, L., Edgerton, S., & Kypros, B. (2003). Teachers speak out on assessment practices. *Early Childhood Education Journal, 31*, 23–31.

Melograno, V. J. (1994). Portfolio assessment: Documenting authentic student learning. *Journal of Physical Education, Recreation, and Dance, 65*(8), 50–55, 58–61.

Meyer, C., & Schuman, S. (1990). *White paper on aggregating portfolio data.* Lake Oswego, OR: Northwest Evaluation Association.

Moersch, C., & Fisher, L. M., III. (1995). Electronic portfolios—some pivotal questions. *Learning and Leading with Technology, 23*(2), 10–15.

New standards project. (2006). Retrieved December 13, 2006, from http://www.ncrel.org/sdrs/areas/issues/methods/assment/as7nsp.htm

Paulson, F. L., & Paulson, P. R. (1996). Assessing portfolios using the constructivist paradigm. In R. Fogarty (Ed.), *Student portfolios: A collection of articles* (pp. 27–45). Palatine, IL: IRI/Skylight Training and Publishing.

Paulson, F. L., Paulson, P. R., & Meyer, C. A. (1991). What makes a portfolio a portfolio? *Educational Leadership, 48*, 60–63.

Pellegrino, J. W., Chudowsky, N., & Glaser, R. (Eds.). (2001). *Knowing what students know: The science and design of educational assessment.* Washington, DC: National Academy Press.

Perry, N. E. (1998). Young children's self-regulated learning and contexts that support it. *Journal of Educational Psychology, 90*, 715–729.

Pintrich, P. R., Marx, R. W., & Boyle, R. A. (1993). Beyond cold conceptual changes: The role of motivational beliefs and classroom contextual factors in the process of conceptual change. *Review of Educational Research, 63*, 167–199.

Posner, G., Strike, K., Hewson, P., & Gertzog, W. (1982). Accommodation of a scientific conception: Toward a theory of conceptual change. *Science Education, 66*, 211–227.

Royer, J. M., Cisero, C. A., & Carlo, M. S. (1993). Techniques and procedures for assessing cognitive skills. *Review of Educational Research, 63*, 201–243.

School of education benchmarks. (2005). Retrieved July 12, 2007, from http://www.baylor.edu/SOE/ps/index.php?id=20108

Seidel, S. (2006). *Project Zero/Massachusetts school network.* Retrieved December 13, 2006, from http://www.pz.harvard.edu/Research/MSN.htm

Shaklee, B. D. (1993). Preliminary findings of the Early Assessment for Exceptional Potential project. *Roeper Review, 16*, 105–109.

Shaklee, B. D., Barbour, N. E., Ambrose, R., & Hansford, S. J. (1997). *Designing and using portfolios.* Needham Heights, MA: Allyn & Bacon.

Shaklee, B., & Viechnicki, K. (1995). A qualitative approach to portfolios: The Early Assessment for Exceptional Potential Design. *Journal for the Education of the Gifted, 18*, 156–170.

Sternberg, R. J., & Grigorenko, E. L. (2002). *Dynamic testing: The nature and measurement of learning potential.* Cambridge, England: Cambridge University Press.

Strike, K. A., & Posner, G. J. (1985). A conceptual change view of learning and understanding. In L. H. T. West & A. L. Pines (Eds.), *Cognitive structure and conceptual change* (pp. 211–231). Orlando, FL: Academic Press.

Strike, K. A., & Posner, G. J. (1992). A revisionist theory of conceptual change. In R. Duschl & R. Hamilton (Eds.), *Philosophy of science, cognitive psychology, and educational theory and practice* (pp. 147–176). Albany, NY: SUNY.

Stuhlmann, J., Daniel, C., Dellinger, A., Denny, R. K., & Powers, T. (1999). A generalizability study of the effects of training on teachers' abilities to rate children's writing using a rubric. *Journal of Reading Psychology, 20*, 107–127.

Swicegood, P. (1994). Portfolio-based assessment practices. *Intervention in School and Clinic, 30*(1), 6–15.

Texas Education Agency (2001). *Gifted and talented performance standards project.* Austin, TX: Author.

Valencia, S. (1992, January). *Implementing literacy portfolio assessment.* Paper presented at the meeting of the Southwest Regional International Reading Association, Tucson, AZ.

Valencia, S. W., & Place, N. (1994). Portfolios: A process for enhancing teaching and learning. *The Reading Teacher, 47*, 666–669.

Vygotsky, L. S. (1962). *Thought and language.* Cambridge, MA: MIT Press. (Original work published in 1934)

Vygotsky, L. S. (1978). *Mind in society: The development of higher psychological processes.* Cambridge, MA: Harvard University Press.

Walters, J., Gardner, H., & Seidel, S. (2006). *APPLE project.* Retrieved December 13, 2006, from http://www.pz.harvard.edu/Research/APPLE.htm.

Wiggins, G. (1989). Teaching to the [authentic] test. *Educational Leadership, 46*(7), 41–47.

Wiggins, G. (1993). *Assessing student performance: Exploring the purpose and limits of testing.* New York: Jossey-Bass.

Wiig, E. H. (2000). Authentic and other assessments of language disabilities: When is fair fair? *Reading and Writing Quarterly, 16*, 179–210.

Wright, L., & Borland, J. H. (1993). Using early childhood developmental portfolios in the identification and education of young, economically disadvantaged, potentially gifted students. *Roeper Review, 15*, 205–210.

Product Assessment

Joseph S. Renzulli & Carolyn M. Callahan

Introduction and Rationale for Product Assessment

The basic rationale for using product assessment in evaluating student outcomes in programs for the gifted lies in the recognition of the importance of using valid assessments to measure student achievement. That is, a significant proportion of the goals and objectives that appropriately represent elevated expectations for gifted students cannot be assessed validly by traditional paper-and-pencil tests. Any goals that suggest the integration of sophisticated, complex, and in-depth understanding; creative productivity; the investigation of authentic problems; the use of alternative means of expression; or performance that emulates or represents that of professionals must be assessed using performance and product assessments.

Many of the models of curriculum and instruction recommended for gifted students include one or more of these elements and product development is woven into the fabric of both the instructional design and the expected outcomes of those models. For example, as early as 1977, Renzulli proposed Type III Enrichment as the hallmark of appropriate instructional programming for gifted students and has continued to stress the importance of products in the Schoolwide Enrichment Model

259

and the Secondary Triad Model (Renzulli, 1977; Renzulli & Reis, 1985, 1986). The expected outcome of Type III Enrichment is a product that addresses a real problem, using the methodology of professionals in the discipline to produce a real product for a real audience. Betts' Autonomous Learner Model includes a component identified as Investigations, whose expected outcome is a product with a presentation to an appropriate audience (Betts, 1986), and Kaplan's layering approach used to guide development of differentiated curriculum for gifted students includes product differentiation as a key dimension (Kaplan, 1986, 2005). Further, The Purdue Three Stage Model (Feldhusen & Kolloff, 1986; Moon, 1994; Moon, Feldhusen, Powley, Nidiffer, & Whitman, 1993) and Purdue Secondary Model (Feldhusen & Robinson, 1986) both include the expectation that students will create products akin to those described by Renzulli as Type III products.

The Integrated Curriculum Model (ICM) also offers opportunities for creative product development as a part of its overall design (VanTassel-Baska, 1986; VanTassel-Baska & Little, 2003; VanTassel-Baska & Stambaugh, 2006). The recently developed model of differentiation offered by Tomlinson (1995) clearly provides guidelines for differentiation of products for gifted students, and the Parallel Curriculum Model has specifications for product development in the Core Curriculum Parallel, the Connections Parallel, the Practice Parallel, and the Identity Parallel (Tomlinson et al., 2002). Finally, the International Baccalaureate Program (2000) requires students to produce an extended essay on an independent study topic and individual courses require completion of research projects involving the formulation of a problem, generation of a hypothesis, collection and analysis of data, and presentation of results. The pervasiveness of product expectations is summarized by Stephens and Karnes, "Creative products are essential to curricula for the gifted" (2005, p. 215).

In some of the models, products or performances are elicited by very specific task descriptions or performance prompts that require reflection of increased depth, complexity, abstractness, and/or sophisticated understanding of state or local curriculum standards. In others they may be used to assess specific goals that are derived from enrichment of the traditional curriculum. Or, they may be much more open-ended tasks/product expectations that reflect outcomes of independent study or in-depth investigation of problems or issues selected by students. In any case, products should allow for all students to engage in the demonstration of their learning and achievement based on clear standards that represent appropriate expectations for gifted students and ways of dealing with advanced content, sophisticated processes, and authentic production.

Product Assessment and the Instructional Cycle

The process of planning and implementing instruction must be looked at as a cyclical process rather than a linear one, with the results of one instructional cycle forming the basis for the next set of decision making. Product assessment most often is viewed as the summative or cumulative assessment of student outcomes. But, product assessment also can inform the next instructional steps. Evaluation of criteria specified on the scoring rubrics for products can provide important information on areas of student strengths and weaknesses, current status of knowledge and understanding, metacognitive skills, and habits of mind. As with any goals or objectives of instruction, it is critical to examine past accomplishments in order to ascertain the "level of proximal development" described by Vygotsky (1978). The zone of proximal development is that band representing the potential to learn wherein a child can complete a task with the help of an adult or a more advanced peer. To create lessons that are in a student's zone of proximal development, teachers must determine where the student currently stands—that level of understanding that represents the difference between what a student can do independently and what the student can do with guidance. The planning process should incorporate tasks that are just beyond the point where the student can do the task without any assistance and should incorporate learning activities that may require some guidance by an adult or peer in execution so that new learning will occur. Ideally, such learning will lead to the student acquiring the knowledge, understanding, and skill to carry out a parallel task independently and complete products that reflect achievement of the learning. Hence, teachers need to take special care in the development of instruction leading to the products that are specified as outcomes of models such at the Schoolwide Enrichment Model or the Autonomous Learner Model to assess students' past product production to ensure that the current instructional activity leading to a product represents new accomplishments.

As a brief example, one fifth-grade student who had completed a very sophisticated game reflective of strong mastery of basic principles of gaming strategies and probability with well-written directions as a Type III product simply submitted the same product when he moved on to middle school because of the failure of teachers to communicate and preassess student knowledge, skills, and past achievement/performance levels. To assume that particular goals and objectives of gifted programs—including product objectives—have been met is as unwise as assuming that gifted students have not met the objectives of the traditional curriculum. It is quite possible that some gifted students already have mastered some or all of the knowledge, understandings, or skills related to the production of particular products outlined in gifted program goals. In other cases, gifted students may have achieved some level of accomplishment, but the goals provide for a very high ceiling of achievement. The higher levels at which these goals can be defined can then be used to set higher levels of expected outcomes for students in terms of the depth, complexity, and difficulty of the content, the sophistication of the skills, or the quality of products that would be used to demonstrate learning.

Students who already have mastered a given level of performance on an objective should not be spending their valuable learning time engaged in activities to achieve those same outcomes. Hence, teachers of gifted students need to assess current levels of performance and strive to set the standards or goals for the gifted student so that he or she ascends to the next level of performance in product production as in any other area of achievement.

Although gifted students often learn at a faster pace, there still is considerable variability among them in the complexity of their learning, their organizational skills, and mastery of prerequisite skills for successful completion of a product. Therefore, developing strategies for monitoring learning and performance as product development progresses is important to ensure that the learning process is proceeding appropriately. Checking on the progress of learning allows for acceleration of pace or the addition of increased levels of complexity. Such monitoring also provides guidance for adjustments if there are misunderstandings, a need for support, or unexpected gaps in prerequisite skills or knowledge. Further, teaching students to monitor or assess their own learning, progress toward product completion, and quality of product is critical in developing independent, self-directed learners.

Reliability and Validity of Product Assessments

A discussion of the particulars of how to approach product assessment must be based on addressing the fundamental concepts of reliability and validity. The *reliability* of an instrument used to assess a product is the degree to which the scores on the measure are consistent. In all assessment, the scores must be as free of random error as possible. That is to say, the measure of a student's success in creating a product that meets the specified criteria for success should not vary greatly from day-to-day due to factors unrelated to the criteria being measured (e.g., factors such as luck, unclear directions, mood, fatigue, boredom, the teacher's mood when scoring the product, or unclear scoring guidelines should not influence the score a student earns). Two individuals rating the product should produce similar scores. For example, if an assessment of a student product includes a dimension that evaluates a student's skill in locating and interpreting credible primary source material, the score should not be based on how an individual interprets "never," "sometimes," "often," or "always." To achieve reliability of a scoring protocol, all criteria must be clearly defined and levels of proficiency clearly specified.

Even more important than reliability is the *validity* of protocols to assess products. It is crucial that the specified criteria relate to the underlying goals and objectives of the unit or task rather than some other variable. For example, in assessing a student's products, raters must take care not to be so distracted by the presentation of the product that they do not accurately assess the quality of content presented, even though presentation may be an important dimension.

Formative Product Assessment

Brief and Informal Formative Assessments

Even formative assessments that are informal and brief can provide reliable and valid information. Quick, informal responses can be gathered simultaneously within the ongoing instructional process. For example, to assess the degree to which students are progressing in the development of their products, a teacher may ask students to turn in a card at the end of each day, indicating the degree to which they made expected progress during the class session. Students are provided *Yes, No,* or *Maybe* cards that they turn in, or during the class they may keep cards on their desk that might be colored green ("I am moving right along."), yellow ("Caution, I feel like I am getting stuck and may be getting lost."), or red ("Things are not going well. I am not making much progress."). If students are working independently or in small groups, they might be given chips of those same colors to hand to teachers as they move around the room, or they might be provided colored pencils to color a small dot on their paper to reflect their status. Groups working on a task together might be provided "group chips" to represent the progress of the group in achieving their goal or finishing the task.

More Formal and More In-Depth Formative Assessment

Having students complete journal entries at the end of a class session might provide more comprehensive data.

Questions such as "Describe your progress on completing your project today and the way you went about completing the task for today. What did you do first? What was the most effective strategy you used today? What problems did you encounter along the way?" will provide information on student progress and give students practice in metacognition. Questions such as "Describe what you will do next to move you closer to completing this project. What help do you need? What materials do you still need?" will provide specifics on student progress toward completion of projects. For science products, outlining the components of an experimental journal as used by scientists and then having students keep such a journal as they explore a topic—recording how their understanding of the concepts have changed, results of their own experimentation, possible interpretations of the data—will provide useful information about student knowledge, skills, and understanding, as well as sophistication of information processing.

Summative Product Assessments

The Dimensions of Product Assessments

One dimension along which products can range is in the specificity of the task given to the student. The product may emanate from a very specific and definitively prescribed task or it may originate from a student-generated idea. Other variations in product assessments stem from differences in the type of rubric used (holistic vs. analytic), and amount of time allocated to product completion (short or extended; teacher or student determined).

Whatever the level of specificity of the task, it is very important to be sure that performance assessments are used to assess outcomes that are not measured adequately by paper and pencil assessment. Hence, performance assessments should focus on application of complex understanding and integration of knowledge and skills; be authentic; focus on deeper meanings; raise other questions or lead to other problems; allow for multiple approaches, solutions, and answers; and not have one clear path of action (Lantz, 2004).

Tasks

Highly Structured Tasks

The range of products that might be produced as reflective of the goals and objectives of instructional units for gifted students range from those that are indicative of achievement of very highly specified goals and objectives across content, process, and product dimensions to those that are reflective of student products evolving from independent choice of task. The curricular models of Tomlinson (1995), Kaplan (1986, 2005) and some dimensions of the Parallel Curriculum Model (e.g., the Core Curriculum Parallel; Tomlinson et al., 2002) call for the creation of very specific products in response to specific tasks designed to elicit outcomes to assess achievement of specific goals.

Callahan (2002) outlined criteria for developing such highly structured performance tasks:

1. Address the goals and objectives of the instruction. Be sure the task will elicit evidence of what students know, understand, and are able to do.
2. Balance and integrate assessment of content, process, and product in the creation of the task. Ensure that the tasks focus on the application of significant and important content that is complex and deep; represents the highest level of expertise in the discipline that is developmentally appropriate; and requires students to demonstrate application of process to content.
3. Create tasks that reflect integration of concepts, principles, generalizations, and skills across disciplines.
4. Detail the expectations for performance in the task description (and in the rubric). Explicitly delineate the dimensions along which student performance will be evaluated.
5. Find ways to express the highest level of quality performance.

6. Generate options within the task, when valid, that respect the learning profiles of the students, but still require demonstration of expected outcomes.
7. Ensure authenticity of the task. Look for ideas for tasks in the world around you. "How do professionals in the field use this knowledge and skill?" "How do they apply this knowledge?"

Wiggins (1993) offers a list of possible roles to consider in the creation of performance tasks across disciplines. Stephens and Karnes (2005) also offer lists of product ideas.

Moon, Callahan, Brighton, and Tomlinson (2002) demonstrated that following these procedures can lead to tasks that receive positive evaluations of content validity.

Semistructured or Unstructured Tasks

Other products or performances to be evaluated may result from long-term assignments or projects that meet the requirements of models such as the Schoolwide Enrichment Model (Renzulli & Reis, 1985), which requires students to produce solutions to real problems and present those products to authentic audiences. The Schoolwide Enrichment Model includes Type I activities that are exploratory activities designed to expose students to a wide variety of disciplines not ordinarily studied in school. One goal is to stimulate new interests in students. Type II activities in the model are designed as process or skill-building activities in the cognitive and affective domain. In these activities, students might learn how to use critical thinking skills; they might be involved in activities to develop their creative thinking or to develop skills in written, oral, or visual communication. The Type I and Type II activities both are designed to help create ideas for and to solidify interests in involvement in Type III Enrichment, which focuses on individual and small-group investigations of real problems. The products created in these instructional situations are defined by the student (with teacher approval) and the path to success is defined by the problem posed by the student.

Products from the Purdue models and the Autonomous Learner Model described above also would fall into this category, as would typical products produced as part of independent study projects.

Rubrics Used in Rating or Scoring Products

Wiggins (1996) has provided general dimensions along which products for gifted students should be scored. The first important criterion he identifies is *impact*. Within this general category, he provides guiding questions for evaluating the degree of effectiveness, the level of quality of the product, and the process of creating the product:

- Does the product created solve the problem? Does it persuade an audience? (Degree of effectiveness)
- Is the product outstanding in its class? Is it novel? Is the product ethical? (Level of quality)
- Is the process of creation purposeful? Was the process efficient? Was it adaptive? Was the creator self-critical? (Process)
- Was the process of creation thoughtful (considerate, responsive, inquisitive)?
- Does the student use the appropriate skills? These skills would be those linked to the task and product and would be situation-specific for each product.

Wiggins (1996) also recommends that the *form* of the product be rated by the degree to which the product is well-designed. Does form follow function? Is the product authentic? Is it elegant? Is it clever? To determine whether a product is well crafted, he provides guidelines for considering organization, price, clarity, and mechanical soundness, among other criteria. *Style* is the third dimension Wiggins identifies as important in rating gifted student products. He recommends consideration of the voice on such aspects as authenticity and grace. And, as expected, Wiggins considers the *content* to be important. He includes accuracy (correctness, validity), sophistication (depth, insightfulness, power, expertise), and aptness (focus) within this category (1996).

Wiggins (1996) also provides examples of ways in which exemplary models have been collected that set the highest level of performance required for gifted students. By looking at the products of older students and examining the models of experts, ascending levels of expertise can be articulated. Students also might identify accomplished works and derive the criteria from their own understanding of excellence. Other ideas for creating tasks for gifted students and generic rubrics for performance-based assessments are outlined by Lewin and Shoemaker (1998), Marzano, Pickering, and McTighe (1993), and Karnes and Stephens (1999).

It is not sufficient to create a task and leave the definition of expectations and standards to chance or to comparative evaluation. It is critical that standards and rubrics used to evaluate student products reflect the highest level of performance in the domain (Wiggins, 1996). Once appropriate standards of excellence or expert performance have been identified, educators must ensure that the rubrics used to evaluate the student clearly describe the progression of development from novice level performance to expert performance.

Creating Rubrics for Evaluating Highly Specified Products

In outlining criteria to be used to ensure that these standards are met in highly specified tasks, Callahan (2002) recommended the following:

1. Clearly delineate the dimensions along which you will evaluate student performance and be sure these dimensions reflect instructional goals across content, process, and product. You also may choose to include habits of mind. Establish levels of performance based on clear indicators of quality, not numbers (e.g., of references, of spelling errors).

2. Find a way to express the highest level of quality on each criterion. Help students learn the difference between "best in class," "best that I can be," and "expertise."

3. Help students understand the new assessment structure.
4. Judge students by what they actually produce, not what you expect of them. Avoid "halo" effects that come from giving students the benefit of the doubt or rate effort rather than productivity, or negative assessment that comes from rating students lower because teachers "expected more." If more is expected, it should be specified in the rubric.

Using tasks and rubrics for specific product assignments, Moon and colleagues (2002) established levels of interrater reliability ranging from .55 to .95 and provided evidence that both teachers and students respond positively to the demands of authentic assessment.

Creating Rubrics for Semistructured and Unstructured Tasks

The creation of rubrics for evaluating the outcomes of student efforts to complete semistructured and unstructured tasks also should follow the protocol of reflecting the dimensions of important content, process, and product qualities. Schack (1994) has outlined effectively such a rubric for adolescent research projects. The dimensions along which she suggests evaluating research projects include:
- formulating the research question,
- generating hypotheses,
- determining sample selections,
- selecting and implementing data gathering techniques,
- representing and analyzing data,
- drawing conclusions, and
- reporting findings.

In the section that follows, we will present the steps that need to be taken to develop a valid and reliable product assessment instrument by reviewing an instrument developed by Reis (1981) entitled the Student Product Assessment Form (SPAF).

Case Study in Instrument Design

Content Validity

Description of the Student Product Assessment Form

The first stage in the development of the Student Product Assessment Form (Reis, 1981) was to outline the content around which the instrument was to be constructed. Toward this end, letters were sent to coordinators of 50 long-established gifted programs throughout the country. Program coordinators and teachers were asked to provide the researchers with any forms or instruments used to evaluate student products. Every response indicated that formal product evaluation rarely occurred; when it did, the instruments used were locally developed and lacked reliability and validity information. Most of the product rating forms were very brief and sketchy, consisting of questions students were asked to answer upon completion of a product, such as, "What did you learn by doing this project?"

A review of literature also was undertaken in an effort to identify methods of evaluating student products completed in gifted programs. As was pointed out earlier, a shortage of instruments designed for this purpose was found. Few of the instruments available were evaluated in terms of reliability, validity, or field test research. Additionally, all available forms and scales that were examined either were geared toward adult products (Besemer & Treffinger, 1981) or geared to specific products such as inventions (Westberg, 1990), or were judged to be sketchy, inadequate, and incomplete for use in the evaluation of gifted students' products.

Based upon the examination of the literature and our years of familiarity with the outstanding products developed by gifted students, a new form was designed (see Summary Sheet in Figure 13.1) to provide raters with a valid and reliable basis for assessing the quality of products completed in gifted and talented programs. Fifteen items were generated that assess both individual aspects, as well as the overall excellence of the product. Each item represents a single characteristic on which raters

Name: _____ Date:_____
District:_____ School:_____
Teacher: _____ Grade: _____
Product (Title and/or Brief Description): _____
Number of Months Student(s) Worked on Product: _____

Factors	Rating*	Not Acceptable
1. Early statement of purpose		
2. Problem focusing		
3. Level of resources		
4. Diversity of resources		
5. Appropriateness of resources		
6. Logic, sequence, and transition		
7. Action orientation		
8. Audience		

9. Overall assessment
  A. Originality of the idea
  B. Achieved objectives stated in plan
  C. Advanced familiarity with subject
  D. Quality beyond age/grade level
  E. Care, attention to detail, etc.
  F. Time, effort, energy
  G. Original contribution		

Comments: _____

Person Completing This Form: _____

* Rating Scales
    Factors 1–8:
    5 = To a great extent
    3 = Somewhat
    1 = To a limited extent

    Factors 9A–9G:
    5 = Outstanding
    4 = Above average
    3 = Average
    2 = Below average
    1 = Poor

Figure 13.1. Student Product Assessment Form summary sheet.

DIVERSITY OF RESOURCES

Has the student made an effort to use several different types of resource materials in the development of the product? Has the student used any of the following information sources in addition to the standard use of encyclopedias: textbooks, record/statistic books, biographies, how-to books, periodicals, films and filmstrips, letters, phone calls, personal interviews, surveys, polls, catalogs, and/or others?

For example, a fourth-grade student interested in the weapons and vehicles used in Word War II read several adult-level books on this subject, including biographies, autobiographies, periodicals, and record books. He also conducted oral historical interviews with local veterans of World War II, previewed films and filmstrips about the period, and collected letters from elderly citizens sent to them from their sons stationed overseas.

5	4	3	2	1	NA
To a great extent		Somewhat		To a limited extent	

Figure 13.2. Example of SPAF Item 4.

should focus their attention. Items 1 through 8 are divided into three related parts:

1. *The Key Concept.* This concept always is presented first and is printed in large type. It should serve to focus the rater's attention on the main idea or characteristic being evaluated.

2. *The Item Description.* Following the Key Concept are one or more descriptive statements about how the characteristic might be reflected in the student's product.

3. *Examples.* In order to help clarify the meaning of the items, an actual example of students' work is provided. These examples are intended to elaborate upon the meaning of both the Key Concept and the Item Description. The examples are presented in italics following each item description. An example of Item 4 is included in Figure 13.2.

Item 9 has seven different components that deal with an overall assessment of the product. No examples of students' work are provided for Item 9. When completing the ratings for the overall assessment of a student's product, raters should attempt to evaluate the product in terms of their own values and certain characteristics that indicate the quality such as aesthetics, utility, and function of the overall contribution. In other words, raters are encouraged to consider the product as a whole (globally) in Item 9 and to use their own judgment and rely upon their own guided subjective opinions when rating this item.

Because of the difficulty of developing a single instrument that will be universally applicable to all types of products, instances occur when some of the items do not apply to specific products. For that reason, a category entitled "Not Applicable" was added to the 1–5 Likert-type scale of Items 1–8. For example, in a creative writing product (play, poem, novel) either the Level of Resources (Item 3) or the Diversity of Resources (Item 4) might not apply if the student is writing directly from his or her own experiences. This Not Applicable category is very rarely used in most rating situations and was not included in the overall assessment of the product (Item 9), which uses a 14-point Likert-type scale.

To examine content validity further, the form was evaluated by several recognized national authorities in the field of education of the gifted and in educational research. It also was distributed to 20 experienced teachers of the gifted in Connecticut. The authorities were asked carefully to assess the content of the form for omissions, clarity, and duplications. They also were asked for suggestions that would improve the form. Very few suggestions or omissions were mentioned by the experts, and the form was modified only slightly.

Reliability

Interrater Agreement

Interrater agreement was determined in two separate phases. In the first phase, 19 raters familiar with the field of education of the gifted (many of the raters were resource room teachers of the gifted) rated an original book on skunks, the product of a first grader. No explanations of the scale or the instructions were given; raters were simply given a copy of the SPAF and the product. They also were asked to assess the SPAF for language clarity, duplication, ease of instructions, and omissions (a further check on content validity). In other words, rater training was accomplished through the three pages of instructions that accompanied the form. This was considered to be important for future use of the instrument, which is intended to be independent of formal in-service training.

After the Phase One field test, the Student Product Assessment Form was revised according to interrater agreement percentages. Items 2, 6, and 7, which did not receive an agreement percentage of 80%, were revised and refined; one key concept in Item 9 was eliminated and replaced with an item that three raters had listed as an omission. In the Phase Two field test, 22 raters (19 of the Phase One group and 3 additional teachers of the gifted) rated a second product (an original local historical walking tour of a Connecticut city) and a third product (a novel written by a sixth-grade student). On the second product, interrater agreement of 100% was achieved for 12 of the 15 items. The other three items achieved agreement percentages of 86.4, 90.9, and 95.5. The nature of the third product (the novel) made it more difficult to attain interrater agreement above 80% in two areas, level of resources and diversity of resources. However, all other agreement percentages were above 80%, and 90% agreement was achieved for 10 of the 15 items.

Stability

An additional consideration addressed was the extent to which the ratings would be stable over time. Stability reliability was determined by having the same raters assess the second product (the historical walking tour) approximately 2 weeks after the first assessment. Almost identical responses and percentages were recorded. A correlation of +.96 was achieved between the first and second assessment of the second product.

Interrater Reliability

A final phase of the reliability check was the generation of interrater reliabilities for 20 different products listed in Table 13.1. The products represented five different product types including Scientific ($n = 7$), Creative Writing ($n = 5$), Social Studies ($n = 5$), Audio-Visual ($n = 2$), and Interdisciplinary ($n = 1$). The products were submitted for assessment to staff members in three public school programs for gifted students in Connecticut. Four experienced teachers of the gifted were asked to evaluate the products using the Student Product Assessment Form. The products varied in format, subject matter, age of the student who completed them, and final form. Some products were accompanied by a completed management plan (a contract-like form used in some programs for the gifted). The completed student guide (an optional segment of the SPAF) accompanied other products.

In some instances, the raters interviewed the student who had completed the product before evaluating it. Other times the raters evaluated the final product simply by examining it without interviewing the student. This was considered essential for the generalizability of the instrument because it will be used in all of these situations.

To obtain interrater reliabilities, the technique described by Ebel (1951) was utilized that intercorrelates the ratings obtained from different raters (see Guilford, 1954, pp. 395–397). The ratings of the four separate raters were correlated for each item presented in the SPAF, as well as on the subtotals of Items 1–8, Item 9's subitems A–G, and on the total rating of the items. Because each of the raters rated 20 products on 15 different traits, intercorrelations of the ratings of the products from all possible pairs of ratings were obtained. The interrater reliability results of the mean reliability for one rater, as well as four raters, on the nine different items ranged from .390–1.000 for one rater to .718–1.000 for four raters; the results were .961 for one rater across all items and .990 for the four raters. Total ratings obtained interrater reliability for the Student Product Assessment Form.

Table 13.1
Listing of Products by Type Used to
Generate Interrater Reliability

Type*	Product
4	1. A weekly television show, "All Kinds of Kids," which is directed, produced, and filmed by a group of gifted students.
1	2. A filmstrip on topology.
2	3. A short story.
1	4. A nonfictional book on pond life in Connecticut.
1	5. A book on skunks.
3	6. A genealogical investigation of a family and resulting book.
1	7. A scientific investigation of mapping pond life resulting in a photo essay and book.
3	8. An historical investigation and recreation of the Battle of the Bulge.
1	9. A model solar home.
1	10. A reflector telescope.
5	11. A filmstrip on computers and their history.
3	12. A study on the attitudes of school and community toward the E.R.A.
3	13. An historical walking tour of a city.
2	14. A short novel.
2	15. An autobiographical creative writing effort.
3	16. An investigative study of a political issue in a community.
2	17. A book of poetry.
2	18. A novel entitled Slave Boy.
1	19. A solar collector.
4	20. A documentary film on sign language.

*Scale for Types of Products
1 = Scientific
2 = Creative writing
3 = Social studies
4 = Audiovisual
5 = Interdisciplinary

From *The Schoolwide Enrichment Model: A How-to Guide for Educational Excellence* (p. 266), by J. S. Renzulli and S. M. Reis, 1997, Mansfield Center, CT: Creative Learning Press. Copyright © 1997 by Creative Learning Press. Reprinted with permission.

It should be noted that two key concepts, Audience and Original Contribution, had lower reliability when evaluated by one rather than when evaluated by four raters. Because SPAF often will be used by single raters in the future, those two areas will need further examination.

The higher interrater reliability should be examined with the realization that the products submitted for evaluation were from three outstanding programs for gifted and talented students. The teachers who submitted products often chose them for their high quality. It could be that fewer superior products would be associated with lower reliabilities. Future data will be collected in this area.

In summary, this section has described the development of the Student Product Assessment Form. Content validity procedures were presented and reliability assessment procedures (interrater agreement, stability, and interrater reliability) were described.

Uses of the Student Product Assessment Form

An almost universal characteristic of students of all ages is a desire to know how they will be evaluated or graded. We would like to begin by saying that we strongly discourage the formal grading of students' creative products. No letter grade, number, or percent can accurately reflect the comprehensive types of knowledge, creativity, and task commitment that are developed within the context of a creative product. At the same time, however, evaluation and feedback are an important part of the overall process of promoting growth through this type of enrichment experience, and students should be thoroughly oriented in the procedures that will be used to evaluate their work.

The best way to help students understand the ways in which their work will be evaluated is to conduct a series of orientation sessions organized around SPAF. Two or three examples of completed student products that highlight varying levels of quality on the respective scales from the SPAF instrument will help students to gain an appreciation for both the factors

involved in the assessment and the examples of the manifestation of each factor.

The evaluation of student products in many gifted programs has been carried out in a random and rather haphazard
manner. Often, no evaluation occurs and a valuable opportunity to provide feedback and to discuss future ideas for subsequent work is lost. If SPAF is used to evaluate completed
student products, the summary sheet (see Figure 13.1, p. 272)
could be filed in students' permanent record folders, providing an academic portfolio of their creative products from the
primary grades through high school. Because so many gifted
programming models include the development of student
products (Betts, 1986; Clifford, Runions, & Smyth, 1986;
Feldhusen & Kollof, 1986; Feldhusen & Robinson, 1986;
Kaplan, 1986; Renzulli & Reis, 1985; VanTassel-Baska &
Little, 2003), the evaluation of such products would seem not
only logical, but advisable.

Student Use of Rubrics

Although all of these rubrics were designed for teacher
assessment of student progress, students should be encouraged
to use these scales to evaluate their own work and that of their
peers. Skills in self-evaluation provide a base for students to
develop intrinsic standards of performance. Using the scales to
evaluate the work of others can be valuable in helping students
understand the high quality levels of productivity by seeing
models of each level and discussing the meaning of the levels of
performance.

Other Dimensions of Rubrics

Although many process dimensions have been included in
the assessments described above as summative evaluations, process skills may be assessed independently as part of either formative or summative evaluation. The evaluation of work habits,
ability to contribute to group productivity, and the development of higher level thinking and questioning skills may be part
of a rubric on a product.

Coming Full Circle

When student products from a unit of instruction are measured, the obvious next step is consideration of how such data will be used. Of course, reporting to parents and students on the degree to which students have achieved the goals of instruction is the primary purpose of summative data collection. Product assessment should constitute one component of the full range of assessment used to assess gifted students' achievement. If a wide range of assessment tools have been used that allowed students to demonstrate their highest level of accomplishment, then all parties will have a clearer understanding of the achievements and progress of students. These data also can serve to inform the new instructional cycle as it provides data on knowledge, understanding, skills, and such affective dimensions as habits of mind, attitudes, emerging interests, and favored learning styles.

When each stage of the instructional process has been supported and enhanced by acting on knowledge from an assessment process that reliably and validly gathers data on students' aptitude, prior achievement and readiness, interests, and learning styles, student learning is enhanced. Investment in learning about the student and responding to that knowledge with learning activities that are engaging, motivating, and within the appropriate range of difficulty is rewarded with learners who maximize the use of instructional time to produce outcomes that are reflective of the highest possible accomplishments.

References

Besemer, S. P., & Treffinger, D. J. (1981). Analysis of creative products: Review and synthesis. *Journal of Creative Behavior, 15*, 158–178.

Betts, G. T. (1986). The autonomous learner model for the gifted and talented. In J. S. Renzulli (Ed.), *Systems and models for developing programs for the gifted and talented* (pp. 27–56). Mansfield Center, CT: Creative Learning Press.

Callahan, C. M. (2002). The ABCs of creating a performance assessment task and scoring rubric. *Gifted Education Communicator, 33*(2), 12–15.

Clifford, J. A., Runions, T., & Smyth, E. (1986). The learning enrichment service (LES): A participatory model for gifted adolescents. In J. S. Renzulli (Ed.), *Systems and models for developing programs for the gifted and talented* (pp. 92–125). Mansfield Center, CT: Creative Learning Press.

Ebel, R. L. (1951). Estimation of the reliability of ratings. *Psychometrika, 16,* 407–424.

Feldhusen, J. F., & Kolloff, P. B. (1986). The Purdue three-stage model for gifted education at the elementary level. In J. S. Renzulli (Ed.), *Systems and models for developing programs for the gifted and talented* (pp. 126–152). Mansfield Center, CT: Creative Learning Press.

Feldhusen, J. F., & Robinson, A. (1986). The Purdue secondary model for gifted and talented youth. In J. S. Renzulli (Ed.), *Systems and models for developing programs for the gifted and talented* (pp. 153–179). Mansfield Center, CT: Creative Learning Press.

Guilford, J. P. (1954) *Psychometric methods.* New York: McGraw-Hill.

International Baccalaureate Program. (2000). *Diploma Program* [Brochure]. Geneva, Switzerland: Author.

Kaplan, S. N. (1986). The grid: A model to construct differentiated curriculum for the gifted. In J. S. Renzulli (Ed.), *Systems and models for developing programs for the gifted and talented* (pp. 180–193). Mansfield Center, CT: Creative Learning Press.

Kaplan, S. N. (2005). Layering differentiated curricula for the gifted and talented. In F. A. Karnes & S. M. Bean (Eds.), *Methods and materials for teaching the gifted* (2nd ed., pp. 104–131). Waco, TX: Prufrock Press.

Karnes, F. A., & Stephens, K. R. (1999). *The ultimate guide to student product development and evaluation.* Waco, TX: Prufrock Press.

Lantz, H. B., Jr. (2004). *Rubrics for assessing student achievement in science grades K–12.* Thousand Oaks, CA: Corwin.

Lewin, L., & Shoemaker, B. J. (1998). *Great performances: Creating classroom-based assessment tasks.* Alexandria, VA: Association for Supervision and Curriculum Development.

Marzano, R. J., Pickering, D., & McTighe, J. (1993). *Assessing student outcomes: Performance assessment using the dimensions of learning model.* Alexandria, VA: Association for Supervision and Curriculum Development.

Moon, S. M. (1994). Using the Purdue three-stage model: Developing talent at the secondary level. *Journal of Secondary Gifted Education, 5,* 31–35.

Moon, S. M., Feldhusen, J. F., Powley, S., Nidiffer, L., & Whitman, M. W. (1993). Secondary applications of the Purdue three-stage model. *Gifted Child Quarterly, 16,* 2–9.

Moon, T. R., Callahan, C. M., Brighton, C. M., & Tomlinson, C. A. (2002). *Development of differentiated performance tasks for middle school classrooms* (RM02160). Storrs: University of Connecticut, National Research Center on the Gifted and Talented.

Reis, S. M. (1981). *An analysis of the productivity of gifted students participating in programs using the revolving door identification model.* Unpublished doctoral dissertation, University of Connecticut, Storrs.

Renzulli, J. S. (1977). *The enrichment triad model: A guide to developing programs for the gifted and talented.* Mansfield Center, CT: Creative Learning Press.

Renzulli, J. S., & Reis, S. M. (1985). *The Schoolwide Enrichment Model: A comprehensive plan for educational excellence.* Mansfield Center, CT: Creative Learning Press.

Renzulli, J. S., & Reis, S. M. (1986). The enrichment triad/revolving door model: A schoolwide plan for the development of creative productivity. In J. S. Renzulli (Ed.), *Systems and models for developing programs for the gifted and talented* (pp. 217–152). Mansfield Center, CT: Creative Learning Press.

Schack, G. D. (1994). Authentic assessment procedures for secondary students' original research. *Journal of Secondary Gifted Education, 6,* 38–43.

Stephens, K. R., & Karnes, F. A. (2005). Product development for gifted students. In F. A. Karnes & S. M. Bean (Eds.), *Methods and materials for teaching the gifted* (2nd ed., pp. 211–244). Waco, TX: Prufrock Press.

Tomlinson, C. A. (1995). *How to differentiate in mixed-ability classrooms.* Alexandria, VA: Association for Supervision and Curriculum Development.

Tomlinson, C. A., Kaplan, S. N., Renzulli, J. S., Purcell, J., Leppien, J., & Burns, D. (2002). *The parallel curriculum: A design to develop high potential and challenge high-ability learners.* Thousand Oaks, CA: Corwin Press.

VanTassel-Baska, J. (1986). Effective curriculum and instructional models for talented students. *Gifted Child Quarterly, 30,* 164–169.

VanTassel-Baska, J., & Little, C. A. (2003). *Content-based curriculum for high-ability learners.* Waco, TX: Prufrock Press.

VanTassel-Baska, J., & Stambaugh, T. (2006). *Comprehensive curriculum for gifted learners* (3rd ed.). Needham Heights, MA: Allyn & Bacon.

Vygotsky, L. S. (1978). *Mind in society: The development of higher psychological processes.* Cambridge, MA: Harvard University Press.

Westberg, K. L. (1990). *The effects of instruction in the inventing process of students' development of inventions.* Unpublished doctoral dissertation, University of Connecticut.

Wiggins, G. P. (1993). *Assessing student performance: Exploring the purpose and limits of test.* San Francisco: Jossey-Bass.

Wiggins, G. P. (1996). Anchoring assessment with exemplars: Why students and teachers need models. *Gifted Child Quarterly, 40,* 66–69.

Using Performance-Based Assessment to Document Authentic Learning

Joyce VanTassel-Baska

Although performance-based assessment has been seen as promising for the identification of gifted learners (see Chapter 7), it clearly represents an indispensable approach for assessing gifted student learning. Only through challenging performance tasks do gifted learners have the opportunity to reveal both their considerable intellectual capacity and energy. Only through performance tasks can they provide insights for teachers about their true level of capability in a domain of knowledge. Thus, the incorporation of performance-based assessment in core content areas would appear a necessary part of designing effective programs for gifted learners.

The Process of Creating Performance Tasks

Performance assessment requires those individuals designing tests and other assessments to be creative designers, much like architects. As in the latter profession, the design issues relate to decisions about content and scope, decisions about processes to be employed, and decisions about overall effect in respect to coherence. Wiggins (1992) outlined important considerations in this process. In the task development phase, designers need to be aware of contextualizing the tasks so that the situations are authentic to the field being studied, as opposed to consisting of many unrelated items. Scoring rubrics need to represent the traits that are being tested, instead of what is easiest to score. Administration factors also need to be considered, including making the constraints of the testing process as realistic as possible. Once the tasks are developed, templates of the tasks, exemplary tasks, and design criteria should be pulled together to create a tool kit to ease creation of tasks in the future. Finally, tasks should be piloted and revised, in order to reveal difficulties or lack of clarity for the students or assessors. After the piloting, revisions should take place, based on the feedback received, and then tried again.

The Literature Base

Specific subject area assessment studies and related literature provide useful bases for considering the dimensions of performance assessment development. The National Council of Teachers of Mathematics (NCTM) presented six standards for assessment that could be used to guide development. These standards focused on mathematics learning, equity, openness, inferences, and coherence (Schulman, 1996). Specific questions recommended to developers included the following:

- What important mathematical ideas does this assessment task address?
- How can responses to this task inform instruction?
- How does the task allow for a variety of responses and modes of response?
- What references do students have for knowing what is expected of them in this task?
- What other sources of evidence exist to support inferences made?
- How does this task fit with learning goals and procedures?

Solano-Flores and Shavelson (1997) advocated a strong conceptual framework in developing science performance assessments (SPA). Their three core components were as follows: (1) a task that posed a well-contextualized problem that requires the use of materials, (2) a response format in which the student responses were captured, and (3) a scoring system that was able to score the scientific reasonableness and accuracy of the responses. SPAs also can be thought of as tasks that attempt to recreate the conditions in which scientists work and that try to elicit the types of reasoning and thinking that they use to solve scientific problems. The authors called attention to the competing priorities between assessment dimensions as a major issue in the task development process. For example, task developers need to reconcile the tensions between such elements as the cost-benefit relationship with materials—the need to have materials behave consistently but still be economically feasible, or between interrater reliability and scorer training time. These tensions between the range of elements never are solved entirely, as changes made in one element create consequences, often unpredictable ones, in a range of other elements.

With performance assessment, the range of tasks given in the assessment becomes very important. Direct assessments of the complex performances usually found in performance assessment do not tend to generalize well from one task to another, even within the same domain. For example, a writing assessment that only uses one prompt and one type of writing does little to assess how well a student is able to perform in the domain of writing. A wider range of tasks within a domain needs to be used to prevent the problems that may arise when assessments use too few tasks. However, studies suggest that a point of diminishing returns occurs, where more tasks or more raters do little to improve the reliability or validity of the assessment (Dunbar, Koretz, & Hoover, 1991).

As performance assessments have gained more popularity, concerns have developed around their reliability. Jiang, Smith, and Nichols (1997) conducted a meta-analysis to investigate and identify sources of poor reliability for performance assessments. Their meta-analysis of 22 studies looked at four sources of error and the way these sources contributed separately or jointly to the reliability of the process. These error sources were: (1) the particular set of items; (2) the set of judges or raters; (3) particular occasions of administration; and (4) momentary inattention from the test takers or other persons. The results showed that the greatest segment of variance came from the task/item and occasions dimensions. The person (test taker) also contributed significant variance. The judges or raters, however, did not contribute a major portion of error variance. This minimal variance can be reduced even more with rigorous training procedures for judges/raters. A three-way interaction, between person, task/item, and judge/rater, contributed the most variance, namely 35% of the total.

Technical adequacy studies also have been conducted on large-scale performance assessment protocols (Lane, Liu, Ankenmann, & Stone, 1996). The QUASAR (Quantitative Understanding: Amplifying Student Achievement and Reasoning) Cognitive Assessment Instrument (QCAI) was developed and used to measure student reasoning and mathematical skills. The questions were open-ended items and asked students not only for the answers, but also to explain their answers and show their solution processes. The QCAI was designed to measure program outcomes and growth in mathematics, rather than individual student outcomes. In examining the outcomes on this assessment for middle school students (grades 6 and 7), researchers found evidence for some generalizability and validity for the QCAI assessment. The generalizability results suggested that rater error was minimal and the greatest differences tended to lie in student performance across tasks. A stronger relationship was found between QCAI scores and the problem solving and conceptual subtest scores on the Iowa Tests of Basic Skills (ITBS) than between the QCAI and the ITBS mathematics computation subtest. Other studies based on this project have focused on item differential responses (Wang & Lane, 1996).

Based on these studies, it may be fair to conclude that performance-based assessments can be developed that honor the integrity of good test construction principles and good curriculum design principles, and achieve their stated purpose of demonstrating authentic student behavior.

Rationale for the Use of Performance Tasks to Assess the Learning Levels of Gifted Students

The criteria for the creation of good performance assessment items parallel several criteria for the development of sound curriculum for gifted learners. Such criteria call for being open-ended, focusing on higher level thinking and problem solving, and stressing articulation of the thinking processes employed (i.e., metacognition). These features then, incorporated into an assessment protocol, should provide evidence of the level of performance in gifted program classrooms because these same features are cornerstones of most curriculum development efforts, regardless of type of program approach. Thus, a high score on performance assessment items should represent well high-level classroom performance in a gifted program focused in a given domain of learning.

Another reason for trying this approach is that it provides an alternative way of looking at student ability via contextual performance. The item prototypes developed not only represent the scope of the domain under study, they also represent the major modes of thinking in that domain. The assessment features of use of manipulatives, lack of emphasis on speed, and preteaching all contribute to optimizing performance for inexperienced learners.

Finally, research evidence suggests that economically disadvantaged and minority learners perform better on tasks that emphasize fluid over crystallized intelligence (Mills & Tissot, 1995), and spatial reasoning over verbal and mathematical (Naglieri, 1999). By employing an assessment approach that contains a strong spatial component, disparities by socioeconomic status (SES) levels or ethnic group may be reduced (Bracken, 2000). Table 14.1 summarizes the features of performance assessment and the corresponding characteristics associated with economically disadvantaged and minority gifted learners. The relationship between task features and population behaviors would suggest a strong match.

Table 14.1
Relationship of Low-Income/Minority Populations to Features of Performance Assessment

Features of Performance Assessment	Characteristics of Economically Disadvantaged and Minority Learners
Rewards fluency and complexity over speed	Capacity for fluency and elaboration in learning situations where time limits do not inhibit quality of response (Torrance, 1977).
Rewards multiple right responses; is reductionistic	Preference for creative responses, nonopen-ended activities, and synthetic thinking (Baldwin, 1989).
Uses manipulation of materials as a pathway to solution finding	Preference for hands-on activities and projects (VanTassel-Baska, 1992).
Employs preteaching (dynamic assessment)	Need exposure to tasks prior to being tested due to fewer relevant environmental experiences outside of school (Rito & Moller, 1989).
Focuses on higher level thinking and problem solving	Capacity to demonstrate real-world skills that show fluid intelligence (Frasier, 1989).
Is metacognitive in that students reflect on the process	Preference for expressive activities and modes of learning that allow for reflection based on repeated practice (Ford, 1996).

Considerations in Developing Performance-Based Assessment Tools

Performance-based assessment, as an authentic tool for judging learning, offers many advantages for enhancing instruction. These include: (1) the use of results as a diagnostic to determine what curriculum needs to be taught and at what level, (2) the use of results for flexible grouping within subjects, and (3) the use of results for instructional emphases or even reteaching of core concepts. However, constructing good performance-based assessments requires attention to important details in the design process. Several considerations important in developing and implementing more authentic and performance-based assessment systems with high–ability learners are addressed below.

Target High-Level Skills

Given the depth and complexity of gifted learners' cognitive abilities, tests for this population should emphasize high-level thinking and processing skills. That is, the test should go beyond simple recollection of knowledge or facts and require students to operate at higher levels of application, analysis, synthesis, and evaluation. Task demands for gifted learners can make use of thinking processes, often identified as central to differentiation, such as comparing, classifying, induction, deduction, constructing support, abstracting, decision making, investigation, problem solving, and invention (Marzano, Pickering, & McTighe, 1993). By the same token, expectations for students' performance conveyed, for instance, through scoring rubrics should reflect the same high standards for complexity and sophistication to bring out the best products that gifted learners are capable of generating.

Use Multiple Approaches

To monitor student performance and inform instruction, a teacher needs to collect student performance data all the way through a learning module or unit, using formative and summative assessments. Formative assessments are used to monitor student progress during instruction, while summative assessments are given at the end of instruction for the purpose of certifying mastery or assigning grades (Gronlund, 1998). While some approaches are more suitable for one type of assessment (e.g., portfolios may be used for formative, rather than summative, assessment), some approaches can be used for both. In order to examine a student's performance from various perspectives and under different conditions, it is desirable for teachers to employ multiple assessment approaches in both oral and written form. A combination of approaches generally works to both the teacher's advantage and the student's advantage because different approaches can supplement one another to provide a more comprehensive picture of a student's performance.

Clarify Purpose

An emphasis on performance-based tasks does not replace standardized tests when the latter may function effectively. For instance, although a performance task can allow students to demonstrate their actual writing ability, students also may construct their own sentences in such a way as to bypass their weak areas in sentence structure. If language mechanics are the purpose for an assessment, then a standardized test can better cover a large number of grammar and language points in a relatively short time. It is a more efficient tool for examining students' mastery in key areas. The appropriate assessment approach always should be based on the purpose of the assessment. Generally, if content mastery is being assessed, a paper-and-pencil test with close-ended items may be preferable. If higher order thinking and problem solving are being assessed, a more performance-based approach would be appropriate.

Think Through How to Use Assessment Results

Differentiation for gifted learners typically calls for the use of advanced content, deep processing, and quality products. Where differentiation is occurring, gifted students tend to get harder books to read and more challenging projects to complete than their regular classmates. How do teachers assess their learning outcomes in such a way that these students feel properly rewarded for their extra labor? How can we encourage gifted students to strive for a higher level when they always compare favorably with their peers in the classroom? And, in attempting a challenging project, how should teachers appropriately weigh the emphasis on their efforts and final results? A disturbing finding that emerged from two districtwide evaluations of gifted programs was that gifted students are not evaluated regularly for their learning in programs (VanTassel-Baska, 2006). Not only is it difficult to provide challenges for the gifted, often we do not document how they handled those challenges in order to know more about restructuring curriculum the next time. Teachers must consider how to document results and use them for future planning and for evidence of student growth.

Creating Performance-Based Assessment Task Demands

The process for constructing performance-based measures can be lengthy, yet shortcuts are possible if we deliberately apply techniques used in earlier efforts (see VanTassel-Baska, Johnson, & Avery, 2002). These techniques provide ways to construct meaningful tasks that align with curriculum standards and meet technical adequacy considerations.

Selection of Prototypes

In order to find appropriate prototypes that encompass verbal, math, and spatial spheres, educators need to review several sources. Off-level assessments such as the Scholastic Aptitude Test (SAT) can be examined, as these tests are designed to give students opportunities to reason in verbal, spatial, and mathematical contexts. Other print sources to be consulted include books on problem solving that contain examples of interesting problems and mathematical games and puzzles. The Curriculum and Evaluation Standards of the National Council of Teachers of Mathematics (1989) and other national group content standards may be used to make a realistic judgment about what content students should know. Aligning performance-based assessments with content standards also is a critical step in the process.

Based on the input gained from all of the sources mentioned above, the following mathematical prototypes may be selected as a starting point for task development: *arithmetic problem solving, number concepts, logic, proportional reasoning, patterns,* and *number theory.* Additional spatial prototypes may include: *spatial reasoning and visualization, spatial patterning, geometry,* and *transformations.* In the verbal area, the following prototypes may be identified for development of individual tasks: *verbal reasoning and problem solving, persuasive writing,* and *analogies and word relationships.*

Criteria Used for Task Development

A core set of criteria are essential building blocks in creating strong performance-based tasks to assess the learning of gifted students. One criterion is an emphasis on thinking and problem solving in order to tap fluid rather than crystallized abilities in a domain. A second criterion is to develop off-level tasks, ones that would be challenging to high-ability learners. A third criterion involves the use of an open-ended format to encourage more creative responses and ways of thinking. A fourth criterion deals with the use of manipulatives, a strategy found useful in aiding students in "figuring out" hard problems and especially recommended for use with at-risk students (Ford, 1996; VanTassel-Baska, 1992). Lastly, the criterion of "thinking made visible" should be applied to each task in order to encourage students to reflect on their problem-solving approaches and self-correct as needed.

On the sample math task "Krypto" (see Figure 14.1), students are asked to solve a challenging problem that requires the development of strategies and recognition of patterns. Knowledge of number facts is a prerequisite, but the real heart of the task is in reasoning quantitatively to solve an open-ended problem.

In the sample verbal task on humor (see Figure 14.2), students have to interpret and write about a picture according to specific parameters. Like the math task, it is open-ended, yet requires verbal reasoning applied to pictorial material to solve the problem.

Krypto
Tear apart the numbers on the paper strip
that you have been given: 1, 5, 6, 4, 12, and
8. Use some or all of the first five numbers to
get an answer of 8. You may change the order
of the numbers and you may use addition, sub-
traction, multiplication, or division. Show
all the solutions you can find:

Using 3 numbers:
Using 4 numbers:
Using 5 numbers:

Figure 14.1. Krypto exercise.

Create a humorous title for the following picture and write a
descriptive paragraph about the picture, explaining why it is funny.

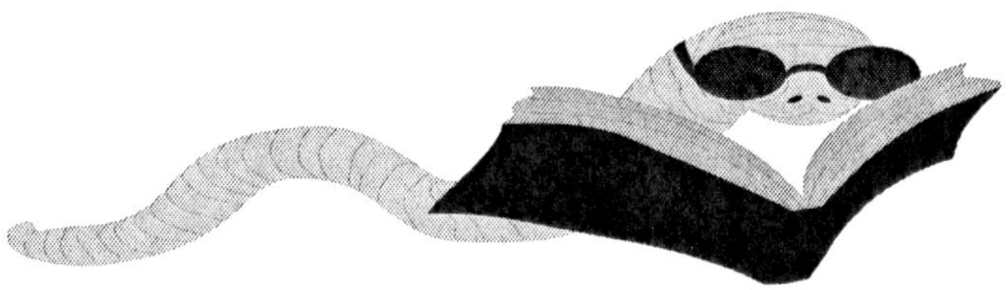

Title:_____
Description:_____
_____
_____
_____
_____

Figure 14.2. Verbal task on humor.

Off-Level/Advanced Tasks

Because the population of interest is high–ability learners,
the criterion of developing "off-level" tasks is crucial. The

power of the tasks ultimately lay in the ability to challenge the learner at an authentic level. The Krypto task illustrates the challenge level that performance tasks should be designed to reach. Even though the task gives students a chance to respond at a simpler level by allowing solutions that use only three or four of the five given numbers, the last part asks for solutions that use all five numbers. By using an advanced and open-ended task, students are not in danger of bumping up against an artificial ceiling, a common problem with traditional in-grade achievement tests for these learners. In the verbal humor task, students have the opportunity to demonstrate sophistication in their thinking through their writing—a common approach for assessing reasoning ability (Paul, 1992). Moreover, they are encouraged to be fluent in their ideas and to represent them in elaborate language.

Open-Ended Format

All tasks should be open-ended, either because multiple answers are possible or because different approaches to answers are possible. When the former case is operant, students are instructed to write as many solutions as they can find. This fluency aspect is illustrated in the Krypto task. It prompts students to find multiple solutions at three levels of complexity. Students are given a fairly wide framework within which they can show how well they can see patterns. In the verbal humor task, students must construct a written response that is of their own devising. Multiple responses are judged equally effective as long as basic parameters of the problem are honored. Elaboration of response also is encouraged and rewarded.

Emphasis on Articulation of Thinking Processes

In performance assessments, students are expected to provide some evidence of the thinking processes used in obtaining a solution for verbal, mathematical, and spatial-visual tasks. In some tasks, students are asked to show in words, pictures, or symbols how they reached their solutions. In other tasks, articulating the solution to a nonverbal problem by writing it out is an important part of the task. An example of this case is the Krypto task. Students are not explicitly prompted to explain their thinking, but they need to express their solutions in ways that convey meaning to the reader of the paper. A single mathematical equation or a collection of equations representing steps in the solution might be given. Because the sample verbal humor task requires a written response, the thinking processes used by students are self-evident. However, the additional prompt to comment on how they "thought about" the picture as humorous requires a deeper probing of their capacity to articulate their ideas.

Development of Rubrics and Exemplars

The rubric development process also involves a careful delineation of a range of responses obtained on a 0–4 scale from a high-level response (4), to a low-level response (0). Rubric scores are used to discriminate among student performances. Once pilot test data are obtained, a set of exemplars can be developed for each point total value to aid in both understanding and scoring the tasks. Answer sets for each task can be constructed and used as a basis for each rubric score. Sample rubrics developed for Krypto and the verbal humor task may be found in Figure 14.3.

Using Existing Models for Performance-Based Assessment

Although creating new assessments can be accomplished by using the steps outlined above, many educators may wisely opt to use or adapt existing performance-based assessments that already meet technical adequacy and have a history of successful use. The examples that follow provide performance-based assessment tools that have been and continue to be employed effectively with gifted learners. The first example is for use at the elementary level, and the second model is for use at the secondary level.

Rubric for Verbal Task (Pictorial/Verbal Humor)				
4	3	2	1	0
Both title and paragraph reflect strong understanding of pictorial humor.	Both title and paragraph reflect good understanding of pictorial humor.	Title is humorous, but paragraph is limited in being able to explain humor.	Both title and paragraph lack understanding of pictorial humor.	No response.

Note to scorers: There are many possible responses to this prompt. You may wish to sort the set of student papers into two piles (strong vs. weak) and then sort into four piles in order to apply the rubric effectively. Students may write an analytical explanation of their title or a humorous story. Either approach should receive full credit.

Rubric for Problem-Solving Task (Krypto)

4	3	2	1	0
Must have at least one 5-card solution and at least 18 points.	Must have at least one 5-card solution and 11–17 points.	7–10 points or above 10 without a 5-card.	3–6 points or solutions attempted, but none correct.	No response.

Note to scorers: Give 3 points for each 3-number solution, 4 points for each 4-number solution, and 5 points for each 5-number solution. Some possible solutions include:

5 cards	4 cards	3 cards
$(6 + 12) - (1 + 5 + 4) = 8$	$(5 + 6) - (12/4) = 8$	$(12/6) \times 4 = 8$
$(12 + 5 + 1) - (6 + 4) = 8$	$(12/6) \times 4 \times 1 = 8$	$5 + 4 - 1 = 8$

Figure 14.3. Sample rubrics.

A Performance-Based Science Assessment: The Diet Cola Test

One example of the use of performance-based assessments may be found in the research on curriculum effectiveness in science, conducted by the Center for Gifted Education at the College of William and Mary (VanTassel-Baska, Bass, Ries, Poland, & Avery, 1998). This research employed a performance-based measure called the Diet Cola Test to assess the capacity of students using the William and Mary curriculum to design experiments and document their understanding of the integrated science processes involved.

The following commentary analyzes the assessment instrument used in the science study, with exploration of key features that influenced the selection of the instrument and its incorporation into the curriculum. Each form of the instrument is presented along with scoring procedures, content validity and reliability data, student exemplars, and instructional inferences to be made from the results.

Description of the Instruments and Scoring

The Diet Cola Test was developed by Marilyn Fowler Cain (1990) to assess students' understanding of experiments. It is an open-ended test that requires students to design an experiment to determine whether or not bumblebees are attracted to diet cola. A parallel form to the Diet Cola Test, the Earthworm Test, asks students to design an experiment to find out whether or not earthworms are attracted to light (Adams & Callahan, 1995). Both instruments were adopted for use on a pretest and posttest basis for their adequate reflection of the unit objectives to develop student experimental research skills, the similar age range targeted, and their sufficiently high ceilings (VanTassel-Baska et al., 1998).

Students' responses are scored according to a checklist of science process skills, with points assigned for addressing each skill and additional points for skills addressed in greater detail: plans for *safety,* stating the *problem* or *question, giving a hypothesis* describing three *steps* or more, arranging steps in a *sequential order, listing materials* needed, plans to *repeat testing, defining terms,* plans for *observation,* plans for *measurement,* plans for *data collection,* plans for *interpreting data,* plans to make *conclusions based on data,* and plans to *control variables.*

Reliability of the Instrument

The National Research Center on the Gifted and Talented at the University of Virginia conducted reliability and validity studies on the Diet Cola Test. The study included 180 students in grades 4–8 who were nominated by their teachers as good in science and employed the method of test–retesting (10-week interval) with alternate forms. Researchers established the reliability of stability and equivalency of the instrument as .76 (Adams & Callahan, 1995).

Validity of the Instrument

The same study investigated the instrument's content and construct validity. The purpose of content validation is to assess whether or not the items adequately represent a performance domain of specific interest (Crocker & Algina, 1986). In this respect, the instrument was said to "exhibit content validity with a clear match between the task and its indicators and the criteria of science aptitude suggested by the literature" (Adams & Callahan, 1995, p. 16). The science portion of the Iowa Tests of Basic Skills, the Group Figures Test, and the Test of Basic Process Skills showed low correlations with the Diet Cola Test, with varied degrees of statistical significance, suggesting that the assessment had little in common with these other measures.

Match Between the Instrument and Unit Objectives

In light of the findings from the analysis of the National Education Longitudinal Study (NELS) data (Hamilton, Nussbaum, Kupermintz, Kerhoven, & Snow, 1995) that the instructional variables of working on experiments in class, problem solving, and promoting scientific understanding were the best predictors of achievement in quantitative science by 10th grade, the William and Mary units focus on developing student abilities to explore a new scientific area, identify meaningful questions within that area, demonstrate good data as appropriate, evaluate results in light of the original problem, make predictions about similar problems, and communicate understanding to others (VanTassel–Baska et al., 1998). The Diet Cola Test, being a performance test that requires students to design an experiment in order to study a given problem, was a good match to curriculum objectives.

Match Between the Instrument and the Instructional Approach

The specific approach used for instruction in the science units is problem-based learning (PBL). Each unit presents students with a problem scenario and proceeds to have them define the problem and ways to solve it. The related scientific experiments are introduced in the process of students' exploring and investigating the problem. This problem-based approach is reflected well in the Diet Cola Test, a desirable feature that adds to the authenticity of the instrument.

Match Between the Instrument and Targeted High-Level Thinking

As a science curriculum developed for high-ability learners, the units provide materials and instruction that are sufficiently challenging, in-depth, and varied to meet learning needs. Through an integrated approach to teaching scientific topics and processes within an overarching concept of *systems,* the units aim to train students in their ability to perform systems thinking and apply what they have learned in an intradisciplinary or interdisciplinary way. Accordingly, the assessment for this kind of learning should give due emphasis to higher level thinking skills, clearly demanded in the Diet Cola Test.

Students' Pretest and Posttest Performance

Most units (four out of six on which data were collected) showed a statistically significant difference when treatment students were compared with their own prior performance or with their peers who received no special curriculum intervention (see VanTassel-Baska et al., 1998). To illustrate students' increased understanding in experimental design and data collection after their exposure to the units, a sample response from a fifth grader is presented in Figure 14.4.

Treatment Effect and Revealed Instructional Needs

The science unit implementation results showed that, compared with students who did not use the unit, those who participated in unit instruction performed significantly better on the posttest after taking into consideration the pretest difference between the treatment and comparison groups. Content

Pretest Response	Posttest Response
I don't think earthworms like light, because most of them live underground unless it rains or something and they get washed out of the dirt. I could always do an experiment to make sure, thow. [*sic*] For an experiment, I might taken an earthworm, with some kind of light, an dirt, and see if it stays out in the light, or trys to get away from the light by going under the dirt. Score: 5	<u>Title:</u> "Are bees attracted to diet cola?" <u>Hypothesis:</u> I don't think bees are attracted to diets just to regular. For example: coke, sprite, Dr. Pepper <u>Materials:</u> Bee, diet cola, container <u>Description of what I would do:</u> Take one can of diet cola and pour about 1 cup of it into a dish, bowl, etc. Then release a bee about a foot away and see if it moves toward the diet cola. If it does–you know bees like diet cola, but if it moves away from the diet cola, or doesn't respond to it you know bees don't like diet cola. When you are done with your experiment carefully release you bee, pour out your soda, and put back the way you found them. <u>What will you record:</u> If the bees are attracted to the diet cola or if they are attracted to the none diet liquids. Score: 12

Figure 14.4. Sample fifth-grade response.

Note. Errors were left in figure to preserve authenticity of the student's response.

analysis of student performance, however, showed that students were weak in (a) stating a plan for interpreting data, (b) stating a plan for making conclusions based on data, (c) planning to control variables, (d) planning to repeat testing, and (e) planning to practice safety (VanTassel-Baska et al., 1998).

This analysis of the Diet Cola Test provides a research-based pathway to demonstrate the technical adequacy and appropriate use of a performance-based measure. The Diet Cola Test is one effective tool that may be used to assess learning gains for gifted learners in science.

Models for Secondary Performance-Based Assessments: IB and AP

At the high school level, the academic provisions for high-ability learners often primarily consist of International Baccalaureate (IB) and Advanced Placement (AP) courses. These courses are calibrated to be "advanced" in a typical college-level course at a selective school in core subject areas. Because of their emphasis on advanced-level work, the assessment approaches employed in IB and AP programs are illustrative of assessments commonly used with academically oriented learners.

The IB assessment model measures the performance of students against the main objectives of the program by using a combination of external and internal assessment methods in both written and oral modes. External assessments are provided and scored by the International Baccalaureate Organization (IBO). Internal assessments, which also are provided by the IBO, are scored by classroom teachers who are required to send representative scores of high, low, and average levels to the IBO for verification of their having correctly used the scoring rubric. The purpose of this is to ensure that students are assessed fairly according to international standards. The IB Language A1 externally assessed exam includes the components of commentary and essay papers on seen and unseen texts and two written assignments of comparative and imaginative/creative nature. The external assessments account for 70% of the overall Language A1 assessment. The internally assessed component consists of two compulsory oral activities, one commentary on a teacher-selected reading, and one oral presentation on a student-selected topic. The oral component accounts for 30% of the total assessment (IBO, 1999). Scoring rubrics for the written work typically contain six levels to differentiate the degrees of *none, little, some, adequate, good,* and *excellent* demonstration of required ability, skills, or presentation. These assessments demand such abilities as appreciation, interpretation, comparison, critique, analysis, evaluation, and creativity.

The Advanced Placement exam for each of its 38 courses provides another example of a performance-based approach, seeking carefully constructed and scored responses that require depth of knowledge and thought. The exams generally contain two question types: multiple choice and free response. The multiple-choice section emphasizes the breadth of the student's knowledge and understanding of the content. The free-response section emphasizes the application of these core principles in greater depth in solving more extended problems, or analyzing complex issues and texts (e.g., College Board Advanced Placement Program, 1999a, 1999b, 1999c, 1999d). For example, a student taking an exam in English Language and Composition might be asked to analyze the rhetoric of a given passage; a student taking English Literature and Composition might be asked to use examples from literature selections he or she has read to support a generalization about a character or theme in literature. Students taking a science or statistics exam may be given a situation and asked to design an experiment to answer a question of interest. In general, the free-response questions are designed so that different students are able to draw upon the different experiences and texts they have encountered in their courses in order to respond to the question, thus allowing choice for both teacher and student while still maintaining a common course framework.

The free-response section is scored against carefully developed guidelines that are drafted by individual item developers, reviewed and revised collectively by a committee, and modified based on student responses. Scorers of the free-response section are trained to apply the guidelines using exemplary student responses. Sample free-response questions for all exams, demonstrating the emphasis on higher level thinking required of students, are available through the College Board at http://www.collegeboard.com.

Along with demonstrating emphasis on higher level thinking and problem-solving skills, the AP and IB exams also illustrate the proper use of different test formats to serve different purposes of assessment. Moreover, these exams are exemplary for high-stakes testing in terms of their careful construction with consideration of the technical concepts of validity, reliability, and ceiling effect. For example, the free-response questions in the AP Physics exam (College Board Advanced Placement

Program, 1999a) were first developed by members of the AP Physics Development Committee, then reviewed and revised by the committee collectively in a meeting, and finally combined with multiple-choice items written by physics content experts at the Educational Testing Service (ETS). Such a detailed and collaborative development helps to ensure the quality of questions.

Although the resources available to the College Board and IB for developing their assessments far exceed those available to the average classroom teacher or district curriculum developer, the procedures used by these organizations are useful for developing even small-scale classroom assessments. The emphases on determining key principles, concepts, and content for assessment; using multiple formats for question development; encouraging review by a group of educators and content experts; and revising careful scoring guidelines based on the test framework and student response are important considerations that educators may use as foundations for adapting their own assessments.

Conclusion

Developing effective and reliable assessment is not an easy task, and to create meaningful assessment for gifted students is even harder, given the nature of the learner and the nature of the expectations in the program. Creating performance tasks, based on sound principles of technical adequacy and test design, hold great promise for elevating authentic assessment to its rightful place as a partner with traditional assessment in understanding what gifted learners know and are able to do.

References

Adams, C. M., & Callahan, C. M. (1995). The reliability and validity of a performance task for evaluating science process skills. *Gifted Child Quarterly, 39*, 14–20.

Baldwin, A. Y. (1989). The purpose of education for gifted Black students. In C. J. Maker & S. W. Schiever (Eds.), *Critical issues in gifted education: Defensible programs for cultural and ethnic minorities* (Vol. 2, pp. 237–245). Austin, TX: ProEd.

Bracken, B. (2000, April). *An approach for identifying underrepresented populations for G/T programs: The UNIT test.* Presentation at the College of William and Mary, Williamsburg, VA.

Cain, M. F. (1990). The diet cola test. *Science Scope, 13*(4), 32–34.

College Board Advanced Placement Program. (1999a). *Released exams: 1998 AP Physics B and Physics C.* New York: College Entrance Examination Board and Educational Testing Service.

College Board Advanced Placement Program. (1999b). *5-year set of free-response questions: 1995–1999 English.* New York: College Entrance Examination Board and Educational Testing Service.

College Board Advanced Placement Program. (1999c). *Released exam: 1997 AP statistics.* New York: College Entrance Examination Board and Educational Testing Service.

College Board Advanced Placement Program. (1999d). *Released exam: 1998 AP environmental science.* New York: College Entrance Examination Board and Educational Testing Service.

Crocker, L., & Algina, J. (1986). *Introduction to classical and modern test theory.* New York: Holt, Rinehart, & Winston.

Dunbar, S. B., Koretz, D. M., & Hoover, H. D. (1991). Quality control in the development and use of performance assessment. *Applied Measurement in Education, 4,* 289–303.

Ford, D. Y. (1996). *Reversing underachievement among gifted Black students: Promising programs and practices.* New York: Teachers College Press.

Frasier, M. M. (1989). Identification of gifted black students: Developing new perspectives. In C. J. Maker & S. W. Schiever (Eds.), *Critical issues in gifted education: Defensible programs for cultural and ethnic minorities* (Vol. 2, pp. 213–225). Austin, TX: ProEd.

Gronlund, N. E. (1998). *Assessment of student achievement* (6th ed.). Boston: Allyn & Bacon.

Hamilton, L. S., Nussbaum, E. M., Kupermintz, H., Kerhoven, J. I. M., & Snow, R. E. (1995). Enhancing the validity and usefulness of large-scale educational assessments: II. NELS: 88 science achievement. *American Educational Research Journal, 32,* 555–581.

International Baccalaureate Organization. (1999). *International Baccalaureate Language A1 guide.* Geneva, Switzerland: Author.

Jiang, Y. H., Smith, P., & Nichols, P. (1997, March). *Error sources influencing performance assessment reliability or generalizability: A meta-analysis.* Paper presented at the annual meeting of the American Educational Research Association, Chicago.

Lane, S., Liu, M., Ankenmann, R. D., & Stone, C. A. (1996). Generalizability and validity of a mathematics performance assessment. *Journal of Educational Measurement, 33,* 71–92.

Marzano, R. S., Pickering, D., & McTighe, S. (1993). *Assessing student outcomes: Performance assessment using the dimensions of learning model.* Alexandria, VA: Association for Supervision and Curriculum Development.

Mills, C., & Tissot, S. (1995). Identifying academic potential in students from underrepresented populations: Is using the Ravens Progressive Matrices a good idea? *Gifted Child Quarterly, 39,* 209–217.

Naglieri, J. A. (1999). *The essentials of CAS assessment.* New York: Wiley.

National Council of Teachers of Mathematics. (1989). *Curriculum and evaluation standards for school mathematics.* Reston, VA: Author.

Paul, R. (1992). *Critical thinking: What every person needs to survive in a rapidly changing world.* Sonoma, CA: Foundation for Critical Thinking.

Rito, G. R., & Moller, B. W. (1989). Teaching enrichment activities for minorities: T.E.A.M. for success. *Journal of Negro Education, 58,* 212–219.

Schulman, L. (1996). New assessment practices in mathematics, *Journal of Education, 178,* 61–71.

Solano-Flores, G., & Shavelson, R. J. (1997). Development of performance assessments in science: Conceptual, practical, and logistical issues. *Educational Measurement: Issues and Practice, 16,* 16–25.

Torrance, E. P. (1977). *Discovery and nurturance of giftedness in the culturally different.* Reston, VA: Council for Exceptional Children.

VanTassel-Baska, J. (1992). *Planning effective curriculum for gifted learners.* Denver: Love.

VanTassel-Baska, J. (2006). A content analysis of evaluation findings across 20 gifted programs: A clarion call for enhanced gifted program development. *Gifted Child Quarterly, 50,* 199–215.

VanTassel-Baska, J., Bass, G., Ries, R., Poland, D., & Avery, L. D. (1998). A national study of science curriculum effectiveness with high-ability students. *Gifted Child Quarterly, 42,* 200–211.

VanTassel-Baska, J., Johnson, D., & Avery, L. D. (2002). Using performance tasks in the identification of economically disadvantaged and minority gifted learners: Findings from Project STAR. *Gifted Child Quarterly, 46,* 110–123.

Wang, N., & Lane, S. (1996). Detection of gender-related differential item functioning in a mathematics performance assessment. *Applied Measurement in Education, 9,* 175–199.

Wiggins, G. (1992). Creating tests worth taking. *Educational Leadership, 49*, 26–33.

Epilogue: What Do We Know About Identifying and Assessing the Learning of Gifted Students?

Joyce VanTassel-Baska

This book has presented multiple perspectives on an issue that has plagued the field of gifted education for more than 30 years. How can we identify gifted learners in ways that are equitable, efficient, and effective? How can we assess their authentic learning? These myriad voices have achieved some degree of consensus on these important questions. The following generalizations appear warranted, based on the material presented here:

1. Nonverbal assessment tests must be used in combination with verbal and other assessment measures to ensure finding top students who will succeed in diversified gifted programs (Lohman & Lakin; Bracken; Naglieri).

2. Off-level group standardized assessment tests are essential to find and assess highly gifted learners (Olszewski-Kubilius & Kulieke).

3. Individual assessment tests must be carefully selected, administered and interpreted to ensure that highly gifted students and learning-disabled students are not overlooked (Rimm, Gilman, & Silverman).

4. Traditional measures of assessment should continue to be employed in the identification and assessment of learn-

ing of all gifted learners (Robinson; Lohman & Lakin; Rimm, Gilman, & Silverman; VanTassel-Baska).

5. The inclusion of diverse learners in gifted programs requires the use of alternative measures of assessment in combination with traditional ones to maximize the finding of potential (Ford; Feng & VanTassel-Baska).

6. The use of multiple measures that assess multiple abilities, achievements, and provide clinical judgment on application capacity in classrooms may be perceived as best practice in identification (Lohman & Lakin; VanTassel-Baska).

7. The use of multiple measures that assess both short-term and long-term authentic performance of gifted learners in programs may be perceived as best practice in assessing learning outcomes for the gifted (Johnsen; Renzulli & Callahan; VanTassel-Baska).

8. Assessments that require creative production enhance the chances of diverse learners being included and authentic learning potential being tapped (Cramond & Kim; Renzulli & Callahan).

9. The predictive validity of different combinations of measures should be monitored over time to ensure that the results are in line with expectations (Lohman & Lakin).

10. Different measures must be employed for making identification decisions than for learning assessment judgments (Bracken; Naglieri).

11. Because the purpose of all assessments is essentially diagnostic, program, curriculum, and instructional inferences need to be able to be made from the selection of any assessment measure (Bracken; VanTassel-Baska).

12. A strong system of assessment for gifted learners includes identification, intervention, and assessment of learning linked together and established at the front end of program design and development (VanTassel-Baska).

Just as these principles apply to the learnings accrued from reading our authors in this volume, so too must we see that these principles need to be operationalized into a comprehensive model for program design and development. In making decisions about who should be in gifted programs, we also need to make related decisions about their intervention, both at the programmatic level of the school and district but also at the curriculum and instructional level of the classroom. Moreover, we also need to design how we will assess their learning for the short term, as well as longitudinally, in traditional cognitive areas and in affective arenas.

Identification

In assessing gifted students for identification purposes, we need to be aware of three levels of concern. One such level of concern is the *screening level*, where both verbal and nonverbal measures should be considered to ensure that a wide net of possible candidates is procured. Use of a teacher rating scale at this stage also may be desirable. Any tool may include students in a pool for further assessment, and the score on any of these measures does not exclude them.

The second level of concern is the *selection level* and the tools to be used at this stage of the process. At this stage, the relationship of the program and curriculum to be offered must be considered and used as a basis for selecting appropriate final selection measures. The tools also must have plenty of ceiling to ensure that the most gifted students in an area of intervention are properly assessed and served. Specific aptitude and performance measures may be the most appropriate for this level of assessment.

The third and last level of concern in the identification aspect of the system is the *selection process* itself. At this stage, all data have been collected and aggregated at a group and individual level of analysis so that student profiles have been developed for perusal by a selection committee at the school level, representative of teachers, a school psychologist, a counselor, and an administrator. All assessment results are examined with an eye to selecting students who have the greatest chance of success in the specified outcomes of the program and who represent culturally and linguistically diverse elements of the learning community. Individual profile analyses allow the committee to see peak areas of performance, as well as just averages, in rendering decisions. The selection committee also must decide how many students may be included in the program, based on pupil-teacher ratios, size of the facility, and special considerations for the type of program to be administered.

Interventions

As important as identification is to the process of program development, equally important is the planned intervention for students. This planned intervention must occur at three levels. District planning must involve decisions at the program level, the curriculum level, and the services level.

The *program level* should represent a multidimensional approach to ensuring that all gifted learners are appropriately served within the school system. Many districts adopt two distinct approaches to ensure that students are best served. One basic approach is the Schoolwide Enrichment Model (SEM) that provides some experiential options to all learners and specialized options to others in a multitiered system. Another is the accelerated learner approach that assumes that all gifted learners require some degree of advancement in their learning rate and pace of instruction in key areas and plans accordingly, adopting an acceleration policy that encourages content acceleration, grade skipping, and telescoping of learning at all levels. Program emphases must be carefully organized over time to provide a comprehensive articulated set of experiences for any learner identified from K–12.

The *curriculum level* of planning requires a framework of goals and learner outcomes to be developed that addresses the aspects of differentiation required for these learners in key areas of the curriculum. It also must delineate the value-added enrichment emphases so valued as a part of gifted student learning at key stages of development. Curriculum planning also must translate these goals and outcomes into practices at each stage of development by citing strategies, materials, and specific task demands that address the framework components.

The *services level* of planning provides the necessary supports for special needs learners including the personalized services of tutoring, mentoring, and counseling. All of these services ideally are required in some form for all gifted learners during their schooling. However, for students of poverty and color, these are lifeline services to being successful in school and in gifted programs. Interest-based options such as clubs and other co-curricular activities also provide more specialized opportunities tailored to specific needs. Staffing these services in such a way that gifted learner needs are addressed is a challenge for program planners yet approaches must be found to ensure that students have affective opportunities, as well as cognitive ones, in the gifted program.

Assessing for Impact on Learning

Although identification and intervention may be planned in tandem and fit together, it is less likely for school practice in gifted programs to assess the impact on learning of the specialized program and curriculum. Yet, in the absence of such data, we have no capacity to defend the efficacy of what we are doing in gifted education. Thus a system of assessment also must focus on how we know that students have benefited from the special programs and services provided them.

In thinking about assessing learning impacts, program developers must come to terms with the need for multiple measures and types of measures to get a true picture of authentic learning for these students. One approach would be to use *multiple cognitive tools for short-term judgments.* These tools might include creative products, curriculum-based assessment, and portfolios, all tools that could be used pre- and postassessment across a semester or year to judge growth in meaningful learning that is differentiated. Moreover, the ongoing use of state and national achievement measures can supplement these data by providing a portrait of specific content-based proficiency. The goal of any gifted program would be to work toward gifted student proficiency in all areas and advanced proficiency in areas of strong aptitude.

A second approach would be to focus on *affective tools* for making short-term program impact judgments. Examining ways for gifted learners to enhance their motivation, to develop positive attitudes about themselves as learners, and to inventory their values and interests provides important understandings about gifted program benefits that can augment the cognitive gains made. For students of poverty and color, monitoring progress in these affective areas is vital to ensuring they continue in programs past the shoals of transition periods like middle school and high school into college.

A third way to assess learning impacts, and perhaps the best way for making a strong case for gifted programs is the use of *longitudinal assessment tools* that would document learning gains over 3 or more years. Longitudinal assessment also allows for tapping into both cognitive and affective issues, over time through questionnaire data, portfolios, and artifacts that speak to a philosophy of life and learning. High-stakes tests that speak to high-level performance such as the Advanced Placement examinations and the International Baccalaureate exam also contribute important information about the quality of programming over time in specific areas of learning. Specific critical and creative thinking measures also can document enhanced performance in these higher level thinking dimensions.

This comprehensive model then provides a way to think about the dual purposes of assessment in gifted programs and to have a way to link them together (see Table 15.1). Comprehensive programming for the gifted involves the bookends of fair and accurate assessment, at the front end to find the best students for programming, and at the back end to decide if they have learned what we had hoped. The system also allows us to study whether our selection of students is well-matched to the programs we deliver or whether course corrections are needed in the intervention phase of the program. Moreover, it offers a way of providing us with data for making programmatic decisions at critical junctures. Should we continue to provide the same programs and services to new groups of gifted learn-

Table 15.1
A System for Assessing Students for Gifted Programs

Assessing for Identification	Interventions	Assessing for Impact on Learning
Screening tools • verbal • nonverbal • teacher clinical assessment	Programs • Schoolwide Enrichment Model • Acceleration Model	Tools for short-term judgments • Creative products • Performance-based tasks (Curriculum-based assessment) • Portfolios • State and national standardized measures of proficiency by subject area
Selection tools • Linked to program emphases (tests, inventories, teacher judgment) • Off-level	Curriculum • Content-based adaptations in all areas • Value-added enrichment emphases	
Processes • Selection committee • Student profile of multiple assessment results	Services • Mentoring • Tutoring • Interest-based clubs • Counseling	Affective tools for short-term judgments • Motivation scales • Attitude scales • Values inventories • Interest inventories
		Longitudinal cognitive and affective tools • Portfolios • Critical thinking tests • PSAT/SAT scores • AP/IB course-taking and performance • Philosophy of learning and life

ers or should we develop new models that can more sharply impact learning? Are some groups of gifted learners doing better than others and can we discern why? Are there developmental differences in the learning curve for these learners and what accounts for it? Such questions as these should be able to be answered if we mount a comprehensive system of assessment for gifted programs.

Alignment With NCATE Assessment Standards

Any book on alternative assessment must be aware of and connected to the new NCATE standards for gifted education, adopted for use in 2006 by the professional organizations for the gifted, CEC-TAG and NAGC. These standards provide important guidance to the field in what teachers of the gifted need to know and be able to do. In the area of assessment, the standards indicate the need for knowledge and skill in selecting and applying multiple assessment approaches to working effectively with gifted learners.

This book serves as a beacon for those wishing to fulfill the NCATE requirements for the knowledge and skills associated with assessment of gifted learners. It is organized to provide important understandings about both identification and learning assessments appropriate for this population. The Bracken, Lohman and Lakin, and Naglieri chapters taken together present the case for the use of nonverbal assessments as a part of the identification protocol for these learners. The Ford chapter speaks to the importance of considering issues of diversity in selecting identification processes. The Feng and VanTassel-Baska chapter and the Sternberg chapter present models for performance-based value-added approaches to using alternative assessments linked to creativity and practical intelligence. The Robinson chapter emphasizes the value of traditional assessments as a key part of any identification model, and the Olszewski-Kubilius and Kulieke chapter remind us of the importance of using off-level tools for making group decisions about gifted learners. Advantages and disadvantages of assessment models for both identification and learning are explored in Chapter 1, as well as individual chapters. Technical adequacy concerns are raised and discussed in context. Specific strategies for the use of alternative assessments also is provided, especially in the Lohman and Lakin chapter.

In the area of selecting assessments for learning, the Cramond and Kim chapter and the Renzulli and Callahan chapter focus on the role of creative products in judging the depth of student learning. The Johnsen chapter highlights the power of portfolios as a way to judge growth over time in a variety of dimensions and on a number of outcomes. The VanTassel-Baska chapter on performance-based assessment provides guidance on the development of differentiated curriculum-based assessments for use as diagnostics, as well as in a pre-post design to document growth. Each of these chapters provides examples of the approach discussed and a process for construction.

The NCATE standard for assessment follows in Table 15.2 to illustrate the alignment just described (also see VanTassel-Baska & Johnsen, 2007).

Final Thoughts

No topic has received greater attention in our literature or the popular press than identifying gifted learners. We clearly have enough evidence to suggest the power of alternative assessment to help us do a better job of finding underrepresented groups of learners and assessing their true potential for talent development. Yet, the real work begins once such learners are identified, the work of providing the optimal matches in programs and services and assessing their impact on gifted student learning. Here too alternative assessments provide a better map of the territory of authentic student learning than traditional measures. Thus, the role of alternative assessment in gifted program design is crucial to consider because the effectiveness of our systems in gifted education are at the core of our efforts to find and serve special populations of gifted learners. May readers of this book find the guidance necessary to use alternative assessments appropriately for the dual purposes of identification and assessment of learning.

Table 15.2
NCATE Assessment Standard

Standard 8: Assessment

   Assessment is integral to the decision making and teaching of educators of the gifted as multiple types of assessment information are required for both identification and learning progress decisions. Educators of the gifted use the results of such assessments to adjust instruction and to enhance ongoing learning progress. Educators of the gifted understand the process of identification, legal policies, and ethical principles of measurement and assessment related to referral, eligibility, program planning, instruction, and placement for individuals with gifts and talents, including those from culturally and linguistically diverse backgrounds. They understand measurement theory and practices for addressing the interpretation of assessment results. In addition, educators of the gifted understand the appropriate use and limitations of various types of assessments. To ensure the use of nonbiased and equitable identification and learning progress models, educators of the gifted employ alternative assessments such as performance-based assessment, portfolios, and computer simulations.

K1	Processes and procedures for the identification of learners with gifts and talents.
K2	Uses, limitations, and interpretation of multiple assessments in different domains for identifying learners with gifts and talents, including those from diverse backgrounds.
K3	Uses and limitations of assessments documenting academic growth of individuals with gifts and talents.
S1	Use non-biased and equitable approaches for identifying individuals with gifts and talents, including those from diverse backgrounds.
S2	Use technically adequate qualitative and quantitative assessments for identifying and placing of individuals with gifts and talents.
S3	Develop differentiated curriculum-based assessments for use in instructional planning and delivery for individuals with gifts and talents.
S4	Use alternative assessments and technologies to evaluate learning of individuals with gifts and talents.

Note. From Standard 8 of the *NAGC-CEC Teacher Knowledge & Skill Standards for Gifted and Talented Education* by the National Association of Gifted Children (2007). Reprinted with permission from the National Association for Gifted Children, Washington, DC.

References

National Association for Gifted Children. (2007). *NAGC-CEC teacher knowledge & skill standards for gifted and talented education.* Washington, DC: Author.

VanTassel–Baska, J., & Johnsen, S. (2007). Teacher education standards for gifted education: A vision for the future. *Gifted Child Quarterly, 51,* 289–299.

Appendix: Alternative Assessment Tools for Gifted Learners

Nonverbal Assessments

Title: Universal Nonverbal Intelligence Test (UNIT)
Author: Bruce A. Bracken; R. Steve McCallum
Publisher: Riverside Publishing
Publisher Address: 3800 Golf Rd., Ste. 100,
Rolling Meadows, IL 60008
Telephone: 800-323-9540
Fax: 630-467-7192
Web site: http://www.riverpub.com
Purpose: To provide fair assessment of general intelligence, measured nonverbally.

Title: Naglieri Nonverbal Ability Test-Individual Administration (NNAT-I)
Author: Jack A. Naglieri
Publisher: PsychCorp, a brand of Harcourt Assessment
Publisher Address: 19500 Bulverde Road, San Antonio, TX 78259
Telephone: 800-211-8378
Fax: 800-232-1223
Web site: http://www.PsychCorp.com
Purpose: To provide a brief nonverbal measure of general ability in children.

Title: Test of Nonverbal Intelligence, Third Edition (TONI-3)
Author: Linda Brown; Rita J. Sherbenou; Susan K. Johnsen
Publisher: PRO-ED
Publisher Address: 8700 Shoal Creek Blvd.,
    Austin, TX 78757-6897
Telephone: 800-897-3202
Fax: 512-451-8542
Web site: http://www.proedinc.com
Purpose: To assess aptitude, intelligence, abstract reasoning, and problem solving in a completely language-free format.

Title: Comprehensive Test of Nonverbal Intelligence (CTONI)
Author: Donald D. Hammill; Nils A. Pearson; J. Lee Wiederholt
Publisher: PRO-ED
Publisher Address: 8700 Shoal Creek Blvd.,
    Austin, TX 78757-6897
Telephone: 800-897-3202
Fax: 512-451-8542
Web site: http://www.proedinc.com
Purpose: To measure nonverbal reasoning abilities in those for whom other mental tests are biased or inappropriate.

Title: Raven's Progressive Matrices
Author: J. C. Raven; J. H. Court; J. Raven
Publisher: PsychCorp, a brand of Harcourt Assessment
Publisher Address: 19500 Bulverde Road, San Antonio, TX 78259
Telephone: 800-211-8378
Fax: 800-232-1223
Web site: http://www.PsychCorp.com
Purpose: To provide a nonverbal assessment of perception and thinking skills.

Title: Cognitive Abilities Test, Form 6 (CogAT)
Author: David F. Lohman; Elizabeth P. Hagen
Publisher: Riverside Publishing
Publisher Address: 3800 Golf Rd., Ste. 100,
    Rolling Meadows, IL 60008
Telephone: 800-323-9540
Fax: 630-467-7192
Web site: http://www.riverpub.com
Purpose: To assess students' abilities in reasoning and problem solving using verbal, quantitative, and spatial (nonverbal) symbols.

Off-Level Assessments

Title: College Board SAT
Author/Publisher: College Board
Publisher Address: 45 Columbus Avenue,
    New York, NY 10023-6992
Telephone: 888-SAT-HELP
Web site: http://www.collegeboard.com
Purpose: To measure the developed verbal and mathematical reasoning abilities related to successful performance in college; includes both the SAT Reasoning Test and the SAT Subject Tests.

Title: EXPLORE
Author/Publisher: ACT
Publisher Address: ACT, 500 ACT Drive, P.O. Box 168,
    Iowa City, IA 52243-0168
Telephone: 319-337-1000
Fax: 319-339-3021
Web site: http://www.act.org
Purpose: To measure the academic progress of eighth and ninth graders in four areas: English, mathematics, reading, and science reasoning; helps students explore the range of career options; and assists them in developing a high school coursework plan.

Creativity Assessments

Title: Abbreviated Torrance Test for Adults (ATTA)
Author: Kathy Goff; E. Paul Torrance
Publisher: Scholastic Testing Service
Publisher Address: 480 Meyer Road, Bensenville, IL 60106-1617
Telephone: 800-642-6787
Fax: 630-766-8054
Web site: http://www.ststesting.com
Purpose: To assess creative thinking ability in adults.

Title: Torrance Tests of Creative Thinking (TTCT)
Author: E. Paul Torrance
Publisher: Scholastic Testing Service
Publisher Address: 480 Meyer Road, Bensenville, IL 60106-1617
Telephone: 800-642-6787
Fax: 630-766-8054
Web site: http://www.ststesting.com
Purpose: To identify and evaluate creative potential.

Title: Thinking Creatively With Sounds and Words, Research
  Edition (TCSW)
Author: E. Paul Torrance; Joe Khatena; Bert F. Cunnington
Publisher: Scholastic Testing Service
Publisher Address: 480 Meyer Road, Bensenville, IL 60106-1617
Telephone: 800-642-6787
Fax: 630-766-8054
Web site: http://www.ststesting.com
Purpose: To assess creative thinking by measuring responses to
  abstract sounds and onomatopoeic words.

Title: Thinking Creatively in Action and Movement (TCAM)
Author: E. Paul Torrance
Publisher: Scholastic Testing Service
Publisher Address: 480 Meyer Road, Bensenville, IL 60106-1617
Telephone: 800-642-6787
Fax: 630-766-8054
Web site: http://www.ststesting.com
Purpose: To assess creativity in young children or others with lim-
  ited verbal and drawing skills.

Title: Gifted Rating Scales (GRS)
Author: Steven I. Pfeiffer; Tania Jarosewich
Publisher: PsychCorp, a brand of Harcourt Assessment
Publisher Address: 19500 Bulverde Road, San Antonio, TX 78259
Telephone: 800-211-8378
Fax: 800-232-1223
Web site: http://www.PsychCorp.com
Purpose: To assess observable student behaviors indicating gifted-
  ness and to help identify children for placement in gifted pro-
  grams.

Title: Group Inventory for Finding Creative Talent (GIFT)
Author: Sylvia B. Rimm
Publisher: Educational Assessment Service
Publisher Address: W6050 Apple Road,
  Watertown, WI, 53098-3937
Telephone: 920-261-1118
Fax: 920-261-6622
Web site: http://www.sylviarimm.com
Purpose: To identify students with attitudes and values usually asso-
  ciated with creativity.

Performance-Based Assessment Projects in Gifted Education

VanTassel-Baska, Johnson, D. & Avery, L. (2002). Using performance tasks in the identification of economically disadvantaged and minority gifted learners: Findings from Project STAR. *Gifted Child Quarterly, 46*, 110–123.

This paper discusses the rationale for developing performance assessment tasks to augment the identification of more economically disadvantaged and minority students for gifted programs in one state; provides a blueprint for the development protocol, including preteaching, rubrics, and exemplars; and shows major findings for use of the protocol with intended students. The performance assessment tasks were developed and revised based on try-out, pilot, and field test data collected across multiple districts with more than 4,000 students at the primary and intermediate grades. Appropriate technical adequacy data were used for decision making on task and rubric revisions. Criterion levels of performance within domains were developed to ensure inclusion of populations of interest without compromising the integrity of the task protocols. The performance assessment tasks of Project STAR resulted in finding an additional group of students who were 12% African American and 14% low-income children using the field test of the instrument. These students represent those who would not have qualified for gifted programs using traditional measures. In that sense, the assessment approach yields a "value-added" component to the state identification system. Thus, Project STAR provides an effective and innovative approach to finding more low-SES and minority gifted students for programs.

Maker, C. J. (1997). DISCOVER Problem-Solving Assessment. *Quest, The Journal of the Division of Research and Evaluation, National Association for Gifted Children, 8*(1), 3, 5, 7, 9.

After a brief description of the DISCOVER assessment, Maker presents a review of research on its development, reliability, and validity for its two intended purposes: identifying the strengths of all students in a classroom and identifying students who are gifted in a way that is equitable across gender, language, economic, and cultural groups.

Maker, C. J., Rogers, J. A., Nielson, A. B., & Bauerle, P. (1996). Multiple intelligences, problem solving, and diversity in the general classroom. *Journal for the Education of the Gifted, 19,* 437–460.

This article is a report on a pilot study of the effectiveness of the DISCOVER approach to curriculum design and teaching strategies when used in regular (homogeneous) classrooms with young children from culturally diverse backgrounds. It contains a short description of the DISCOVER assessment, a description of the curriculum and teaching strategies developed to build upon student strengths and interests, an explanation of the pilot study, and the impact of the teacher classified as a "high implementer" on the students' growth in problem solving in spatial, logical-mathematical, and linguistic intelligences.

About the Editor

Joyce L. VanTassel-Baska is the Jody and Layton Smith Professor of Education and Executive Director of the Center for Gifted Education at The College of William and Mary in Virginia, where she has developed a graduate program and a research and development center in gifted education. Formerly, she initiated and directed the Center for Talent Development at Northwestern University. She has also served as the state director of gifted programs for Illinois, as a regional director of a gifted service center in the Chicago area, as coordinator of gifted programs for the Toledo, OH, public school system, and as a teacher of gifted high school students in English and Latin. She has worked as a consultant on gifted education in all 50 states and for key national groups, including the U.S. Department of Education, National Association of Secondary School Principals, and American Association of School Administrators. She has consulted internationally in Australia, New Zealand, Hungary, Jordan, Singapore, Korea, England, Germany, The Netherlands, and the United Arab Emirates. She is past-president of The Association for the Gifted of the Council for Exceptional Children, the Northwestern University Chapter of Phi Delta Kappa, and the National Association for Gifted Children.

Dr. VanTassel-Baska has published widely, including 22 books and more than 500 refereed journal articles, book chapters, and scholarly reports. Recent books include: *Comprehensive Curriculum for Gifted Education* (3rd ed.; 2006) with Tamra Stambaugh; *Curriculum for Gifted*

Students (2004); *Designing and Utilizing Evaluation for Gifted Program Improvement* (2004) with Annie Feng; *Content-Based Curriculum for Gifted Learners* (2003) with Catherine Little; and *Curriculum Planning and Instructional Design for Gifted Learners* (2003). She also served as the editor of *Gifted and Talented International*, a publication of the World Council on Gifted and Talented, from 1998–2005.

Dr. VanTassel-Baska has received numerous awards for her work, including the National Association for Gifted Children's Early Leader Award in 1986, the State Council of Higher Education in Virginia Outstanding Faculty Award in 1993, the Phi Beta Kappa faculty award in 1995, the National Association of Gifted Children Distinguished Scholar Award in 1997, and the President's Award, World Council on Gifted and Talented Education in 2005. She has received awards from Ohio, Virginia, Colorado, South Carolina, and Illinois for her contribution to the field of gifted education in those states. She was selected as a Fulbright Scholar to New Zealand in 2000 and a visiting scholar to Cambridge University in England in 1993. Her major research interests are on the talent development process and effective curricular interventions with the gifted. She holds her bachelor's, master's, and Ed.D. degrees from the University of Toledo.

About the Authors

Bruce A. Bracken is professor at The College of William and Mary, in the Center for Gifted Education. Bracken has published more than 120 articles, reviews, book chapters, tests, books, curricula, training CDs, and videos. He cofounded and coedited the *Journal of Psychoeducational Assessment* for more than 20 years, and currently sits on the editorial boards of eight national and international educational and psychological journals. Dr. Bracken chaired the American Psychological Association's Committee on Psychological Testing and Assessment, and served as APA's President of the International Test Commission. He is a Fellow of the American Psychological Association and the American Board of Assessment Psychology, and served on a panel for the National Academies of Science.

Carolyn M. Callahan is Commonwealth Professor of Education at the University of Virginia, where she has been a principal investigator on projects of the National Research Center on the Gifted and Talented for the past 17 years. She has published more than 180 refereed articles and test reviews and 50 book chapters across a broad range of topics including the areas of identification of gifted students, program evaluation, the development of performance assessments, and curricular and programming options for highly able students. Dr. Callahan received recognition as Outstanding Faculty Member in the Commonwealth of Virginia, Outstanding Professor of the Curry School of Education, Distinguished Higher Education Alumna of the University of

Connecticut, and was awarded the Distinguished Scholar Award and the Distinguished Service Award from the National Association for Gifted Children. She is a past-president of The Association for the Gifted and the National Association for Gifted Children.

Bonnie Cramond is professor of gifted and creative education in the Department of Educational Psychology and Instructional Technology at the University of Georgia where she is also the Director of The Torrance Center for Creativity and Talent Development. A member of the Board of Directors of the National Association for Gifted Children, and former editor of the *Journal of Secondary Gifted Education*, she currently is on the review board for several other journals. Dr. Cramond has had experience teaching and parenting gifted and creative children, has published papers, chapters, and a book on creativity, and has presented at local, national, and international conferences. Her research interests are in creativity assessment and the nurturance of creative abilities.

Annie Xuemei Feng was Research and Evaluation Director of the Center for Gifted Education at The College of William and Mary until the fall of 2007 when she began employment as a researcher at the National Institute of Health in Bethesda, MD. Her research interests include curriculum effectiveness studies, program evaluation research, gender-related studies, and cross-cultural research.

Donna Y. Ford is professor of Education and Human Development at Vanderbilt University, in the Department of Special Education. Dr. Ford has been a professor of special education at The Ohio State University, an associate professor of educational psychology at the University of Virginia, and a researcher with the National Research Center on the Gifted and Talented. She also taught at the University of Kentucky. She earned her Ph.D. in urban education (educational psychology), master's degree in education (counseling), and bachelor's degree in communications and Spanish from Cleveland State University. Dr. Ford conducts research primarily in gifted education and multicultural/urban education.

Barbara ("Bobbie") Gilman assesses gifted children, makes educational recommendations, and consults with families worldwide about gifted advocacy, as associate director of the nonprofit Gifted Development Center in Denver. She trains professionals in the intricacies of gifted assessment, and holds degrees in psychology from

Duke University and child development from Purdue University. Gilman helped create Colorado's Summit Middle School, a charter school in the Boulder Valley Schools, and shape its highly successful, accelerated curriculum. Her book, *Empowering Gifted Minds: Educational Advocacy That Works* (2003), won both the Legacy Award and ForeWord Magazine's Book of the Year Silver Award in *Parenting*. She has just completed her newest book for educators, *Challenging Highly Gifted Learners*.

Susan K. Johnsen is professor in the Department of Educational Psychology at Baylor University. She directs the Ph.D. program and programs related to gifted and talented education. She has written more than 150 articles, monographs, technical reports, and books related to gifted education. She is a frequent presenter at international, national, and state conferences. Dr. Johnsen is editor of *Gifted Child Today* and serves on the boards of *Gifted Child Quarterly, Journal for the Education of the Gifted,* and *Roeper Review*. She is the author of *Identifying Gifted Students: A Practical Guide,* coauthor of the *Independent Study Program,* and coauthor of three tests that are used in identifying gifted students: *Test of Mathematical Abilities for Gifted Students* (TOMAGS), *Test of Nonverbal Intelligence* (TONI-3), and *Screening Assessment for Gifted Students* (SAGES-2). She is president-elect of The Association for the Gifted, Council for Exceptional Children and past-president of the Texas Association for Gifted and Talented.

Kyung Hee Kim is assistant professor in the Department of Teacher Education, Eastern Michigan University. She received her Ph.D. in gifted and creative education from the University of Georgia, where she worked in The Torrance Center for Creativity and Talent Development. Dr. Kim has received awards for her research from the National Association for Gifted Children, the American Creativity Association, and the International Council of Psychologists. Her research interests include understanding the nature of creativity and the characteristics of creatively gifted students; assessing creativity (with the TTCT and other measures); and nurturing creativity, particularly concerning environmental and cultural interactions with creativity.

Dr. Marilynn Kulieke is Senior Vice President for Research and Development at the National Study of School Evaluation, the research and development division of AdvancED. She worked at the Midwest Talent Search as a program evaluator and has served as an officer in the

Illinois Association of Gifted Children. Her current research interests are formative and summative assessment, standardized testing, and school improvement.

Joni Lakin is a doctoral student in educational psychology at the University of Iowa. Her research interests include cognitive and non-cognitive predictors of academic achievement and the use of assessments to identify gifted students, especially gifted students who are English language learners.

David Lohman received his doctoral degree from Stanford University in 1979 and joined the faculty of the University of Iowa in 1981. From 1993 to 1997, he served as chair of the division of Psychological and Quantitative Foundations in the university's College of Education. He was a Fulbright Fellow at the University of Leiden, the 2003 recipient of the University of Iowa Regents Award for Faculty Excellence, and the recipient of the 2007 Distinguished Scholar award from NAGC. He currently directs the Institute for Research and Policy on Acceleration at the Belin-Blank International Center for Gifted Education and Talent Development. David is a fellow of the American Psychological Association and of the American Psychological Society. He serves on several national boards including the Committee on Tests and Assessments of the American Psychological Association and chairs the Design and Analysis Committee for the National Assessment of Educational Progress. His academic interests have embraced a wide range of topics. Since 1998, he has worked with Elizabeth Hagen on the *Cognitive Abilities Test*. Much of his recent research has concerned procedures for identifying academically gifted children, especially those who have historically been underrepresented in programs for the gifted.

Jack A. Naglieri is professor of psychology and director of the school psychology program at George Mason University. He is a Fellow of APA Division 16, recipient of APA Division 16 2001 Senior Scientist Award, and holds an appointment as a senior Research Scientist at the Devereux Foundation's Institute for Clinical Training and Research. Dr. Naglieri worked as a school psychologist in the New York area, obtained his Ph.D. in Educational Psychology from the University of Georgia, and taught school psychology at Northern Arizona University and The Ohio State University. The author of more than 250 publications, he has emphasized nonverbal assessment, cognitive processing, cognitive interventions, and measurement of psychopathology and resilience. He has published a number of books including *Essentials of CAS Assessment* and *Helping Children Learn* and tests such as the *Cognitive Assessment System*, *Wechsler Nonverbal Scale of Ability*, and the *Naglieri Nonverbal Ability Tests*.

Paula Olszewski-Kubilius is currently the director of the Center for Talent Development at Northwestern University and a professor in the School of Education and Social Policy. She received both her master's degree and Ph.D. from Northwestern University in educational psychology. She has worked at the Center for almost 25 years during which time she has conducted educational programs of all types for learners of all ages including programs for underrepresented gifted students. She has conducted research and published more than 80 articles or book chapters on issues of talent development, particularly the effects of accelerated educational programs and the needs of special populations of gifted children She currently serves as the editor of *Gifted Child Quarterly*, previously served as coeditor of the *Journal of Secondary Gifted Education*, and has served on the editorial review board of *Gifted and Talented International*, *Roeper Review*, and *Gifted Child Today*. She also serves on the board of trustees of the Illinois Mathematics and Science Academy.

Joseph Renzulli is a Board of Trustees Distinguished Professor at the University of Connecticut where he also serves as director of the National Research Center on the Gifted and Talented. His work has focused on the development of theories and research related to broadened conceptions of human potential, the identification and development of creativity and giftedness in young people, and on organizational models and curricular strategies for differentiated learning environments and total school improvement. Dr. Renzulli's most recent work is a technology-based program [http://www.renzullilearning.com] that applies the pedagogy of gifted education to enrichment learning and teaching for all students.

Sylvia B. Rimm is a psychologist; directs the Family Achievement Clinic in Cleveland, OH; and is a clinical professor at Case Western Reserve University School of Medicine. Her clinic specializes in guiding gifted children toward achieving to their potential. Dr. Rimm has authored many articles and books related to gifted children and coauthors, with Gary A. Davis, a frequently used introductory textbook, *Education of the Gifted and Talented* (2003). Dr. Rimm served for 9 years as a contributing correspondent to NBC's Today Show, hosted a long-running parenting program nationally on public radio, and writes a parenting column syndicated nationally through Creators Syndicate. She currently serves on the Board of Directors of the National Association for Gifted Children.

Nancy M. Robinson is Professor Emerita of Psychiatry and Behavioral Sciences at the University of Washington and former director of what is now known as the Halbert and Nancy Robinson Center for Young Scholars. Known previously for her work in mental retardation, her research interests since 1981 have focused on the effects of marked academic acceleration to college, adjustment issues of gifted children, and verbal and mathematical precocity in very young children. Dr. Robinson received her Ph.D. from Stanford University. She continues her work in assessment and counseling with gifted children and their families through the Robinson Center. Dr. Robinson is chair of advisory committees to the U.S. State Department Office of Overseas Schools and the Advanced Academy of Georgia. She also is on the board of the Open Window School. She received the 1998 Distinguished Scholar Award from the National Association for Gifted Children and the Ann Isaacs Award in 2007.

Linda Kreger Silverman is a licensed psychologist. She directs the Institute for the Study of Advanced Development, and its subsidiary, the Gifted Development Center in Denver, CO, which has assessed more than 5,200 children in the last 28 years. Her Ph.D. is in educational psychology and special education from the University of Southern California. For 9 years, she served on the faculty of the University of Denver in counseling psychology and gifted education. She served on the Advisory Panel of the fifth edition of the *Stanford-Binet Intelligence Scale*, organized a "gifted summit meeting" for Riverside Publishing, organized the first international symposium on assessment of the gifted at the World Council for Gifted Children, and cochairs the NAGC Task Force on Assessment. She has been studying the assessment, psychology, and education of the gifted since 1961 and has written more than 300 articles, chapters, and books in gifted education, including *Counseling the Gifted and Talented*, *Upside-Down Brilliance: The Visual-Spatial Learner*, and *Advanced Development: A Collection of Works on Gifted Adults*.

Robert J. Sternberg is dean of the School of Arts and Sciences and professor of psychology at Tufts University. Prior to accepting this position, he was IBM professor of psychology and education in the Department of Psychology, professor of management in the School of Management, and director of the Center for the Psychology of Abilities, Competencies, and Expertise at Yale University. Dr. Sternberg also was the 2003 President of the American Psychological Association. He is the author of more than 1,100 journal articles, book chapters, and books, and has received more than $20 million in grants and contracts for his research that has been conducted on 5 continents. The central focus of his research is on intelligence, creativity, and wisdom, and he also has studied love and close relationships, as well as hate.